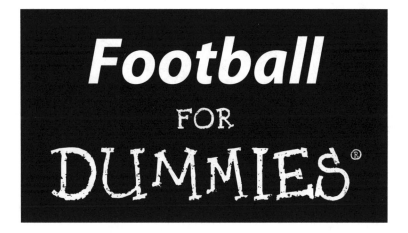

Football FOR DUMMIES®

by Scott Murray

WILEY

A John Wiley and Sons, Ltd, Publication

Football For Dummies®

Published by
John Wiley & Sons, Ltd
The Atrium
Southern Gate
Chichester
West Sussex
PO19 8SQ
England

E-mail (for orders and customer service enquires): cs-books@wiley.co.uk

Visit our Home Page on www.wiley.com

For general information on our other products and services, please contact our Customer Care Department within the U.S. at 877-762-2974, outside the U.S. at 317-572-3993, or fax 317-572-4002.

For technical support, please visit www.wiley.com/techsupport.

Wiley also publishes its books in a variety of electronic formats. Some content that appears in print may not be available in electronic books.

British Library Cataloguing in Publication Data: A catalogue record for this book is available from the British Library

ISBN: 978-0-470-68837-3

Printed and bound in Great Britain by Bell & Bain Ltd., Glasgow

10 9 8 7 6 5 4 3 2 1

WILEY

About the Author

Scott Murray is a freelance writer and former sports editor of guardian.co.uk. He writes regularly for guardian.co.uk, the Guardian, the Fiver, and FourFourTwo. He also has written for the Observer, GQ, Men's Health, GQ Sport, Shortlist, the Evening Standard, and Arena. He is co-author of the football miscellany *Day Of The Match: A History Of Football In 365 Days*, and an upcoming biography of Maurice Flitcroft, the world's worst golfer: *Phantom Of The Open*. The club he supports has won quite a lot of trophies, but then he also has to follow Scotland, so it all balances out.

Acknowledgments

I would like to thank everyone at Wiley, especially Simon Bell for his help and never-ending patience, especially upon being quizzed about the managerial merits of Frankie Gray. I would also like to thank Annabel Merullo and Tom Williams at PFD.

Publisher's Acknowledgements

We're proud of this book; please send us your comments through our Dummies online registration form located at www.dummies.com/register/.

Some of the people who helped bring this book to market include the following:

Commissioning, Editorial, and Media Development

Development Editor: Simon Bell

Content Editor: Jo Theedom

Acquisitions Editor: Wejdan Ismail

Assistant Editor: Jennifer Prytherch

Copy Editor: Charlie Wilson

Technical Editor: Ollie Jones

Publisher: David Palmer

Production Manager: Daniel Mersey

Cover Photos: © PBWPIX / Alamy

Cartoons: Ed McLachlan

Composition Services

Project Coordinator: Lynsey Stanford

Layout and Graphics: Nikki Gately, Joyce Haughey, Christine Williams

Proofreaders: Melissa Cossell, Lauren Mandelbaum

Indexer: Slivoskey Indexing Services

Contents at a Glance

Table of Contents

Part III: Exploring the World of Football..................... 153

Chapter 10: The World Cup...................................155

Chapter 11: Surveying the International Scene 169

Introduction

Congratulations! You've got a copy of *Football For Dummies* in your hands. This book has been written specially for people who want to know all they can about the greatest and most popular sport on the planet: association football. *Football For Dummies* aims to satisfy your curiosity, help you to understand the basics of how to play the game, arm you with knowledge so you can enjoy watching it to the full and show you that you have a whole world of football to be explore. There's a reason football has taken off all around the globe, after all!

Millions are passionate about the sport, from fans of the 'beautiful game' in Brazil to lovers of 'soccer' in the US. And none more so than fans in the British Isles, where the game as you know it today took off back in the mid 1800s. It's the simplest of sports in principle – in the final analysis, all you need to know is that one team has to score more goals than the other to win. Nevertheless, a plethora of laws, tactics and skills exist that can easily flummox the beginner.

That's where this book comes in. I wrote it so that anyone who wants to enjoy football – whether by playing it or watching it – can get to grips with the sport quickly and easily, without feeling overwhelmed or intimidated. And I promise it won't be long before you've become something of an expert on the most talked-about sporting pastime in the world. You'll never look back!

About This Book

The simple aim of *Football For Dummies* is to provide you with all the basic skills and help you remember every scrap of crucial knowledge that you need to become a football fan. All the information you need is between the covers of this book. But although it's all crammed in here, don't feel daunted: you certainly don't have to read every word, from start to finish, to get the most from the book.

Each chapter covers a separate topic about football, so you can easily dip into the chapters to find out about something you don't quite understand. Say you're watching a Champions League game on television, but don't really know much about the history of the competition; just turn to the chapter that talks about important football competitions and *Football For Dummies* will fill the gaps in your knowledge.

If you fancy getting up off the sofa and turning out for a team yourself, *Football For Dummies* explains how you can set about getting involved as a player. The book offers plenty of handy hints and practical skills you can develop. Maybe you'd even like to become a referee. Well, that's no problem. I even help you find a whistle.

And even if you're not an absolute beginner, I'm confident that *Football For Dummies* can still help you discover plenty that's new and fascinating from the long history of association football.

Foolish Assumptions

Assumptions are indeed foolish, so I'm not making any of them. Don't worry if you feel you know absolutely nothing about football. Chances are you already know more than you think, and this book helps you gain confidence in your knowledge.

But even if you don't have a scrap of understanding about the game to start off with, never mind! *Football For Dummies* soon gets you up to speed. And remember: even folk who think they know everything about the game have some gaps in their knowledge. Soon enough, I'm confident *Football For Dummies* will make an expert of you.

At the moment you might ask:

- Why do some teams kick the ball up in the air but others pass it around the floor?
- What on earth are the crowd singing?
- Why are there two people dressed in black running up and down the side of the pitch waving flags?
- What on earth is the offside rule?
- Who was the greatest footballer who ever played the game?

This book answers those questions – and many, many more. My only assumption – and this one isn't so foolish! – is that you know nothing about the game to start with. I take it from there, and it won't be long before you understand all there is to know about football.

How This Book Is Organised

This book is organised into six distinct parts. Each section focuses on a different – but important – part of the world of association football.

Part I: Kicking Off

If you're a complete beginner, this part gives you a basic grounding in what football is all about. This part describes what football is and why people love playing and watching the game so much. It tells the history of the sport, from its early days in China to the modern game that's showcased in stadiums and on televisions all across the globe. And I show you how to get ready to join in, whether you'll be getting your boots dirty or just watching from the stands!

Part II: Playing the Game

I don't waste any time getting to the nitty-gritty here. The first chapter in this part explains the rules of the game – which are the same whether you're having a kickaround in the local park or playing in the World Cup final! The part goes on to explain what each player on the pitch is expected to do, the tactics they're told to employ and the skills they need to play the game. This part also includes tips on coaching and management, how to keep fit and where you can put it all into practice – on the pitch.

Part III: Exploring The World of Football

Football is the biggest sport in the world, and this part explains everything about the professional game. I explain all about the biggest show on earth – the FIFA World Cup – and other international tournaments such as the European Championships, Copa America and the African Cup of Nations. The part also details how club football is organised across the world, from the English Premier League to Major League Soccer in the US. I run down all the important international and club sides, so you know your Brazils from your Barcelonas and your Argentinas from your Arsenals. Plus there's an in-depth look at women's football – a fast-growing sport in its own right.

Part IV: The Fans' Enclosure

If you love watching the game, this is the part for you. Chapters go through the routine of going to the match, as well as pointing you in the right direction of the best television programmes, Internet sites, newspapers, magazines, books, films and DVDs. I even explain what to do if you fancy a flutter, or just enjoy controlling a virtual match on your video-game console.

Part V: The Part of Tens

The part without which no *For Dummies* book would be complete. This part is packed full of nuggets of information you can squirrel away for use later, when you need to impress someone with your football knowledge. Was there really someone more talented than Pelé in the famous Brazil team of the 1950s and 1960s? The answer's here – along with many other facts that are in turns funny, illuminating, tragic and interesting.

Appendixes

This part contains two really useful collections of information: a roll of honour of the greatest tournaments in football history and a glossary of useful phrases.

Icons Used in This Book

To help you navigate through this book with the ease of Diego Maradona slinking past Terry Fenwick, keep an eye out for these icons, the little pictures that sit in the margin. They help you spot particular snippets of information. This list tells you what the icons mean.

This highlights small pieces of advice that can help you become a better player or a more knowledgeable football expert.

This information is especially useful to remember. If you only remember one thing from each page, make sure it's this bit!

Hopefully, this won't come up too much – but when it does, take heed, because the information accompanying it ensures you don't come a cropper.

The great thing about football is the amount of random trivia it generates. There's lots of trivia in *Football For Dummies*, and you'll quickly become an expert if you commit all these facts to memory!

Where to Go from Here

So here you are, ready for kick off. Exactly what you get out of *Football For Dummies* depends on your needs. If you're a complete beginner the book gets you up and running. If you already know a bit about the game the book soon fills in the gaps in your knowledge. And even if you fancy yourself as a bit of an expert, well, everyone's still learning, so hopefully you'll find something new and fascinating in here too.

But although I'd advise beginners to start at the beginning, even they don't have to. This book is designed for you to dip in and out of – so if you want to find out about the world's most famous clubs first, turn to that chapter. You can always turn to a different chapter to bone up on the laws of the game. Or its history. Or its most famous stadiums. Or the hardest tricks to pull off down the five-a-side court. Or . . .

Part I
Kicking Off

In this part . . .

To break you in gently to the great game of association football, this part provides an introduction to the game, covering how it began, and what it is all about. Those of you who are new to football receive a comprehensive rundown of the whys and wherefores of the game right here.

In this part of the book, I describe how football has become the most widely played and watched team sport on the globe. I explain the basic aims of football, the pitch on which the game is played, and, last but not least, what gear you need to have to play it.

Chapter 1

Welcome to Planet Football

. . . .

. . . .

A ssociation Football is the most popular sport in the world. Depending on where you hail from, you may know it as football, footy, soccer, *fitba*, *fútbol*, *calcio*, *futebol*, *voetbol*, *le foot*, *foci*, *sakka* or *bong da*, but the game remains the same: two teams of 11 players, each one trying to kick a spherical ball into a goal more times than the other.

Football is fiendishly addictive, whether you watch or compete. Across the planet more supporters and spectators follow the professional game than any other sport, and at grass-roots level more amateur participants enjoy the game than any other athletic pastime.

Football arouses passion in spectators and players like no other game in the world – and perhaps like nothing else known to humankind. It has done so ever since some English rule-makers formalised the pastime of kicking a ball around into a sport during the late 1850s and early 1860s. (That's 150 years and counting *and it's still getting more popular by the day*.) But why have billions of men and women, boys and girls, adults and children been enthralled by this simplest of sports for such a long time? What makes football so special?

Football: the Simplest Game

John Charles Thring was bang on the money when, in 1862, he wrote a set of draft rules for the game that later became known as 'Association Football'. With the sport yet to be christened, Thring decided to entitle his rules *The Simplest Game*.

Thring's rules were tweaked before being ratified by the newly founded Football Association the following year, but the new sport of Association Football remained 'the simplest game'. Because no game – with the possible exception of running in a straight line, and that's not really a game, is it? – is less complicated than football.

The basic aim: it really is that simple!

The object of the game is simple: for a team of 11 players to guide a ball into a goal and do it more times than the opposition team can manage.

That's it!

So why is football so popular?

Pop psychologists have written more words attempting to explain why football is so popular than on any other subject (except organised religion, maybe, although some supporters will tell you that's pretty much the same thing).

The truth is, nobody's ever been able to quite put their finger on why the game is so popular, so I'm not going to pretend to give you a definitive answer. There simply isn't one. The best I can do is offer you the following three suggestions:

- ✓ **Its simplicity makes it readily accessible.** You only have to watch a couple of minutes' worth of action to work out what the teams are trying to do.

- ✓ **Goals have a rarity value and are at a premium.** Cricket involves scoring hundreds of runs and a tennis player might win a point every 30 seconds. But you can watch 90 minutes of football and not see a single goal scored by either team. So when you do see one, the excitement is palpable.

- ✓ **The teams belong to the people.** Despite its public-school origins, organised football quickly became a working-class sport, a release from the tedium of everyday life. Results really began to matter. Following a team became tribal, with a sense of belonging and a commitment to a cause.

Having said that, thousands of other, better reasons may exist. After you've watched a few matches, or played a few games, you'll no doubt have a few theories of your own. Actually, that's another great thing about football: everyone's got an opinion about it.

Soccer: not an Americanism

One of the great myths in football is the origin of the word 'soccer'. It's generally considered to have been coined in the United States of America – where the game commonly known as 'football' in the United Kingdom is indeed called 'soccer'. But in fact the word is a creation of the English upper classes!

In universities and public schools well-spoken students had the habit of abbreviating nouns and then appending them with the suffix 'er', to create a new informal word. For example, someone with the surname 'Johnson' would be known as 'Johnners'. Similarly, the game of rugby union was called 'rugger'.

According to legend, in the mid-1880s someone asked an Oxford student called Charles Wreford-Brown whether he wanted to play a game of 'rugger'. Preferring to play football, he shortened the 'association' of 'association football' to 'soc' and tacked on the usual matey suffix – quipping back that he'd rather have a game of 'soccer'.

This tale may well be apocryphal, but what's definitely true is that Wreford-Brown went on to captain the England national football – sorry, soccer – team.

Where do people play footie?

Everywhere, basically. The game, in a very basic form, is thought to have started out in China over 2,000 years ago, with the ancient Greeks, the Romans and indigenous Australians playing variations on a theme over the centuries.

It wasn't until the mid-1800s that the game as you know it today developed in England, but by 1900 it had spread all over Europe and to South America. Fast-forward another 110 years and every country and continent in the world is now playing the game. That includes the United States of America, a country that held out for so long but is now slowly falling for its charms, with major men's and women's leagues now established Stateside.

Explaining a Few Rules

So how does this team of 11 players actually go about playing the game and scoring these elusive goals? I go into further detail about the laws of the game in Chapter 4, but first here's a brief overview of how you play a football game.

The pitch

You usually play football on grass, occasionally on artificial surfaces, but always on a pitch no bigger than 73 metres (80 yards) wide and 110 metres (120 yards) long. Figure 1-1 shows you how the pitch looks.

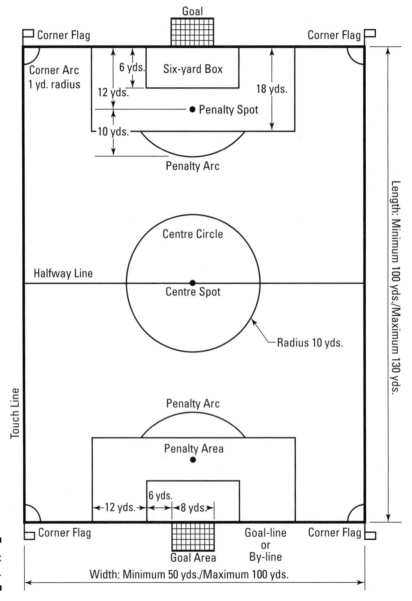

Figure 1-1: The pitch.

Each end of the pitch has a goal, comprising two upright posts 7.3 metres (24 feet) apart and 2.43 metres (8 feet) high, topped with a horizontal crossbar. One team tries to score in one goal and the other team tries to score in the other goal. While both teams are trying to score they also try to stop the other team scoring.

The ball isn't allowed to leave the pitch. If a player in one team kicks the ball off the pitch then a player in the opposing team must throw or kick the ball back in.

The players

Each team has 11 players. Ten of these players aren't allowed to touch the ball with their arms or hands. They're called *outfield players*. The other member of the team is called the *goalkeeper*; he can use his hands and arms in the penalty area around the goal he's tending.

Four basic positions exist:

- ✔ **Defender:** A defender's job is primarily to defend his goal and stop players from the opposing team scoring.
- ✔ **Forward:** A forward's role is to score goals or create them for other players.
- ✔ **Goalkeeper:** The goalkeeper's job is to stop the ball going in the net at all costs, thus ensuring the opposing team don't score a goal. He can do so by using any part of his body.
- ✔ **Midfielder:** A midfielder – usually the team's most adaptable players – covers a lot of ground, helping the defenders defend and the forwards attack.

These players are arranged in various formations. The most common is 4-4-2: four defenders, four midfielders and two attackers. The goalkeeper isn't listed in the formation; his position is taken as read. Find out more about the fun of formations in Chapter 5.

General behaviour

A referee is on hand to officiate every game, and his decision is final.

Players aren't allowed to barge each other off the ball, or kick each other, or trip each other up or obstruct each other. If they do, they give away a *foul* and the referee awards the other team a *free kick*. See Chapter 4 for more on free kicks.

If one team concedes a free kick close to the goal then the team awarded the kick has a fair chance of scoring direct. If a team concedes a free kick in the penalty box then the ref awards the opposition a *penalty* – a free shot from 12 yards out with only the goalkeeper in the way.

Referees can send off, or banish from taking any further part in the match, players who continually concede fouls. Find out more about free kicks, penalties and obeying the laws of the game in Chapter 4.

Goal!

To score a goal the whole ball has to cross the goal line, going between both of the posts and under the crossbar.

Players are allowed to score by shooting with their feet or heading the ball into the goal. This sounds easier to achieve than it actually is, which is why goals are greeted with such unbridled joy by crowds.

Keeping score . . .

The scoring system in football is simple. If Team A has scored one goal and Team B hasn't scored any then the score is 1-0. If Team B then scores two goals the score is 1-2.

A match may end with neither team scoring a goal. (This score is 0-0 – that's 'nil nil', not 'zero zero' or 'nothing nothing'.)

. . . and keeping time

A match lasts 90 minutes, split into two 45-minute halves. The team with the most goals at the end of 90 minutes wins the game. If both teams have the same number of goals then the match is a draw.

Playing the Game

The beauty of football as a sport is that anyone can play it, anywhere. That's something you can't say about horse racing or Formula One!

Jumpers for goalposts

Everyone who's ever kicked a ball remembers putting down a couple of jumpers for goalposts in the park as a youngster and having a bit of a kickaround with their friends. Usually only four or five kids would play, so you'd have to play some other games in lieu of a proper match.

✔ **Three and in.** One player's the goalkeeper, with the other players competing with each other to become the first to score three times. The winner then takes his turn in goal.

✔ **Headers and volleys.** One player's the goalkeeper, with the other players trying to score, but only with headers and volleys. Players get a point for a goal scored but have to go in goal if their attempts are caught in the air by the keeper.

✔ **World Cup doubles.** The best street football game bar none. You only have one goalkeeper. Everyone else pairs up. Each pair tries to score; whenever they're in possession all the other pairs try to stop them. Upon scoring, a pair qualifies for the next round. Each round sees the last pair yet to score dropping out.

You don't even really need any equipment, apart from a ball – and even then you can improvise. (Famous players, like the Brazilian legend Pelé and Argentinian icon Diego Maradona, both grew up in shanty towns playing with rolled-up newspapers.)

Playing solo

Although football's a team sport, you don't even need anyone else to play it with. Football is a game you can have just as much fun practising alone. Bobby Charlton, who won the 1966 World Cup with England and the 1968 European Cup with Manchester United, used to spend all his spare time as a little boy practising with a tennis ball up against a wall. As well as keeping him fit and healthy, it honed the skills that turned him into one of the greatest players the world's ever seen.

Playing with others

If you do have a few friends to play with, but not enough to make two teams for a match, you can play hundreds of *street football* games, variations on the game that give a kickabout in the park some purpose and a little bit of competition.

But if you want a proper game, don't fret: thousands of organised teams exist, at all age groups and levels of ability, that you can join. And who knows: if you're good enough you may one day get a trial for a professional team. And then . . . well, we're not promising anything, but *somebody's* got to be the next Cristiano Ronaldo, haven't they?

Watching Football – and Supporting a Team

Professional football is the most popular spectator sport in the world. Billions of people follow the game, either by going to a stadium to witness the action in the flesh or watching live coverage or edited highlights, either on television or over the internet.

Following club and country

Most people follow the fortunes of two favourite teams: the club side closest to their heart and their international team that represents the country of their birth or that of a parent's.

Supporters choose club sides for different reasons. Perhaps they were born near the ground. Maybe their father or mother, or some other close family member, was a fan. Or it could be that a child watched a particular match and fell in love with the club immediately.

There could be other reasons. Their favourite player plays for them. They really like the colour of the team shirts. They visited the ground once and especially enjoyed the atmosphere. Anything is possible when people are making emotional attachments.

Who you support is up to you, and you can't change what feels right. One warning, though: if you're a Manchester United fan from Torquay, some fans will accuse you of being a *glory hunter* (someone who follows a club just to associate themselves with its success) and ask why you aren't supporting the side from your home town. You'll never win this argument, so don't bother getting involved in it. Remember, who you support is a personal decision; no right or wrong answer exists.

Remember too that supporting Team X means that you'll automatically dislike Team Y. (Think England/Scotland, Rangers/Celtic, Arsenal/Tottenham, Real Madrid/Barcelona.) These rivalries can generate a lot of pain – but a lot of joy as well. It might not be edifying but it's an important part of the game.

Winning trophies: the be-all and end-all?

At a very basic level football is about winning things, whether watching or playing. Club teams compete to win league championships and cup competitions, and international sides try to win the World Cup.

But it's not just about winning the big trophies, which is just as well because there aren't that many to go round and it's always the big sides and perennially successful nations who land them anyway. Football is also about:

- **Beating your arch rivals.** Your team could end the season relegated while your rivals walk away with the championship. But if you've beaten them home and away – preferably convincingly – you still maintain the most important bragging rights that season. There's logic in there – albeit logic that's a bit twisted.

- **Avoiding relegation.** If your team has looked doomed all season then pulls a couple of late-season victories out of the bag to secure their divisional status, the feeling of relief is so much greater than the joy of lifting a trophy. Seriously.

- **Registering an unexpected win.** Some weekends it's best to write off a result in advance, especially if you're going to the league leaders in full knowledge that they're miles better than you. It insulates you from the pain of defeat – and also makes it 100 times better when your side somehow come away with a ludicrous 4-1 win.

- **Schadenfreude.** It's not necessarily an emotion to be proud of. But few feelings are better in football than letting rip a guttural guffaw after watching a painful defeat befall a club you dislike intensely.

- **Formation and tactics.** Football isn't just a visceral thrill, it can be an intellectual pursuit too. Working out how your team played, and why they won or lost, can be enlightening and frustrating in equal measure.

- **Having an opinion (and an argument).** Apart from the hard facts on the scoresheet, no absolute rights and wrongs exist in football. A heated discussion with fans of either your team or another club over the performance of various teams and the merits of different players can be one of the real joys of being a fan. And a pressure value to let off steam and keep you sane.

- **The game's history.** Football is over 150 years old and there are thousands of fascinating stories to be told. If you're bitten by the bug you may never be able to stop reading about old-school players and what they got up to. Despite what Sky Sports want you to think, football didn't begin with the Premier League in 1992!

✔ **A famous jaw-dropping moment.** Everyone remembers where they were when Eric Cantona jumped into the crowd and kicked a supporter, when Zinedine Zidane headbutted Marco Materazzi in the World Cup final and when Liverpool scored three goals in six minutes to come back from 3-0 down in the Champions League final.

✔ **A personal jaw-dropping moment.** Nobody will remember this one apart from you. Maybe it was a moment spent watching the game as a youngster with your dad, or the time a first-goal-scorer bet came in at 50/1.

✔ **Watching the biggest games.** You may never see your team compete in one but still nothing shares the pomp, ceremony and sheer anticipation of the final of a major tournament.

✔ **The pain of defeat.** Because without it, you wouldn't appreciate the good times.

Chapter 2

The Ball Starts Rolling: a Potted History of Football

. . . .

In This Chapter

▶ From China to Covent Garden: football in its infancy

▶ How the English gave birth to the modern sport

▶ From England to Brazil (via Scotland): the game goes global

▶ Football stars take over the world . . . with a little help from television

. . . .

*W*herever you go in the world today you're doing well if you can avoid football for more than 24 hours. Over the years the game has spread to every last nook and cranny on the planet – yes, even the United States of America – and can justifiably claim to be the number one team sport in the world.

But how did footie get so big? And when – indeed where – did it start? This chapter looks into the rich history of the sport, from its inauspicious beginnings to the multi-billion pound behemoth it is today.

The Birth of Football

So did someone kick a ball in anger first? As you'd expect, both the Ancient Greeks and Ancient Romans played games that occasionally involved propelling a ball by hoofing it around with the foot. The Greeks played games called Episkyros and Phaininda, the Romans a sport called Harpastum. However, it seems these sports have more in common with rugby – or, indeed, all-in wrestling – than anything you'd recognise as football.

Want some proof? Here's the Greek comic poet Antiphanes describing a game of Phaininda: 'He seized the ball and passed it to a team-mate while dodging another and laughing. He pushed it out of the way of another. Another fellow player he raised to his feet. All the while the crowd resounded with shouts of "Out of bounds! Too far! Right beside him! Over his head! On the ground! Up in the air! Too short! Pass it back in the scrum!" '

Luckily, other ancient civilisations were partaking in pastimes altogether more refined . . .

Anyone for Cuju?

Far across the seas, in China, the Han Dynasty (206 BC to 220 AD) had come up with a game remarkably similar to modern football. It was called Cuju – a literal Chinese translation of 'Kick Ball'.

The aim of the game was simple. Two teams of up to 16 players tried to kick a ball through a 'goal' – usually a hole in a silk sheet suspended between two bamboo posts. Players could use any part of the body apart from the hand. The game was indeed remarkably similar to today's football, though huge rugby-style scrums and melees still occurred.

Over the centuries the ball – which historians think was usually made out of leather stuffed with feathers – became more lightweight, and finally air-filled. In turn the sport became more refined, less inclined to degenerate into a rabble. As the later section 'England, the Home of Football', explains, this wasn't the last time the sport morphed from a free-for-all into a more skill-based pastime.

But Cuju fell out of fashion during the Ming Dynasty, from the 14th century onwards, and quickly became obsolete.

Kemari, Marn Gook and Calcio Fiorentino

Cuju isn't the only ancient sport with similarities to modern football. In Japan, during the sixth century, an extremely hectic pastime called Kemari became very popular. Possibly more group exercise than sport, the idea was to keep an air-filled ball made of deerskin up in the air using only the feet. All players interacted with each other in order to achieve this goal.

On the other side of the planet indigenous Australians were partaking in a hobby known as Marn Gook ('Game Ball'). Marn Gook is easily as old as Cuju – they played it well into the 1800s and it had been around for at least 2,000 years.

Accounts suggest there was little intrinsic point to the matches, which featured up to 50 players. Keeping the ball off the ground, and showing off elaborate skills while doing so, seemed to be the order of the day. Foot skills earned larger plaudits, so became the focus of the game.

A similar free-for-all developed in Italy in the 16th century. Calcio Fiorentino – or Florentine Kick Game – was basically a psychotic version of modern beach soccer. Set in a huge sandpit, players kicked the ball towards designated goals – though they were also allowed to catch, throw, punch, elbow, head-butt and choke. Kicks to the head were outlawed, mind you. (That's all right, then!)

Many other old ball-kicking sports existed, from matches between Native Americans in deserts to ice-based games between Inuits in Greenland. Other communities in the north of France, Ireland and the Shetlands played kick-and-chase games, whole villages often joining in a massive scrum. But it was only when players in England slowly got themselves organised in the 1850s that the sport of Association Football as you know it today really began to develop.

England: The Home of Football

The English have played football for nearly a thousand years. The earliest record of a match (of sorts) being played in the country is in 1175, when schoolboys in London staged a match in the city streets. There were few rules save trying to hoof the ball to a predetermined point at one end of the street or the other. It was a dangerous pastime indeed, so much so that over the next few centuries the game was regularly declared illegal by royal decree (see the nearby sidebar 'Red card! We've been banned!' for more).

Red card! We've been banned!

The ballyhoo caused by rowdy football matches annoyed more than one King of England. In 1314 Edward II decided that anyone playing the sport was causing a breach of the peace. 'Forasmuch as there is great noise in the city caused by hustling over large balls, from which many evils may arise, which God forbid; we command and forbid on behalf of the King, on pain of imprisonment, such game to be used in the city in future.'

Yet people kept playing matches. Richard II, Henry IV, James III and Edward IV all made football illegal, one statute reading: 'No person shall practise any unlawful games such as . . . football . . . but that every strong and able-bodied person shall practise with the bow for the

reason that the national defence depends on such bowmen'!

But archery was considered a duty, rather than a fun pastime, and ordinary folk kept on playing football, despite the sport being proscribed. The majority of the country could only afford football, and were quite satisfied playing it anyway, despite Sir Thomas Elyot, writer and snooty social commentator, describing it in 1564 as 'beastlike fury and extreme violence'.

The masses kept on playing, even with many individuals getting fined or physically punished for doing so. By the 1800s the authorities seemed past caring and the game had spread all across the country.

The 1850s: time to lay down some rules

The first football clubs in the world were set up in England during the mid-1800s. Public schools and universities in the south founded some, cricket clubs or firms in the industrial north set up others. By 1860 historians estimate that at least 70 clubs existed across the country.

The problem was, everyone was playing to a different set of rules, so football as an organised sport struggled to take off. The first attempt to write some standardised rules came in 1846, when scholars at Cambridge University cobbled some together.

In 1857 the first-ever football-only club was founded in Sheffield. (Other football clubs existed already, but they were either linked to schools, universities, or cricket or rugby union clubs.) The men behind Sheffield FC laid down some rules of their own – the Sheffield Rules – and by 1860 even had another team to play, a new set of local rivals called Hallam.

Enter the FA

But while a burgeoning scene was developing in Sheffield it was the posh lads in the south who finally helped the game to spread all across the country.

In 1863 several London-based clubs – mainly from local public schools – got together at a pub in Covent Garden, London, to pen the definitive set of rules. They formed the Football Association, with the intention of governing the game right across the country.

Governance didn't happen immediately, and for the first decade of the FA's existence their rules co-existed alongside the Sheffield Rules among many others. But it was the FA who kept printing out their rulebook and sending it around the nation's clubs. Eventually, their rules became the standard, as more and more clubs joined the association. (Of course, it also helped when, in 1871, the FA launched the first major football tournament in the world: the FA Cup.)

The FA also helped give the game its name – Association Football – which distinguished it from rugby.

Step aside for the professionals!

The FA Cup – or to give it its full name, the Football Association Challenge Cup – was first held in the 1871/72 season. By this time the FA had fifty members, though only 15 clubs decided to compete. The first final of the first major football competition in history was won by founder members Forest-Leytonstone, who had been renamed Wanderers, and they were the team of the FA secretary Charles Alcock! Hmm.

By 1883 over 100 teams were competing in the FA Cup. In the first 12 years of the tournament's existence a team of amateurs from the South won the cup. But in 1883 Blackburn Olympic won, backed by a local manufacturer who'd controversially paid for the players to take a week off in Blackpool ahead of the final in preparation. Professionalism was on its way.

Being professional in 1883 was, technically, against FA rules. But nobody complained until a team called Upton Park played the pros of Preston North End in 1884. Upton Park – old-school southern amateurs – complained to the FA that their northern industrial opponents had an unfair advantage. The FA banned Preston, along with several other clubs, from competing in the following year's FA Cup – so the teams (from the industrial North and Midlands) simply threatened to form a breakaway professional association.

The FA buckled, allowing professionalism to become legal. So Old Etonians' FA Cup win in 1882 forever remained the last time a fully amateur team won the famous trophy. For more on professionalism and amateurism in the game, check out Chapter 12.

The FA

The Football Association (the FA) is the oldest national governing body in the world. This explains why there's no 'English' in the title: because it was the first the founders felt no need to differentiate.

It was formed on 26 October 1863 when representatives of London public schools, civil service departments and sporting clubs met in a pub in Covent Garden, central London, to agree on a single code for the sport. The founder members were Kilburn, Barnes, War Office, Crusaders, Perceval House, Crystal Palace, Forest-Leytonstone, Blackheath School, Kensington School, Surbiton and Blackheath.

Agreement on rules didn't come immediately – handling the ball, for example, wasn't outlawed for another three years! (Which goes to explain why some of the founder members quickly dropped out to become rugby clubs, going on to form the sport of rugby union in 1871.) The FA kept going, though, beating off challenges from several rival organisations to establish itself as English football's governing body.

The FA runs English football to this day, from the grass roots to the very top of the sport. It organises the FA Cup and FA Premier League, and is responsible for the English national team, Wembley stadium and the National Football Centre academy for the development of young players.

As well as those major men's competitions the FA oversees women's football and the amateur game.

The world's first league

The professional clubs had got their way, but with professionalism came problems. It was all well and good being able to pay players, but you needed money to do so! Fans were willing to pay to watch matches but the FA Cup didn't offer enough competitive football. A club knocked out in the first round would only have one competitive game a year; the rest were less-appealing *friendlies*, games with nothing at stake but the kudos of winning.

So in 1888 William McGregor, the chairman of Aston Villa, wrote to his counterparts at Blackburn Rovers, Bolton, Preston and West Bromwich Albion, suggesting an amazing new idea. 'Ten or twelve of the most prominent clubs in England combine to arrange home and away fixtures each season,' he wrote. 'This combination might be known as the Association Football Union.'

In fact, the organisation, and the tournament, would be called the Football League. Within months it was up and running, beginning on 8 September 1888, and by January 1889 Preston had become the first league champions. McGregor got his reward, though: by the turn of the century Villa had won five league titles of their own!

The first international

Initially, the FA had hoped their cup would be an all-encompassing British competition, but in 1873 Scotland formed an FA of their own – the Scottish Football Association, naturally – and in 1873–4 launched their own cup competition. (Yes, you've guessed it, the Scottish Cup.)

Even so, top Scottish teams such as Queen's Park occasionally travelled down to England to compete in the FA Cup. (They even reached the final twice in the mid-1880s.) Relations between the teams, and the associations, were good, and so in 1872 the two associations decided to stage the world's first international fixture: Scotland versus England.

Romantically, the game was held on St Andrew's Day in Glasgow. Less romantically, it ended 0-0. Scotland soon gained the upper hand in the early annual fixtures, recording 7-2, 6-1 and 5-1 wins during the first decade. English clubs, noting Scotland's dominance, enticed many Scottish players south of the border, and these players became a major factor in the legalisation of professionalism.

Meanwhile in Scotland the game became absurdly popular. The Scots followed the English lead in setting up a league – they set up the Scottish League in 1890 with Dumbarton and Rangers sharing the first title.

Football was beginning to spread around the world.

Dribbling or passing?

Why were the Scots so dominant in the early days of the Scotland/England internationals? It was all down to the different tactics they played.

The English liked to run with the ball and dribble it past opponents, but the Scots realised that passing it around between each other paid dividends. They still dribbled the ball too, but mixed their play up with short and long passes. This was called 'combination play'.

As the British took the game around the world, many countries copied combination play, swiftly adapting it because most Europeans and South Americans were more interested in the skilful side of the game rather than the trademark British physicality.

The World Takes Notice

After the FA set down their rules in 1863, British sailors, soldiers and civil servants started taking them round the world. Often packing a ball in their bag on their travels, they introduced the game first to mainland Europe and later South America.

The game takes over Europe . . .

The first club in mainland Europe actually pre-dated the FA, though it still required a travelling Brit to set it up. The Lausanne Football and Cricket Club was founded in Switzerland in 1860.

In turn, Switzerland helped popularise football in Spain – it was a Swiss, Hans Gamper, who founded the famous FC Barcelona in 1899 – but not before British miners working in copper mines in Andalucia helped to set up Recreativo de Huelva, the oldest club in Spain, in 1889.

Meanwhile British students had taken the game to Portugal, introducing Lisbon to the game in 1866; Belgium, setting up a club in Antwerp in 1880; Austria, forming two clubs in Vienna in 1890; Russia, where they played football in St Petersburg in the same year; and Germany, where a club in Berlin was formed in 1893.

Other countries discovered England's creation for themselves. The Dutch started their own FA in 1889, having witnessed British embassy staff at The Hague enjoying kickabouts. And travelling Italian textile worker Edoardo Bosio, after experiencing football in Nottingham and London, took a ball back to his native Turin and in 1891 formed Italy's virgin club, Internazionale of Torino.

Bosio's club is not to be confused with the famous modern Internazionale, who hail from Milan.

. . . then South America . . .

Many British emigrants already lived in South America due to long-established trading routes, so the game quickly caught on across the continent. Several British boarding schools in Buenos Aires began playing the game in the mid-1860s, not long after the FA was set up.

By 1867 the city had its first team – Buenos Aires FC – and by 1891 a league association had been set up. Outside of England and Scotland this was the oldest league in the world – although for the first few years of its existence it was primarily populated with British ex-pats and not locals.

The game reached Uruguay in 1891, when diplomats and businessmen formed the Montevideo Rowing Club, and Brazil in 1894, when Charles Miller, a former pupil of a Southampton boarding school, arrived in São Paulo with a couple of balls and the FA rulebook. (See the nearby sidebar, 'How Britain gave football to Brazil' for more on Miller).

The British influence had little effect on the more skilful style of play South Americans developed, but English clubs regularly toured the continent for the next 50 or 60 years. It was on Southampton's tour of Brazil in the late 1940s, for example, that future England World Cup winning manager Alf Ramsey, then a player with the Saints, picked up several new tactical ideas.

. . . and finally the world

It wasn't long before football was totally global. Although the Brits were the main players in spreading the word, French, German and Portuguese colonialists ensured football made inroads into Africa.

The first officially recognised international away from the United Kingdom was between Uruguay and Argentina in Montevideo, Uruguay, in 1902. Argentina won 6-0.

Meanwhile Brits took the game to the United States and Canada, where it was picked up by university students. In 1885 the two North American countries played out the first-ever international game outside of Britain and Ireland, in Newark, New Jersey. Canada won 1-0.

The United States avenged the defeat a year later, beating the Canadians 3-2, but didn't play another international until 1916! The game never quite took off in the States (baseball had already taken the mantle of the 'people's game') but there was always grass-roots interest.

How Britain gave football to Brazil

Brazilian football may bear little relation to its more prosaic English cousin, but the game would never have taken off in the country were it not for an English public schoolboy.

Charles Miller was the son of a wealthy Scottish diplomat who'd settled in Brazil. Miller was packed off back to Blighty in his youth and became a skilful footballer while at boarding school. Nicknamed 'Nipper', his tricky dribbling skills won him an invitation to play for St Mary's, the club that later became Southampton FC.

St Mary's hoped Miller would stay and become a professional with them, but Miller returned to Brazil in 1894, taking with him two footballs and the FA rulebook. Disembarking at São Paulo with his goodies, he soon won over the ex-pats in the country with the new game, and in 1901 helped form Brazil's first league.

Miller has a square named after him in São Paulo. Brazil is the most successful country in world football, having won five World Cups.

Then, in the mid-1960s, the NASL – the North American Soccer League – was set up. Within a decade the great Brazilian Pelé was playing in the United States for the New York Cosmos.

Football's Golden Age

Football really began to take off in the middle of the 20th century. Domestic leagues in England, Scotland, Spain, Italy, Brazil and Argentina were becoming huge news. FIFA added to the football fever by launching the World Cup in 1930.

Massive crowds flocked to the games. In Scotland, crowds of over 100,000 were frequent; in 1937, 149,415 flocked to Hampden Park in Glasgow to witness the annual Scotland versus England match.

The story was the same the whole world over: a crowd in excess of 200,000 people watched the final game in the 1950 World Cup between Brazil and Uruguay in the Maracanã, Rio de Janeiro.

Television switches on

The popularity of football made it perfect for the new medium of television. (It was also easy for the cameras to cover.) By the mid-1950s live matches were already a regular fixture on televisions across the globe (if not necessarily for the British, who despite leading the way in live coverage took longer than most to cotton on to the sport's popularity).

FIFA: the world body

By the turn of the century people all over the world were playing football. The need for an all-encompassing governing body was imperative.

Because England had given the game to the world, the world looked to England for guidance. But it got none. Great Britain was an extremely inward-looking island, with a massive superiority complex, and saw little need to get *too* involved in the organisation of the sport across the globe.

So instead the French took the lead, forming the Fédération Internationale de Football Association on 21 May 1904. FIFA – as it became colloquially known – drifted for a while. Few associations bothered joining in its early days, and even when membership increased the First World War got in the way of progress.

After the war the Home Nations – England, Scotland, Wales and Northern Ireland – withdrew from FIFA, citing an unwillingness to play against countries Britain had been at war with. They also fell out with FIFA over 'broken time' payments to amateur players. (FIFA wanted to make sure players who missed work, or incurred expenses, were recompensed.)

In truth, though, the Home Nations simply saw international competition as beneath them, still regarding their teams as the best in the world. It was a ridiculous stance: they missed out on the first three editions of FIFA's new baby, the World Cup, and when they finally returned to the fold in 1950 they found themselves lagging behind the rest of the world.

FIFA today is the international governing body of football. It organises all of football's major worldwide tournaments – the jewel in the crown being the World Cup – and has 208 member associations.

It is based in Zurich, Switzerland.

The first live football match on TV was the 1938 England versus Scotland game. That same year the FA Cup final was televised for the first time.

With huge crowds turning up to grounds and TV further popularising the game, people were making plenty of money, but players weren't necessarily seeing much of it. In Britain, for example, the clubs enforced a maximum wage, which saw some players venturing abroad in search of more money.

The problem wasn't solely a British one either. In South America many players felt poorly paid. At one point in the late 1940s and early 1950s the Colombian league broke away from FIFA and paid players huge sums to play in a breakaway league.

Players become stars

Soon enough, wage restrictions were stripped away. And with TV becoming ever more popular, players became global stars. Pelé – the 17-year-old prodigy in the 1958 Brazilian World Cup winning side – was arguably the game's first major star.

Others soon followed and the concept of *superstar* players really began to take off in the 1960s. In Britain, people treated Manchester United winger George Best – with his good looks, fashionable Beatles haircut and silky skills – like a pop star. And he acted like one, spending as much time in nightclubs and driving around in flashy sports cars as he did on the training pitch.

Players like Best, England World Cup winning captain Bobby Moore and later England striker Kevin Keegan started making large sums of money through endorsements and advertising. Footballers were now celebrities. It's a trend that has snowballed to the present day. A player such as David Beckham, famous from Manchester to Madrid and Milan to LA, is as recognisable as any Hollywood star on the planet.

In the 1950s you'd often see players travelling to matches on public transport along with the fans. Preston winger Tom Finney – at one point the best player in England – worked during the week as a plumber.

As players became more powerful, so did the bigger clubs. Outfits from the big cities – like Manchester United, Liverpool, Celtic, Rangers, Milan, Juventus, Real Madrid and Barcelona – naturally drew bigger support than teams from the provinces.

An imbalance was always bound to occur, though it took many years to become evident. Even as late as 1980 a relatively small provincial club like Nottingham Forest could win the European Cup. But times were about to change.

The Modern Game

The 1990s saw sweeping changes in football as it became a multi-million-pound commercial enterprise. As larger amounts of television money started to pour into the game, clubs also began to realise the marketing opportunities open to them.

How TV changed everything

With the advent of deregulated satellite television, the major European leagues were able to charge vast sums of money for television rights.

In England, for example, the BBC and ITV – operating as a cartel – paid only £3.1m for television rights to the Football League in 1987. In 1992, however, Sky television blasted them out of the water with a five-year £304 million deal for the newly created FA Premier League. And the deals grew and grew: the Premier League rights for 2010 to 2013 sold for a total of £1.78 *billion*.

The big clubs in the big leagues were now vastly wealthy – and with increased worldwide exposure thanks to satellite television, new markets opened up for sales of merchandise such as replica shirts. Football had become a massive industry.

Player power

The players now also became incredibly rich, thanks in no small part to a Belgian player called Jean-Marc Bosman, who took his club, RFC Liège, to the European courts in 1995 after they refused to transfer him to another club when his contract had run out. Citing restriction of his free movement as a worker, Bosman won his case. His victory gave footballers more freedom to move between clubs, and therefore play hardball in contract negotiations.

From this point onwards even the most average top-flight footballer earned tens of thousands of pounds a week in the biggest European leagues, with the top stars earning over £100,000 a week. No longer did they arrive at the ground on the bus, or were they forced to go plumbing during the week!

So is the game better for the changes? Opinions vary: some miss the old-school innocence, others think the game is much improved as a spectacle because players earn their money by becoming fitter, faster and more skilful. Some also express concerns that the amount of money earned by the large clubs makes the game anti-competitive, with the same teams competing for the big trophies every year. The vast sums of money gambled on players and wages also means smaller clubs are in danger of going out of business.

All these views are valid. But one thing seems certain: whether the game is in boom or bust, its worldwide popularity will grow and grow. Football has come a long way since those early games of Cuju!

Chapter 3

Getting Your Boots On: the Gear You Need

*Y*ou need a set of clubs to play golf; a bat, ball, stumps, helmet and pads for a game of cricket; and a whole bag of expensive tackle if you want to go fishing. The beauty of football, however, is in its basic simplicity. To start playing all you need is a football – and as you see in this chapter, if push comes to shove you don't even need that!

Having said that, you can't have an organised game without the right equipment. So in this chapter I look at all the things you need to kit you out and get you up and running. And there's no more obvious place to start than with the thing you'll be kicking around.

Having a Ball

Most people agree that the greatest two players in the history of football are Pelé and Diego Maradona. Amazingly, neither man learned how to play the game using a ball. Brought up in extreme poverty in, respectively, the cities of Três Corações, Brazil, and Buenos Aires, Argentina, neither Pelé nor Maradona could afford a proper ball. Both children had to improvise if they wanted to play, using rolled-up socks, newspapers scrunched up and tied together with string, and even old grapefruits or melons.

How balls have rolled down the ages

The ball is round, but that hasn't always been the case. The oldest football known to be still in existence is over 450 years old. Made in Scotland, it was constructed by inflating a pig's bladder by blowing through it with a pipe, then pulling deer skin tightly around it and stitching the whole thing together. An innovative design, and one that no one improved on for centuries.

In the very early days of organised football – in the early 1800s when only students at British public schools and universities played the sport – the 'balls' were crudely stitched together leather pouches, totally dependent on the shape of the pig's bladder and often almost box-like in shape.

By the 1860s some bright spark had invented inflatable rubber bladders, and the football literally began to take shape. For the best part of a century the design remained the same: a rubber bladder covered by 18 orange leather strips. One part of the casing had a large lace where the ball had been laced together. If a player headed this they sometimes cut open their forehead. The balls also got heavy in wet weather – it was often hard to kick the ball any meaningful distance in torrential weather. Some believed the heavy ball also tragically caused some players brain damage through repeated heading.

But in the 1960s new technology brought synthetic-leather balls. The balls became lighter and easier to play with in all conditions. A new 32-panel design replaced the old 18-strip leather cover, and the modern ball as you know it was here to stay.

Whether that helped their ball skills is a moot point, but what this irrefutably shows is this: you don't need the most expensive ball or the best pieces of kit to enjoy the game or become proficient at it.

You can buy all sorts of balls. As a child you doubtless played with a soft sponge ball before upgrading to light plastic air-filled balls of various sizes. You may have even kicked a tennis ball around.

Playing with smaller balls, such as tennis balls, is a good way to improve your ball control and dribbling skills.

But if you're serious about playing you eventually have to familiarise yourself with a proper football.

Modern footballs are usually made of 32 panels of waterproofed leather (or sometimes rubber): 12 pentagonal, 20 hexagonal. When filled with air they blow out into an (almost) perfect sphere. However, manufacturers are always looking for a new design: the one used in the 2006 World Cup final, for example, had 14 curvy panels.

Still, a ball is a ball is a ball, and as long as it meets the official FIFA Laws of the Game, it'll do the job. A full-size ball must meet the following criteria:

✔ **Material:** The ball should have a leather covering or be covered by 'other suitable material'.

✔ **Pressure:** The ball must be inflated to a pressure of 0.6 to 1.1 atmospheres (600 to 1,100 g/cm^2) at sea level.

✔ **Size:** The ball should have a circumference of between 68 and 70 centimetres (27 to 28 inches).

✔ **Shape:** The ball must be an air-filled sphere.

✔ **Weight:** The ball should weigh between 410 and 450 grams (14 to 16 ounces).

Size is important too, especially in youth football. Three main sizes of ball exist:

✔ **Size 3 (or No. 3) ball:** A small 283-gram (10-ounce) version recommended for children between four and nine years old. This is small enough for their small feet and allows them to dribble, shoot and take throw-ins.

✔ **Size 4 (or No. 4) ball:** A 340-gram (12-ounce) ball for children between 9 and 14 years old.

✔ **Size 5 (or No. 5) ball:** The size of ball outlined in the Laws of the Game, and one the professionals use. At 396 grams (14 ounces) minimum, players of 14 and up can use this ball.

Costs vary wildly depending on quality. You can get a perfectly serviceable leather ball to play and train with for between £5 and £10. Mid-range balls are priced at anything between £10 and £50. A professional standard ball – replicas of the ones players use in the very highest-level games, such as the FA Premier League, Champions League and World Cup – could cost anything between £50 and £100.

The variations in price are often dependent on quality of material and construction – perhaps the stitching or bonding of panels is stronger – and give you a rough idea how much life you'll be able to get from the ball. However, remember that you'll also be paying for aesthetic design and branding: a similar ball to the one used in the Champions League final will obviously be of a higher quality, but you're also paying a premium for the name and sponsor.

It's certainly worth spending money on a good-quality ball for match situations. But you don't need to spend so much on training balls, or balls for everyday use. If you're buying a bag of balls for practice sessions, the cheaper end will suffice.

Balls are usually predominantly white, although you'll always be able to find some more colourful designs. Additionally, all major clubs produce their own branded balls – and of course a Chelsea one is likely to be all-blue, a Manchester United ball red and black.

If you're playing indoor football, such as five-a-side or futsal, you need a bespoke indoor ball. These are smaller than full-size balls – usually Size 4 for five-a-side – and they're usually made from a translucent yellow felt rather than leather panels. A futsal ball is made of synthetic leather and is heavier than the traditional outdoor ball. This helps to absorb impact, making the ball bounce less than a usual felt indoor football.

Skills-based court games such as futsal require even smaller balls. You can get these 'skills balls' in Size 2 and sometimes even Size 1.

One of the most famous worldwide sayings in football is 'the ball is round'. It's an irrefutable fact, but the maxim (uttered by the 1954 World Cup winning coach, West Germany's Sepp Herberger) means 'anything can happen in football', because a ball can roll in any direction.

Getting Kitted Out

If you want to play in an organised match, certain items of kit are mandatory. The following sections take you through what you need.

Shirts

All players on the same side, the goalkeeper apart, must wear identical shirts. Players can decide individually whether they'd like their shirts to have long or short sleeves, but all shirts must have a sleeve of some description.

Cameroon wore a sleeveless 'vest' shirt in the 2004 Africa Cup of Nations. It was popular with players and fans, but later outlawed by FIFA, who refused to let them wear the shirt in that year's World Cup.

Shirts are usually made of a lightweight polyester. Kit manufacturers are constantly coming up with new materials that keep players' bodies as cool and dry as possible because they work up a sweat.

In the past shirts were made of thick cotton and sometimes even wool. They were handy for keeping players warm in cold climates, but often soaked up sweat and became very heavy during matches, requiring players to put in more effort simply to run around.

You can buy shirts in traditional, simple designs, or more contemporary fashionable ones. Cost often dictates choice: as a rule, the simpler and less showy a shirt's design is, the cheaper it is.

Simple shirt designs, suitable for park football, cost between £10 and £30, depending on style and manufacturer.

Remember first and foremost this is a sporting garment. It's important that you can move freely in it – so make sure your kit isn't too tight, even though a slightly looser fit may not be fashionable or contemporary.

Shorts

Players on the same side, goalkeeper apart, must wear identical shorts. The design of shorts is usually quite basic, although there have been various changes in fashion: in the late 1800s and early 1900s shorts were very long, often past the knee in Victorian times. Lengths gradually got shorter, a trend that continued until the 1980s at which point the legs barely reached the top of the thigh. In the 1990s fashion swung back with longer shorts. Today shorts are somewhere in the middle, a happy compromise of style and function.

Shorts should neither be too short (they offer the legs little protection when slide tackling) nor too long (flapping material can hinder movement).

Unlike shirts, which are highly visible and often designed for the purposes of fashion, shorts are functional items and as a result cheap to buy. You can usually pick up a pair in a sports retail outlet for less than £5. Again, if you're buying for an entire team it pays to negotiate a bulk deal.

Make sure your shorts don't clash with your shirts. Although it's not against the rules to wear hideously clashing colours, it could cause you problems when playing other teams – if you wear red shirts and blue shorts you'll almost certainly have to change at least one part of your kit to avoid colour confusion during matches.

Boots

It's vitally important to get the right footwear: your boots are, after all, the ultimate tools of your trade. If you're playing football on grass you need a studded boot.

In the olden days, boots were big lumbering items, hard-leather clogs covering the ankle and a fair bit of the shin. Nowadays the designs are much lighter; the most expensive models slip onto your foot almost like a glove.

First things first: boots need to protect your feet above all else. Make sure the boots fit snugly, but aren't too tight. Most professionals prefer a snugly-fitting shoe because it allows them to feel both the ball and their feet on the ground.

An almost confusing array of designs is available. Narrow down the options by deciding what's best for you. Are you a fast-sprinting striker? Some boots are designed to be as light as possible, with speed and sharp movement in mind. Or are you a midfield enforcer? It may be best to choose a boot offering maximum protection because you'll be making a large number of tackles every game.

You may also want to take studs into the equation. Some cheaper pairs of boots have fixed studs or even moulded plastic studded soles. Others come with a selection of screw-in studs that you should change with a key depending on whether you're playing on hard, firm or soft ground.

Some boots are less performance related, with an eye on fashion: different colours from the usual black are popular, as are retro designs harking back to the 1970s and '80s.

You can get a decent pair of leather boots for around £30. The latest high-end designs can cost anything between £80 and £200.

There's no point buying an expensive boot if you don't play in matches regularly or you're not a particularly proficient player – you simply won't reap the benefit. Many of the cheaper pairs are still very well made boots that protect your feet and make your feet feel good. Remember that although the most expensive boots are obviously of high quality you're also paying a premium for design, manufacturer name and recommendations by famous players.

Trainers

You're allowed to play in training shoes, although without studded boots you may not get the traction you want from the ground. Trainers are also unlikely to offer your foot particularly good protection in a tackle.

You're best having a pair, though – especially if you're playing on hard courts, artificial turf or indoors, where you can't use studded boots.

India have only qualified for the World Cup once, in 1950, but withdrew after several of their players said they'd only play barefoot, which was against FIFA rules.

Shinpads

Shinpads – also known as shin guards – are compulsory. They drastically reduce a player's chance of serious leg injury. Two types of shinpad exist: a hard plastic guard, padded on one side, which fits down the front of your sock and in front of your shin; or a tightly fitting fabric tube, pulled onto the leg, with a guard sewn either into or onto the front, protecting the shin and also supporting the leg muscles.

The more basic, old-fashioned plastic guards cost around £10 for a pair, while the tight-fitting tubular pads cost between £15 and £30 for a pair.

Goalkeeping gear

Goalkeepers are a breed apart, and they need to look different on the pitch as well. This section tells you what you need to know about kitting out your keeper.

Shirts and shorts

Goalkeepers must wear a different-coloured shirt to the rest of their team for purposes of instant identification. Green or black are the traditionally preferred colours, although any colour is permitted as long as players can easily distinguish it.

Goalkeeping shirts are made with protection of the upper body in mind because the keeper has to dive around during the match. They offer more padding than a normal football shirt, especially on the elbows.

You can also purchase elbow pads to wear beneath the goalkeeping shirt, for extra protection.

Goalkeeping shirts are usually priced between £15 and £50.

Goalkeeping shorts, and long trousers, should have padding down the sides of the legs and, in the case of trousers, on the knees. Shorts cost marginally more than outfield pairs, at around £8 to £10, and trousers can cost between £15 and £30.

Don't skimp on quality for goalkeeping kit: make sure all items of kit have sufficient padding in order to keep your keeper injury free!

Gloves

Keepers wear gloves in order to protect their hands from blisters, cuts, ripped nails and other impact injuries. They cost between £20 and £60 – a decent set will probably set you back at least £40.

Just like boots on an outfield player, picking the right pair of gloves is a personal issue. Some keepers want extra padding; others may want extra feel. It's worth trying on a few different pairs to find the pair that fit like, well, a glove!

The referee

The referee's kit is supplied by the league or organisation that is running the competition. If you're refereeing in an informal, friendly match then you don't need any special kit, providing your shirt and shorts don't clash with either side and you have a pocket for your cards and whistle. Even so, you can buy kit especially designed for referees: shirts usually cost around £30, with shorts and socks £5 apiece.

Remember that a referee requires other tools of the trade:

- ✔ **Notebook, pencil and cards:** You need, at the very least, a scrap of paper and a pencil in order to record any bookings. You can buy bespoke referee sets for around £3, and wallets for between £5 and £10.

- ✔ **Stopwatch:** Referees need to time 45 minutes exactly, and may have to pause the clock for lengthy stoppages such as injuries. You can buy a sports timer cheaply at around £7; models with more features may cost between £20 and £40.

- ✔ **Touchline flags:** A set of two flags for the assistant referees costs around £10.

- ✔ **Whistle:** A simple plastic whistle costs around £2. You can pick up a more hard-wearing metal whistle for around £5.

Additional garments

Although not required by the Laws of the Game (see Chapter 4 for these), other items of kit that may be useful include:

- ✔ **Cap:** Outfield players aren't permitted to wear headgear, but the goalkeeper can wear a peaked cap to help him see long balls coming through the air when the sun is in his eyes.

- ✔ **Gloves:** These come in handy on particularly cold days. Long gone are the days when people would accuse you of being soft for wearing them!

- ✔ **Long-sleeved vest or T-shirt:** If your team's shirts are short-sleeved, you can wear a long-sleeved undergarment to keep your arms warm.

- ✔ **Sports bra:** Female players should wear a supportive bra while playing, to reduce the risk of damage to ligaments in the chest.

✔ **Tracksuit bottoms or leggings:** You must always wear shorts over them, but if it's cold you're permitted to wear tracksuit bottoms or some form of leggings. These are also recommended if you're playing on an artificial pitch, where slide tackling can lead to blisters and friction burns. Goalkeepers are allowed to swap their shorts for tracksuit bottoms.

✔ **Training bib:** A bib is a small coloured vest that you can wear over the shirt. You use them in training sessions, when the coach divides a squad of players wearing the same kit into teams for practice matches; one team wears the coloured bibs to distinguish it from the other.

Approaching Equipment

The ball isn't the only piece of equipment you need to stage a proper football match.

Goals and nets

If you're just having an informal kickaround in the park then throwing down a couple of jumpers for goalposts will do. But if you're embarking on a serious training session, or a full-blown match, you need proper goals.

An all-in goal frame locks together a set of posts, crossbar and *runback* (the poles that hold the net up behind the goal). The frames are fully portable and you can easily anchor them to the ground. Small sizes for juniors start at around £40 per goal and full-size league goals cost around £150.

You need nets to hang from them; these cost between £40 and £90 depending on the size of frame. You also need clips to attach the net to the frame; it usually costs around £5 for enough plastic clips to fix one net to a frame. You should also anchor the net to the ground with metal skewers; these cost roughly £5 a pack. Carrying bags for nets, clips and pegs usually come at an additional fee of around £10 to £15.

If you're responsible for the pitch furniture you also need corner flags and poles. A decent set costs around £50.

Check where you're playing before you invest in goals, nets and corner flags. There's a very good chance that all this equipment will come as part of the pitch rental fee and will already be there for you.

First-aid kits

You should always have a first-aid kit at a game or training session. You can cobble one together yourself but it's often easier (and not particularly more expensive) to buy a bespoke sports first-aid kit. Basic kits start at around £15, with bigger kits costing between £25 and £40.

A sponge bag is always handy to carry a sponge and ice onto the pitch; these cost between £5 and £7. And single-use ice or heat packs can help treat injuries; they cost around £1 each but you can buy more cheaply in bulk packs.

Training aids

A wide range of training equipment is available. The following are the most basic and common training aids:

- **Hurdles:** Useful for fitness drills and stride technique, different heights cost between £4 and £6 per hurdle.

- **Marker cones:** Perhaps the most essential training aid, you can pick up a set of 50 flat-disc plastic markers for around £10.

- **Passing arc:** Loops through which you pass balls, they cost around £5 per arc.

- **Slalom poles:** Used to improve dribbling technique, these spiked poles cost around £3 apiece.

- **Traffic cones:** More visible than marker cones, these usually stand a foot high and have a reinforced base. Five cost between £7 and £10.

Other kit and equipment

You can buy a few other items that you may consider useful:

- **Ball bag.** A nylon carrying bag for up to 20 footballs usually costs around £15. Unless you're a juggler as well as a football player, this makes your life a whole lot easier if you have more than two balls to carry.

- **Ball pump.** Essential if your football loses pressure. Sizes are usually universal but make sure the nozzle fits your ball or that you have an adaptor to make it fit. A pump only costs around £10, but if you have a lot of balls you may require an electric pump costing around £80.

  You'll need a ball pressure needle to measure the air pressure of the ball once it has been inflated. Footballs that exceed the recommended amount of pressure could result in injury.

✔ **Drinks bottle.** A plastic drinks bottle costs around £3. You can buy them in sets with carriers.

✔ **Tactic board.** You can buy magnetic wipe-clean whiteboards with numbered counters in a set, usually costing around £30 to £40.

Meeting Up with Merchandise

Football merchandising is now a global industry responsible for raising many millions of pounds annually for the world's bigger clubs. An amazing range of merchandise is on offer for the discerning – and not so discerning – fan.

Replica strips

Football shirts aren't only for playing in. Where fans once went to the games displaying their allegiance with a scarf bearing the club colours, nowadays they wear the team's latest top. All clubs sell replicas of their current shirts. You can buy those of the bigger clubs in the FA Premier League, Championship and Scottish Premier League in sports shops across the country; fans of smaller clubs must go to their club shop.

Up until the 1970s clubs rarely changed their shirts, perhaps updating their strip once a decade with the then slow-moving vagaries of fashion. (For example, v-necked collars were in vogue during the 1950s and round collars defined the 1960s.) Many clubs didn't even have a badge on their shirts. But during the 1970s kits began to carry distinctive embellishments and striking badges.

As a rough rule, clubs change the design of their home strip once every two seasons and change their away strip in the alternate seasons. The home strip always features the club's traditional colours but has enough significant changes in the design to make the previous strip look dated, thus encouraging a new purchase.

Shirts cost between £30 and £50 when they're released, but usually decrease in price during the second season of use. Replica shorts and socks are also on sale, though these are usually only popular in children's sizes.

Don't throw away your old shirt just because you've got the latest strip. Even if it's out of fashion now, tastes are cyclical – in 10 or 20 years' time it'll be a retro classic and possibly even worth some money to collectors! Check out the section 'Retro shirts' for more on the appeal of old-style kit.

Football fans usually buy the shirts of the teams they support, although some companies do a brisk trade in shirts of foreign teams, especially if the design – or even the team – is considered fashionable. The more obscure the team the better, because some fans love to show off their in-depth knowledge of world football!

Numbering and lettering

You can get the name and squad number of your favourite player printed on the back of your replica shirt. Some shops still charge by the letter – which means buying a shirt with Jan Vennegoor of Hesselink's name on it is a pricey affair – but many places now offer a flat fee. Shop around if the price you're quoted is much more than £10.

You can also ask the shirt printers to put your own name and number on the back of the shirt.

Retro shirts

Some fans eschew the modern in favour of classic kits of yesteryear. Retro kit manufacturers such as Toffs (www.toffs.com) offer a huge range of shirts, replicating designs from as far back as the 1800s. Supporters often buy shirts that are synonymous with a certain period of success for their club, that fans consider to be the one true 'classic' design of their club's shirt, that are fashionable or that have some retro-kitsch appeal. Shirts cost between £20 and £40.

One retro shirt that ticks just about all the boxes is the early 1970s Leeds United kit. The all-white shirt has a yellow-and-blue 'LU' badge, which looks like a smiley face. Many consider this shirt a design classic very much rooted in its time, and for fans this their most iconic kit because their best-ever side, the 1973/74 championship-winning team, wore it.

A burgeoning market in second-hand replica shirts produced since the 1970s also exists. Some shirts are very rare and can fetch up to £1,000!

Rightly or wrongly, many fans see retro kits – whether newly manufactured to old design specifications or old replica shirts – as a 'badge of honour' because they either show knowledge of a club's history or prove that the wearer has been a fan of the club for years.

Scarves

In the days before replica shirts became the norm it was de rigueur to wear a long woollen scarf with your club colours on it. (If you were an Arsenal supporter, for example, your scarf may be coloured red, or more likely striped red and white.) Scarf-wearing is now less prevalent, though still popular with some fans who consider the wearing of a replica kit childish or gaudy. You can buy tastefully striped retro scarves from many sports shops, online football stores and club shops. They cost between £10 and £30.

More modern designs, usually bearing the club name in large print, also sell in vast numbers. Some scarves even bear the name of two clubs. These are usually sold to commemorate big European games between two clubs who rarely play each other. Also, fan bases of certain clubs, especially across the England–Scotland border, have friendly but informal ties with each other: it's not uncommon to see Rangers and Chelsea scarves, or Liverpool and Celtic ones. (How close these ties really are can be illustrated by the fact that Celtic are also said to have informal ties with Manchester United!)

Other official merchandise

Clubs are happy to put their branding on just about anything, from quilt covers to bottles of cheap red wine. Some of the less tenuous merchandise offered by football clubs today includes kit bags, enamel badges, caps and hats, branded casual wear such as polo shirts and jackets, tracksuits, sports training gear . . . and footballs!

Knowing Where to Get It All

Most towns have at least one sports retail shop. Many boast several, including larger warehouse-sized hangars usually located in retail parks.

Most shops stock all the latest replica kit, as well as non-club-branded training and playing kit at competitive prices. Not all shops stock a wide range of training equipment – you may have to go to a more specialist retailer or hunt the products down online.

It's worth checking the adverts at the back of football magazines such as *FourFourTwo* for companies selling cheap team strips and training equipment. And of course you can find just about everything on the Internet: Google is your friend here.

For club-specific merchandise the club shop at your team's ground is the best place to visit. Larger clubs also have stores in the centre of their city as well as other towns across the country. Most clubs also have an online shop, which you can find through their official website.

Part II
Playing the Game

'Well, so much for the tactics for
next Saturday's match.'

In this part . . .

In this part, I start off by explaining the Laws of the game (that's *Laws*, not rules: it's a serious business). I also talk you through the different playing positions, and the various tactical formations that have been used through the history of football, and the ones that continue to be used to this day. I also explain in detail the skills you need to acquire in order to excel on the field.

Getting and staying physically fit for football is important, and I give you advice both on how to stay in the game for the full ninety minutes, and how to avoid and deal with injury. And if you who want to be a coach, or even set up your own club, this part describes the steps you need to take.

Chapter 4

Laying Down the Laws

. . . .

In This Chapter

▶ Getting to grips with the basic laws

▶ Everything that's allowed on (and off) the pitch

▶ Clearing up that most contentious of laws: offside!

▶ Other rules and regulations

. . . .

*T*he Laws of the Game – as the rules of football are officially known – may seem daunting to the beginner. The official FIFA (the world governing body) handbook runs to 140 pages!

But you really don't need to worry because the game is as basic as they come. The object of football is beautifully simple: to send a ball by foot, or any other part of the body except for the hands and arms, into your opponents' goal. And that's it!

Well, okay, not quite . . . but the rest is easy to pick up, I promise.

Living by the Laws

Under the auspices of FIFA, the International Football Association Board writes the Laws of the Game. The Board consists of members from the English, Scottish, Welsh and Northern Irish Football Associations, plus representatives of FIFA.

Every season the Board makes changes to the rules. Sometimes they're major changes, such as when it outlawed back passes to the goalkeeper in 1990. And sometimes they're minor alterations; for example, referees are often asked to crack down on a particular rule, such as time-wasting, diving or feigning injury.

The press, websites and television always highlight any changes before the start of a season or major tournament, so keep your eyes peeled.

The simplest game!

Here are the original rules of football, from which today's Laws of the Game are descended. They were written by a Mr J.C. Thring in 1862, and adapted by the nascent Football Association a year later.

The rules were for a sport called The Simplest Game:

A goal is scored whenever the ball is forced through the goal and under the bar, except it be thrown by hand.

Hands may be used only to stop a ball and place it on the ground before the feet.

Kicks must be aimed only at the ball.

A player may not kick the ball whilst in the air.

No tripping up or heel kicking allowed.

Whenever a ball is kicked beyond the side flags, it must be returned by the player who kicked it, from the spot it passed the flag line, in a straight line towards the middle of the ground.

When a ball is kicked behind the line of goal, it shall be kicked off from that line by one of the side whose goal it is.

No player may stand within six paces of the kicker when he is kicking off.

A player is out of play immediately he is in front of the ball, and must return behind the ball as soon as possible. If the ball is kicked by his own side past a player, he may not touch or kick it, or advance, until one of the other side has first kicked it, or one of his own side has been able to kick it on a level with, or in front of him.

No charging allowed when a player is out of play; that is, immediately the ball is behind him.

Much has changed since 1862, but the aim remains the same – to score more goals than the other team!

Law 1: the field of play

The field of play is otherwise known as *the pitch*.

The surface

You can play matches on natural surfaces, such as grass, or artificial ones, such as Astroturf (depending on the rules of the tournament).

The colour of any artificial surface must always be green!

Size, shape and markings

The *pitch* (the green bit in the middle) must always be rectangular, marked out with boundary lines. Check out Figure 1-1 in Chapter 1 for what the playing surface looks like.

The two longer lines down the sides are called *touch lines*. The shorter ones (on which the goals stand) are the *goal lines*.

The touch lines must be a minimum of 90 metres (100 yards) long, with a maximum length of 120 metres (130 yards). The goal lines must be a minimum of 45 metres (50 yards) wide, with a maximum width of 90 metres (100 yards).

Pitches for international matches are more rigidly defined: a minimum and maximum length of 100 metres (110 yards) and 110 metres (120 yards); and a minimum and maximum width of 64 metres (70 yards) and 75 metres (80 yards).

The pitch is divided into two halves by the *halfway line*, which joins the middle of both touch lines. In the middle of this halfway line is the *centre mark* commonly referred to as the *centre spot*. Around it is marked a circle with a 9-metre (10-yard) radius.

The *penalty area* surrounds the goal. Lines are marked starting out from the goal line, 16.5 metres (18 yards) either side of each post, and extending 16.5 metres (18 yards) into the pitch. These lines are joined by a line parallel to the goal line.

A *penalty mark* is drawn 11 metres (12 yards) from the goal, on an imaginary line drawn exactly between the two goalposts.

Flags are placed on each corner of the pitch, and at either side of the halfway line, not less than 90 centimetres (1 yard) outside the touch line.

The goal

The goal must be placed on the centre of each goal line. It consists of two upright posts, joined by a horizontal crossbar at the top.

The goal must be 7.32 metres (8 yards) wide, and 2.44 metres (8 feet) tall. A net must be attached behind the goal.

Law 2: the ball

Think any old ball will do? If you're playing an official match, please think again . . .

Properties

The ball, it surely goes without saying, must be spherical. It has to be made of leather or a similar suitable material, have a circumference no bigger than 70 centimetres (28 inches) and no smaller than 68 centimetres (27 inches), weigh between 410 grams and 450 grams (14 to 16 ounces) and maintain a pressure of 0.6 to 1.1 atmospheres (600 to 1,100 g/cm^2) at sea level.

What if it bursts?

If the ball becomes defective in any way then the referee must immediately stop the game and issue a replacement ball. The match is restarted either with a dropped ball, for which both teams can compete, or with a set piece or throw in if the ball was out of play.

Nobody can change the ball without the referee's say-so.

Law 3: the number of players

Two teams play matches. Each team consists of a maximum of 11 players, one of whom is the goalkeeper. Teams must have at least seven players or they can't play in the match.

(Teams rarely field fewer than the full 11 players from the outset. Should their squad be legitimately decimated by illness or injury, or some other extreme circumstance, a postponement is usually agreed. Teams often have fewer than 11 by the end of a game, though: players can be sent off for foul play, while injuries may outnumber the amount of substitutes allowed.)

Teams can make three *substitutions* during a match. A substitution occurs when a team brings a nominated substitute player into the game to replace one who was already playing. Teams can name between three and seven possible substitutes at the start of a match, depending on tournament rules.

To substitute a player, the assistant referee must inform the referee. This usually happens with the assistant referee signalling to the referee by holding his flag at both ends over his head. (For more on the roles of match officials check out the sections 'Law 5: the Referee' and 'Law 6: the Assistant Referees', later in this chapter. Figure 4-1 shows the signal the assistant referee makes.

Figure 4-1:
An assistant referee signalling an imminent substitution.

Substitution

Before the team can make a substitution, the referee must give the okay in a break in play – the team can't substitute when play is continuing.

The substitute – usually called the *sub*, for short – can only come onto the pitch after the player he's replacing has left it.

The player who's been substituted can no longer take any part in the game. It is possible to substitute the substitute!

Players are allowed to swap places with the goalkeeper, but only if the team informs the referee, makes the change during a natural stoppage in the game and the 'new' keeper wears the keeper's shirt.

Any attempt to substitute a player without the referee's say-so results in a booking for that player. Should a team play more than 11 players then the referee books the extra player(s) and then asks them to leave the pitch.

Law 4: the players' equipment

Players must wear the following basic kit:

- Footwear: boots or trainers
- Shinpads (which must be covered by the socks)
- Shirt with sleeves
- Shorts
- Socks

Colours

The two teams must wear colours that they can easily distinguish, to avoid confusion. They must also not clash with the referee's kit.

Goalkeepers must wear separate colours that distinguish them from both their team-mates and the opposition.

Safety first

Players must not wear, or use, equipment that could cause harm to themselves or any other player on the pitch. This means no jewellery – players must remove all bling. However, players can continue to wear items such as earrings or wedding rings, providing they cover these with medical tape.

Argentina's infamously thuggish Estudiantes side of the late 1960s used to take paper clips and small blades onto the field of play and poke them into opponents at set pieces and corners!

Law 5: the referee

Every match is controlled by a *referee*, a man or woman who has the power to enforce all rules of the game.

It's irrelevant whether players think a referee has made a right or wrong decision: the ref's decision can't be changed. 'The decisions of the referee regarding facts connected with play are final,' state the Laws of the Game. In other words, even if the ref's wrong, he's right.

If you're playing don't bother arguing with the referee's decision. A referee has yet to be born who's changed his mind, and you'll only end up in the book if you argue the toss too much.

Playing to the whistle

The referee is armed with a whistle, a stopwatch, yellow and red cards and a book and pencil. A blast on the whistle means the referee's made a decision, and play must stop. Referees whistle to start and stop the match, call fouls, award free kicks and penalties, book or send off players (the book and pencil!) or pause the game so that an injured player can be treated.

The referee also acts as official timekeeper for the match, hence the stopwatch.

Referees may look as though they're running around like headless chickens, but they usually jog diagonally across the pitch, hopefully covering all angles with the help of their assistant referees.

As I said, referees are always right, even if they're wrong. But sometimes they can be very, very wrong. In the 2006 World Cup English referee Graham Poll showed two yellow cards to Croatian defender Josip Simunic in a match against Australia, but failed to send him off! Simunic only got his marching orders when Poll issued him with a *third* yellow. Oops.

Changing his mind

A referee can only change a decision he's decided is incorrect – usually as a result of intervention by one of the assistant referees – if the game has yet to be restarted. If play has continued, the decision has to stand.

Law 6: the assistant referees

Assistant referees, formerly known as *linesmen* or *lineswomen*, run down the touch lines with flags in their hands, following the path of the ball. They provide the referee, also known as *the man in the middle*, with invaluable assistance.

Assistant referees help the referee by indicating:

- **When the ball has left the pitch:** In doing so they show which team has won a corner, goal kick or throw in. See the later section 'Law 9: the ball in and out of play' for the definition of 'out of play'.
- **When a player is offside:** See the later section 'Law 11: offside' for the intricacies of this thorny subject.
- **When a player is to be substituted:** See the earlier section 'Law 3: the number of players' for more on substitutions.
- **When they've spotted a foul:** Especially if the referee appears to have missed it.

Although not officially part of the Laws of the Game, many matches now have a *fourth official*. They take over many of the sideline duties from the assistant referees (such as substitutions), allowing them to concentrate on the action. They also take over from the referee or an assistant referee should they be unable to continue with their duties.

Law 7: the duration of the match

Football matches are always split into two equal halves, lasting 45 minutes apiece.

The half can be shorter if both teams agree prior to kick-off, but only if competition rules allow it. Which, invariably, they don't. Still, a rule is a rule!

The half-time interval

All matches have one, otherwise you wouldn't get two halves! The interval must be no longer than 15 minutes.

Half-times used to be ten minutes maximum, but over the years they were lengthened, primarily to allow television to show plenty of advertisements in the interval. This continues to be the subject of much speculation – constant rumours abound that intervals may grow to 20 minutes in length for commercial purposes.

At the end of the day . . .

After the 90 minutes are up the referee should bring play to a halt. However, he makes allowances for substitutions, injuries and time-wasting, allowing 'added time'.

On average, referees add on 30 seconds of time for each major incident. So if there have been three substitutions, one player treated for injury on the pitch, another carried off and one incident of time-wasting, the referee will add three additional minutes of play (6×30 secs).

In knockout competitions, such as the World Cup, a game that requires a definitive result may end drawn after 90 minutes. Should this happen, the match either goes to 30 minutes of extra time – played in two 15 minute halves – or straight to a penalty shootout.

Law 8: the start and restart of play

Although the 90 minutes start with a blast of the referee's whistle and a first prod of the ball with a boot, the very first act of a match is the coin toss.

The winner has the option of either kicking off or deciding which way to kick in the first half. In the second half the teams change ends and kick in the opposite direction.

Kicking off

Kick-offs start the match at the beginning of both halves. They also restart play after a team scores a goal; the side who's conceded the goal takes the kick-off. All players must be in their own half when the player takes the kick.

The player may score a goal directly from kick-off, though this has never happened in the professional game. It's illegal to kick the ball a second time without another player touching it – so don't dribble away with the ball from the kick-off!

Weather conditions can play a part in deciding which way to kick in the first half. If it's windy, teams might prefer to play against the wind in the first half, getting the hard part out of the way first. Dazzling sun can also play a part: defenders and goalkeepers hate to look into it because they can lose the flight of the ball, giving the attacking side an advantage.

The dropped ball

If the referee decides to halt the match while the ball is still in play, the game can only be restarted with a dropped ball. This takes place at the exact point the ball was when play was stopped. The referee allows the ball to fall to the ground from shoulder height. When it hits the floor it's back in play.

Usually, one team agrees to pass the ball back to the side that was in possession when play was stopped, but occasionally dropped balls are contested. When they are, it's usually each team's hardest tackler who gets stuck in, hoping to come out with possession!

Law 9: the ball in and out of play

Rules don't get much simpler than this: the ball is out of play if the *whole ball* crosses either the goal line or the touch line, whether rolling along the ground or flying through the air.

If *any part* of the ball, no matter how small, is level with the goal line or touch line, the ball is still in play.

The ball remains in play if it rebounds off a post, crossbar or corner flag. It's also still 'live' if it hits the referee (or one of the referee's assistants should they be on the pitch at the time).

Law 10: the method of scoring

This is what football is all about! A player scores a goal when the entire ball crosses over the goal line, between the goalposts, under the crossbar and into the net, whether in the air or on the ground.

The principle is the same as Law 9: if *any part* of the ball fails to cross the line, no matter how small, the player hasn't scored a goal.

Whoever scores more goals wins. If the teams score an equal number of goals, or no goals, it's a draw. In certain knock-out tournaments the match may then be decided by the away goals rule (in two-legged games), extra time and/or penalty kicks. Check out the section 'Other points to note', at the end of this chapter, for more on these means of settling games.

The most infamous decision regarding whether a ball crossed the goal line or not came in the 1966 World Cup final. With the scores level between England and West Germany in extra time, English striker Geoff Hurst swept a shot onto the underside of the crossbar. The ball bounced down, onto the line, and away, only for the linesman to signal a goal. Replays proved the whole ball never crossed the line, but as Law 5 explains, the referee is right, even when he's wrong!

Law 11: offside

Here's a guaranteed few minutes' worth of fun: go up and ask any football fan to explain the offside law to you. No matter how long they've been watching the game, I guarantee they'll tie themselves up in knots, and then change the subject.

It's possibly the most misunderstood law in the sport, but a bit of careful explanation will clarify this tricky rule.

Why do you need an offside law?

If the offside law didn't exist, players could just hang around the goals, waiting for the ball to be hoofed up to them.

So when is a player offside?

A player is caught offside if he's nearer to the opponents' goal than both the ball and the second-last opponent when his team-mate plays the ball. In other words, a player can't receive the ball from a team-mate unless there are at least two players either level with him or between him and the goal. Figure 4-2 illustrates the offside law.

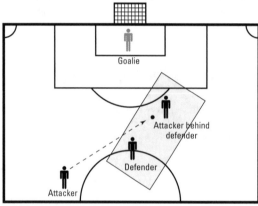

Offside

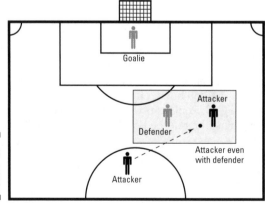

Figure 4-2:
Explaining
offside.

Onside

It is not an offence in itself to be offside. A player is only penalised for being offside if he is deemed to be involved in 'active play'. So a player can only be called offside if he is:

- ✔ In the opposition's half.
- ✔ Interfering with play (that is, he's part of the attacking move).
- ✔ Interfering with an opponent (that is, he's preventing the opponent from defending against the attacking move).
- ✔ Gaining any advantage by being in that position.

A player also cannot be offside from a goal kick, throw in or corner.

When calling an offside, the assistant referee holds his flag upright and then straight ahead of him. The referee awards an indirect free kick to the defending team from the place the offside occurred. Check out the next section, 'Law 13: free kicks', for the differences between direct and indirect free kicks.

The crucial phrase in this rule is 'when his team-mate plays the ball'. The key to beating the offside trap is to time the run forward properly so when a team-mate passes the ball forward the runner is still onside – but by the time the runner receives it he's running clear of the last line of defence!

In recent years the Laws of the Game have encouraged referees and their assistants to give the attacking side the benefit of the doubt. If any doubt exists, the referee won't whistle for offside. So referees often let marginal cases – players are sometimes millimetres offside! – go without punishment.

Law 13: free kicks

Hold on . . . what happened to Law 12? Don't worry, it's coming up next. But first, we're going to explain the difference between direct and indirect free kicks because they're extremely relevant to Law 12 and the awarding of fouls.

Types of free kick

You need to know one thing about free kicks above all else: they're either *direct*, or *indirect*. It's all in the name: if a player kicks a direct free kick straight into the opponents' goal, it's a goal! And an indirect free kick? For a goal to be scored, the ball has to touch another player before it enters the goal. You can either achieve this by passing it to a team-mate and allowing him to have a shot, or by a deflection, however slim, either off a team-mate or an opponent.

Here's a fact not widely known: if a team kicks either a direct or indirect free kick straight into their own goal, the referee doesn't award the opposition with a goal. Instead, the opposition get a corner.

Upon being awarded a free kick . . .

After whistling for a foul, a referee signals for a direct free kick by holding his arm out perpendicular to his body. See Figure 4-3 for how it's done. The referee signals an indirect free kick by holding his arm above his head, as in Figure 4-4. The rules to bear in mind are:

✔ The player must take the free kick from the exact spot the foul was committed. The player must wait for the referee to whistle again before taking the kick.

✔ The ball must be standing still before the player takes a free kick. After taking the kick, a player can't touch the ball again until another player touches it.

✔ A direct free kick awarded to the attacking team in the opposition's penalty area results in a penalty kick (see the later section 'Law 14: the penalty kick').

Figure 4-3:
Referee signalling for a direct free kick.

Direct free kick

Figure 4-4:
Referee signalling for an indirect free kick.

Indirect free kick

If a referee awards a free kick against a team, all that team's players must stand at least 9 metres (10 yards) away from the ball until it's kicked. The section 'Law 14: the penalty kick' tells you where to stand if the referee awards a penalty against you.

Law 12: fouls and misconduct

There are many types of foul but only two types of recompense for the victim: a direct free kick (or penalty, if it's in the penalty box) or an indirect free kick. I deal with penalty kicks (actually a type of direct free kick) in the next section, 'Law 14: the penalty kick'.

Offences resulting in a direct free kick

The referee awards a direct free kick for violent, aggressive or serious offences, such as when a player – either deliberately or clumsily – kicks, trips, charges, jumps at, strikes, holds or spits at an opponent, or handles the ball with his hand or arm.

The player takes a direct free kick from the exact position the offence occurred. If the referee awards a direct free kick in the aggressor's own penalty area, the team will get a penalty kick.

Offences resulting in an indirect free kick

The referee awards an indirect free kick for more technical offences, such as goalkeeping handling errors – goalkeepers aren't allowed to pick up or handle back passes from their own team-mates, or hold onto the ball for more than six seconds – or *obstructions* (when a player deliberately impedes the progress of another with no challenge for the ball).

The player takes an indirect free kick from the exact position the offence occurred. It makes no difference if the referee awards an indirect free kick inside the penalty area; it's still only an indirect free kick and the referee doesn't award a penalty kick.

Yellow and red cards

If a referee thinks a foul is worthy of punishing a player more than by simply awarding a free kick against his team, the referee has the option to caution or send off the player.

The referee awards a *caution* – also known as a *booking* – by showing the player a *yellow card*. This tells everyone playing and watching that the player has been cautioned. Figure 4-5 shows how this is done.

Figure 4-5:
Referee
issuing a
yellow card.

Issuing a yellow card

Players pick up yellows for unsporting behaviour, dissent, persistent minor fouling, time-wasting, encroaching at free kicks, corners or throw ins, or entering or leaving the pitch without the referee's permission.

If a referee shows a player two yellow cards he then shows him a red card and sends the player off. A player who's shown a *red card* is automatically sent off. He must leave the pitch and cannot return to the game. He can't be replaced by a substitute.

The referee shows a player a red card if he commits one of the following six offences:

- Deliberate handball to deny the opposition a chance to score
- Fouling to deny the opposition a chance to score
- Serious foul play
- Spitting at another person
- Using offensive or abusive language or gestures
- Violent conduct

Play on!

Just because a player commits a foul, it doesn't mean the referee will definitely blow his whistle and award a free kick. Referees can *wave play on*, gesturing for play to continue if they think the attacking team will gain an advantage by doing so. Figure 4-6 shows a referee waving play on.

If the referee waves play on, he makes an ostentatious sweeping movement with both hands. This shows he recognises a foul has been committed, but that he'll deal with it later.

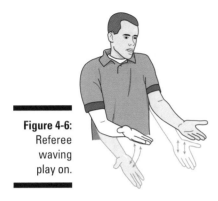

Figure 4-6:
Referee
waving
play on.

Play on

If a referee waves play on after a foul he may well award a yellow or red card when a natural break occurs in play. This could happen several minutes after the foul, depending on how long the game continues without the ball going out of play!

A team doesn't necessarily gain an advantage if a referee awards them a free kick for a foul. For example, a player may be hacked down but one of his team-mates may be able to pick up the ball and burst through on goal. Should the referee whistle for a free kick, the defending team will have time to get players back and organise their defence – and the chance will be gone.

Some players can go through their entire career without ever picking up a booking. The former England striker Gary Lineker played over 500 games for club and country without a referee ever showing him a yellow card.

On the other hand, many players have appalling disciplinary records: a referee once sent off the Aberdeen midfielder Dean Windass three times in one game for separate offences upon leaving the field *after* picking up his first red card!

Law 14: the penalty kick

A referee awards a *penalty kick* – usually referred to simply as a penalty – when a direct free kick is awarded against a team in their own penalty area. The main things to remember about a penalty are:

- ✔ A player may score a goal directly from it.
- ✔ The ball is placed on the penalty spot by a player who's identified to all as the intended taker.

✔ The goalkeeper must stay on his line until the ball is kicked, though he can move along the line beforehand.

✔ All other players must remain outside the penalty area and behind the penalty spot (on either side of the box). They may not enter the area until the player has taken the kick.

After the referee blows his whistle the penalty taker can – wait for it – take the penalty. He must kick the ball forward and can't kick it again until another player has touched it.

Obviously, the plan is to score directly from the kick. More often than not, that happens. But if the keeper saves the shot, the player – or any other on the pitch – is permitted to play the ball again, either in an attempt to score or to clear the ball.

If the ball comes back off the post or crossbar, the penalty taker can't play the ball again until another player has touched it. A team-mate, of course, is allowed to follow up and play it himself.

Players don't necessarily have to go for goal directly from a penalty. Ajax scored one of the most famous penalties of all time in 1982. Johan Cruyff, the taker, surprised everyone by rolling the ball to the left of the spot. As the shocked keeper ran out to claim it, Cruyff's team-mate Jesper Olsen rushed into the box and passed the ball back to Cruyff in the middle, who rolled the ball into the empty net!

Law 15: the throw in

The referee awards a throw-in when the ball leaves the pitch, crossing the touch line. Whoever put the ball out cedes possession; the opposing team gets to throw the ball back in.

The thrower must have at least part of both his feet touching the floor, either outside the pitch or on the touch line. He must throw the ball in using both hands, delivering it from behind and over his head. He must throw the ball in at the point it left the pitch. A player can't throw the ball onto the pitch and then play it himself – it has to touch another player before he can touch the ball again.

You can't score a goal directly from a throw-in.

It's crucial to throw the ball in correctly because players don't get a second chance. A foul throw concedes possession, and the opposition get to throw the ball back in instead.

Sheffield United striker Dean Saunders once scored an ingenious goal from a throw. Chasing a long ball with Port Vale keeper Paul Musselwhite, the goalie put the ball out of play and turned to run back to his goal. Saunders took a quick throw-in – off the back of the retreating Musselwhite! The ball bounced back to him and Saunders was able to curl it into the empty net.

Law 16: the goal kick

The referee awards a goal kick when the ball runs out of play over the goal line and the attacking team were last to touch it.

Either the goalkeeper or a team-mate takes the kick from anywhere within the goal area – the 6-yard box in front of the goal in the penalty. The ball must leave the penalty area before another player can touch it. No players, other than the kicker, are allowed in the area when the kick is taken.

If your keeper doesn't have a big or accurate kick, it's best to let one of the defenders take the goal kick instead.

You can score a goal directly from a goal kick, though this almost never happens.

Law 17: the corner kick

The referee awards a corner kick when the ball runs out of play over the goal line and the defending team were last to touch it.

The kicker must place the ball in the corner arc nearest the point where the ball crossed the goal line. The kicker isn't allowed to move the corner flag, and can't play the ball once kicked until another player has touched the ball.

Players can score goals directly from corners.

Other Points to Note

So those are the 17 laws of association football. But there are one or two other minor points to note.

Extra time

In the section 'Law 7: the duration of the match' I mention that matches last 90 minutes and either end in a win for one side or a draw. But in some tournaments a fixture must be decided one way or the other.

Should a game finish level after 90 minutes, the referee may add on extra time. Extra time usually consists of two periods of 15 minutes. At the end of extra time, whoever is ahead on goals wins. If the scores are still tied, a sudden-death penalty competition may take place.

Between 1996 and 2004 major tournaments such as the World Cup and the European Championship featured *golden goals* and *silver goals* in extra time. A golden goal resulted in an immediate win for the scoring team; a silver goal meant that team would win at the end of either extra-time half, providing the opposition didn't score an equaliser. Golden and silver goals were dropped after Euro 2004 because they were unpopular with fans.

Penalty shootouts

A penalty competition can settle matches requiring a winner that end in a draw or a draw after extra time.

Each team has five penalty kicks. Any player, including the goalkeeper, can take the kicks, providing he was on the pitch at the end of the game. Teams can't make substitutions after the final whistle.

The team who scores more penalties from their five kicks wins. If the scores are level, the teams take sudden death kicks, each team getting one kick apiece. The teams continue to get one kick apiece until one team scores and the other misses.

Teams don't always have to take all the initial five penalty kicks. For example, if Team A score their first three kicks and Team B miss their first three, it's impossible for Team B to win because they only have two kicks left and are 3-0 down!

Away goals

Teams sometimes play ties over two fixtures, home and away. Should the aggregate score – the total of all goals in both matches – be level after the second game, away goals may count as double according to tournament rules. So if a team draws 1-1 at home but drew 2-2 away, scoring more away goals than their opponent, they win the tie.

The technical area

In major – usually professional – matches, a designated area where managers and their assistants can sit or stand is marked out.

Managers aren't allowed to leave the technical area or encroach on the pitch. This is principally to ensure they don't get involved in unseemly arguments with the referee!

Common sense

Referees are technically required to follow the letter of the law, but some-times they turn a blind eye if it's for the greater good. Say a team is losing 5-0, there are two minutes to go and a player already on a yellow card commits a needless foul. A second yellow – and a sending off – is technically right, but the referee may not issue the card.

Some argue that the referee should still pursue a hardline policy, to achieve consistency, and perhaps they're right. But don't be surprised to see refs sometimes showing mercy on already defeated players!

Chapter 5

Players, Positions and Tactics

*F*our basic positions exist in football: goalkeeper, defender, midfielder and forward. Each has a specific duty to perform, although during the course of a match they all have to take on the responsibility of another position at some point. In this chapter I look at each position in detail, and see what players in those positions have to do and how they interact with each other.

Because the tactical approach of a team determines much of what a player is expected to do, I also look at how different tactics and playing styles affect the way in which games develop.

Perusing Positions

Nothing in football is set in stone. Depending on how a game pans out, a player picked as a striker may end the game dropping back to defend a lead, and the losing team's goalkeeper can sometimes be found in the dying minutes of a game going up to contest a corner in desperation!

But as a rule, players concentrate on their specific duties first and foremost. From back to front, the four basic positions are the goalkeeper and the outfield positions of defender, midfielder and forward. You can play each outfield position in many different ways.

The goalkeeper

The goalkeeper (often shortened to 'keeper') is the last line of defence. His job is to protect the goal and make sure the ball doesn't enter it. Each side has only one goalkeeper.

The goalkeeper holds a unique position in that he's the only player on a team who can handle the ball. He's only allowed to handle the ball inside his penalty area. If he does so outside the area, he runs the risk of receiving a red card. See Chapter 4 for more on red cards.

Goalkeepers aren't allowed to handle the ball in their own area if it's been passed back to them by a team-mate who's used his feet to do so. If a goalkeeper does handle such a pass the other teams gets an indirect free kick. The keeper can, however, pick up a headed pass or one played off any part of his team-mate's body above the knee, and do so without penalty.

Goalkeepers are allowed to play the ball with their feet, either on the floor anywhere on the pitch or volleying it from the hand – a drop kick – from inside their area. They can run anywhere on the pitch, but rarely make excursions from their area because this would leave the goal unattended, making it easy for the opposition to score. They're also permitted, like any other player on the pitch, to score goals.

A keeper has the following main responsibilities:

- ✔ Keep goal and stop any shots going in.
- ✔ Constantly organise and chivvy the team's defenders, giving them tactical advice during play (because the keeper, playing at the back, has the advantage of seeing the whole field of play).
- ✔ Organise his team in the defence of free kicks and corners.
- ✔ Collect crosses and passes forward before opposition players can get to them.
- ✔ Take goal kicks and free kicks from inside his own area (or often anywhere in his own half of the field).
- ✔ Distribute the ball to team-mates quickly and efficiently, by either throwing or kicking the ball, in the hope of setting his side on an instant counter-attack.

Keepers effectively have three means of stopping the opposing team scoring a goal: use their hands to stop the shot – parrying it back out into play, tipping it away from goal or holding onto it; hack it clear with their feet; or somehow block it with any other part of their body, usually by spreading themselves as big as possible.

The back-pass rule

In days gone by defenders were allowed to pass the ball back to their keeper, whereupon the keeper was allowed to pick up the ball. Not only did this lead to some strange additional rules – keepers were then required to bounce the ball on the ground every four steps if they wanted to walk around their area with it in their hands – but it also produced negative football. If a team was under pressure at the back, they'd simply give the ball back to their keeper and the danger would be over.

After the 1990 World Cup, which many regarded as the dullest of all time, FIFA decided to speed up the game by introducing the back-pass rule in 1992. This meant goalkeepers could no longer pick up back passes from their own defenders.

If the ball is rolled back to them by a team-mate using his feet, goalkeepers now have to play it with their feet or give away an indirect free kick close to goal.

As a result keepers have had to become far more adept with their feet than goal custodians of generations past. To this day most keepers choose to take no chances upon receiving a back pass, hoofing the ball high up the pitch, turning defence into attack, or into the stands, allowing the defence time to regroup. Some keepers take pride in their footballing skills, however – and crowds always enjoy seeing their keeper roam from his box and outfox an opposition striker.

Keepers must wear distinctive clothing that marks them out from their team-mates, all opposition players and the referee. They can wear padded gloves and are allowed to wear peaked caps – to keep out the sun, making it easier to claim balls dropping from the sky – or padded head-guards.

Teams must field a goalkeeper at all times. So if a goalkeeper is unable to continue through injury or is sent off, they must be replaced by a substitute goalkeeper (who'd either replace an injured keeper or outfield player in the case of the original keeper being sent off). However, if a team has no substitutions left then one of the team's outfield players has to stand in goal.

In general, keepers consider safety first and as a basic rule position themselves in the middle of the goal, in front of the net. However, while their own team is attacking and the ball is in the other half of the pitch, they often wander around their area, sometimes even venturing outside it.

Goalkeepers need to keep their concentration. They could feasibly spend the majority of the match doing absolutely nothing, only to suddenly find the opposition suddenly attacking strongly.

Sometimes, if the opposition breaks quickly upfield after a long ball, leaving defenders in their wake, a goalkeeper rushes out from his area to hack the ball clear before any opposition player can get to it. He is effectively acting as a last-ditch defender, one example of when a player helps out a team-mate in another position.

A numbers game

All players on the pitch has to wear a numbered shirt, to enable the referee – and at professional level, spectators – to identify them.

The methods of numbering have changed over the years since the legendary Arsenal manager Herbert Chapman – and his friend and Chelsea counterpart David Calderhead – introduced them in 1928. On 25 August that year, the Arsenal and Chelsea pair persuaded the teams they were up against – Sheffield Wednesday and Swansea Town respectively – that the players should run out in shirts numbered 1 to 22.

The Football League ordered the teams to stop the practice immediately, considering numbers on the back of shirts a desecration of club colours. But the idea caught on: at the 1933 FA Cup final between Everton and Manchester City, the idea was given another run-out, in order to help BBC radio commentators. Everton wore 1 to 11, City 12 to 22.

Eventually, after the Second World War, a new system of numbering – 1 to 11 for each team – was introduced across the board. Because teams were printed in match-day programmes on a diagram according to their positions on the pitch, numbers were assigned so they read logically across the pitch. 1: goalkeeper; 2 and 3: full-backs; 4, 5 and 6: half-backs; 7, 8, 9, 10 and 11: forwards.

As tactics changed the numbers switched around gradually, but the principle remained the same. It all changed with the advent of the FA Premier League in 1992, when squad numbers were introduced – along with the players' surnames on the backs of their shirts.

Although size isn't always a determining factor in picking a goalkeeper, it's rare to see a team fielding a keeper under 1.8 metres (6 feet). In fact, even 1.8 metres (6 feet) is now seen as an under-average height for a keeper, with many of the top teams fielding players of 1.9 metres (6 foot 6 inches) and above. However, there's one disadvantage of being too tall – it takes a split second longer to get down for low shots!

As the last line of defence, a mistake by a goalkeeper usually ends up in the opposing team scoring a goal. This means the stakes for goalkeepers are high – as are the levels of criticism when things go awry. As a result, keepers have to grow a thick skin and have the sort of mental strength that allows them to put mistakes firmly in the past. This is easier said than done, even at the top level of football, where a single mistake in one match has defined many great professional goalkeepers' entire careers.

Great goalkeepers include Lev Yashin (USSR), Gordon Banks (England), Dino Zoff (Italy), Peter Schmeichel (Denmark), Sepp Maier (Germany) and José Luis Chilavert (Paraguay).

Defenders

The job of a defender is to play in front of the goalkeeper and put a stop to attacks from the other side. If the defender can't stop the attack altogether then his next responsibility is to at least slow down the attack, giving team-mates time to come back and assist.

Over the years defenders have become more and more important to the game. In football's infancy, teams usually fielded seven attackers, with only three outfield players stationed in defence and midfield. Nowadays much has changed, with teams rarely fielding fewer than four defenders (who are undoubtedly supported by at least one defensive midfielder – see the later section 'Midfielders' for more).

A defender usually has a specialist position, although he's often able to play in any position along the back line. Primarily, two types of defender exist: *central defenders* and *full-backs*.

Usually, a team picks four defenders – a left-sided full-back (known as a *left back*), two central defenders and a right-sided full-back (the *right back*). Broadly speaking, central defenders concentrate on defending the area directly in front of the goal, while the full- backs deal with attacks down their respective flanks. Teams may play tactical variations on this theme – usually an extra central defender as part of a back five (or a back three if the full-backs are then instructed to push further forward) – but more often than not in modern football teams place four across the back.

Defenders either play a *man-to-man marking* game or a *zonal defence*. The former sees him follow a particular player closely, tracking him during the game. The latter technique sees defenders pick up players when they come into the particular area, or zone, they're patrolling.

Both tactics have pros and cons. Man-to-man marking keeps things simple, but depending on the opposition, mismatches of speed, strength, height, talent or experience can occur, putting the defender at a disadvantage. Zonal marking takes such pressure off individuals, but requires greater concentration and communication – if two players go for the same opponent, another may be left free to score.

Central defenders

The central defender's job is to patrol the central areas of the defensive third, attempting to stop opposition attacks. He can do this by tackling opposition players, harrying them into making mistakes, winning headers or intercepting passes.

The central defender usually plays as one half of a two-player central defensive partnership. Both central defenders have essentially the same remit, although the two players usually have slightly different skills that complement each other.

Often one of the two central defenders is dominant in terms of height and strength and the other is a more assured ball player and is perhaps a quicker and more mobile runner. This combination theoretically covers all bases: the partnership will not be outmuscled by a tall, strong, bustling striker, and neither will it be caught flat-footed by a nippier and more wily opponent.

For example, the central defensive partnership at Manchester United in their 2008 Champions League winning season was between Rio Ferdinand and Nemanja Vidi⊠. Vidi⊠ had a reputation for being totally dominant in the air, able to head the ball clear easily and strong in the tackle. Ferdinand's game, meanwhile, was more cerebral, dependent on clever positioning. Ferdinand was also the pacier player, able to cope with fast attacks, and a confident passer of the ball, able to set his team off on counter-attacks of their own.

Because they're usually some of the tallest players on the pitch – indeed, the very tallest – you often see central defenders heading into the opposition penalty area to contest corners or free kicks, with a hope of scoring. Central defenders can amass a decent tally of goals per season doing this, the best often scoring ten goals or more per season.

Full-backs

A defensive line usually features two full-backs, one on either side of the central defensive partnership. The one on the left is known as the left back and the one patrolling the right wing is known as the right back.

Their roles are to defend the respective flanks of the pitch from attack. As a broad and basic rule, full-backs don't move from their flanks, though in practice they often cut inside to assist their central defenders should they be pulled out of position.

Full-backs are also increasingly asked to assist in attacks, working in tandem with the midfielder or winger ahead of them on the pitch. They push upfield, offering support to their team-mates and making runs ahead of them down the wing, giving the attackers another passing option. This is known as *overlapping*.

Full-backs who overlap many times during a match may have been given a more attacking remit, and are often referred to as *wing backs*. When full-backs or wing backs are given scope to roam up field, teams often compensate by adding a third central defender, either as part of a back five or 3-5-2 formation (two of the five midfielders, the wing backs, drop back into defence when required).

The captain

All teams name one player as captain. The role of captain carries official responsibilities: he must participate in the coin toss at the start of the match to decide who kicks off and choose ends, and any coin toss prior to a penalty shootout.

Captains also communicate with the referee during a game: should a team regularly break the Laws of the Game in some respect, a referee will have a word with the captain, asking him to sort out the behaviour of his team.

The captain should be the strongest willed, most dominant player on a team. He's expected to encourage or chide his team-mates when necessary, perhaps even making minor tactical changes while play is running.

More often than not, captains are either defenders or midfielders, because players in these positions can see what's going on around them and affect it directly. However, well-respected attackers and goalkeepers have been known to captain sides – 40-year-old goalkeeper Dino Zoff captained Italy's 1982 World Cup winning team.

Captains are usually also one of the more popular players with the crowd, allowing a bond to develop between the support and the team.

Perhaps the most effective attacking full-back of recent years has been Paolo Maldini, who patrolled the right flank for both AC Milan and Italy between 1985 and 2009. He holds the record for the quickest ever goal scored in a European Cup final – 51 seconds against Liverpool in 2005.

Sweeper

A sweeper is effectively a third central defender, though one with a free-floating remit. The two other central defenders may cover either particular opponents or areas of the pitch, but the sweeper is allowed to roam as he sees fit – 'sweeping up' any loose balls and dealing with any difficult situations. To do this, he plays just behind the central defensive pairing, where he can see all the play unfold in front of him.

Extremely talented sweepers possess such good passing skills, dribbling ability and tactical awareness that they're the star players in their team, dictating the way a team plays. In effect, they end up taking the role of playmaker – historically a midfield or attacking role. So difficult is this combination, however, that it doesn't happen very often.

Two of the best exponents of this art were both German internationals. Franz Beckenbauer had the ability to saunter straight down the middle of the pitch almost at will, winning the 1974 World Cup with West Germany and three European Cups with Bayern Munich. Matthias Sammer reprised the role for Germany at Euro 96, where he ran the show from the back of the park and was unquestionably the player of the tournament.

Midfielders

Midfield is the most important area on the pitch, where games are effectively won and lost. Lose control of the midfield and your defence will be over-run. Win the midfield battles and your side will have a platform from which to launch attack after attack and dominate the game, or shut down opposition attacks, frustrating their attempts to score while you run out time.

Several different types of midfield player exist, and not all of them can play together in the same midfield. Midfielders can attack or defend, create or destroy, play near the front or the back, on either wing or with a floating role.

Usually – but by no means exclusively – a team fields between three to five midfielders. A general rule of thumb is that a team with three midfielders plays them all in the central area; a team with four plays two in the centre and one on each flank; and a team with five plays as a team with four, but with an extra free-floating player.

Central midfielder

The central midfielders are often the most crucial players on the park. Their remit is to attempt to control the game, helping out the defence when required and the attack where possible. The most fit and active central midfielders, who are able to run all around the pitch for 90 minutes without tiring, contributing to both attack and defence, are known as *box-to-box midfielders*. Top-quality box-to-box midfielders are as adept at executing a crunching tackle as a sweet 40-yard pass.

Most central midfielders, however, concentrate on one job above all else. They often operate as a partnership with at least one more central defender: usually there's a defensive central midfielder and a more attack-minded partner.

The defensive midfielder patrols the area just in front of his defence, acting as a stopper. He breaks up opposition attacks, harries and hounds opponents and does anything it takes to win the ball – before giving it to a more creatively minded team-mate, often his central midfield partner.

The attacking central midfielder dictates the pace and direction of play, instigating attacks by either passing the ball around to better-positioned team-mates or making runs forward with the ball. He's likely to be a frequent goal-scorer, good free-kick taker and confident dribbler.

Attacking central midfielders are often known as *play-makers* for their ability to change the shape of a game. However, the definition of a play-maker is fairly loose: deep-lying forwards are also often referred to as play-makers, with the line between both positions blurred!

Play-makers (or Number 10s, or *fantasisti*...)

They could be central midfielders, attacking midfielders, even sometimes wingers or strikers, but play-makers are always one thing: head and shoulders above the rest of their teams in terms of ability.

Play-makers are the ones, through their passing and dribbling skills and tactical vision, who can dictate how a match develops. They're the focal point of their side, and are usually so dominant that when they have a poor match their entire team plays poorly. On the other hand, when they play well they can drag any old rabble to victory (as Diego Maradona proved with a very average Argentina side at the 1986 World Cup).

Play-makers are often known as Number 10s – even if, in the days of squad numbering, they may not actually wear that number. That's because nearly all of the great play-makers have worn 10 on their back. Here are ten great Number 10s: Diego Maradona, Pelé, Ferenc Puskás, Gianni Rivera, Sandro Mazzola, Michel Platini, Roberto Baggio, Dennis Bergkamp, Zinedine Zidane... and the only one on this list currently playing today, the Brazilian women's star Marta.

Wingers (or left-and-right-sided midfielders)

In the old days on either side of the pitch in midfield teams fielded *wingers*. Their job was to take up the ball in the middle of the park, race down the touch line and, with a combination of tricky ball skills and pace, beat the full-back and send a dangerous cross into the box. They had little or no defensive responsibilities whatsoever.

However, in the modern game even the most talented wingers – such as Real Madrid's Cristiano Ronaldo – require other strings to their bows. Players positioned on the left and right wings still need to try to beat their man, but they must also be able to link up with their central midfielders, interchanging with them as play unfolds. They also have to track back and assist their full-backs in defensive duties.

Midfielders are usually the fittest players on the pitch because their workloads are – in theory – greater than anyone else's.

Midfielders of all persuasion – but especially central attacking midfielders – are increasingly expected to chip in with a large number of goals, taking some scoring responsibility off the shoulders of the strikers. England under Fabio Capello illustrate this tactic, with starting strikers such as Emile Heskey scoring rarely – but often setting up marauding midfielders like Frank Lampard and Steven Gerrard to hit the net themselves.

Strikers

The job of a striker – or a forward – is to either score goals or help their team-mates score. Modern teams usually field between one and three strikers, with two the most common number but one becoming increasingly common.

Strikers usually work best in a partnership. Teams can field any attacking combinations of centre-forward, deep-lying forward, attacking midfielder or winger.

If a team fields one striker their remit is usually to hold the ball up for midfield runners to come and join in the attack. The striker obviously also looks to score himself, but it's increasingly less important for him to do so – providing the midfield runners score enough goals!

Centre-forward

The centre-forward – also known as a *target man* – spearheads the attack. He receives forward passes, wins headers and keeps possession of the ball – called *holding the ball up* – in order to bring team-mates into play.

Centre-forwards are usually tall and/or physically strong (though exceptions to this rule exist). A top-quality centre-forward expects to score around one goal every other game. However, increasingly a centre-forward's first responsibility is to keep attacks going, bringing other players into the game. He should still notch a healthy number of goals, but providing the team is scoring and the centre-forward is an integral part of that, modern coaches are less concerned about a striker's personal tally. (Fans, however, don't always see it that way, and can give non-scoring strikers some fearful stick.)

Centre-forwards usually work best with a partner. Often the most effective partnerships consist of players with contrasting abilities: tall and small, powerful and mobile, direct and tricky. One of the all-time classic centre-forward partnerships in English football was the one between Kevin Keegan and John Toshack for Liverpool in the 1970s: Toshack was a tall, strong battering ram and Keegan nipped around his feet, bustling and causing havoc.

Deep-lying (or second) striker

A deep-lying striker isn't expected to hold the ball up, but drops back, either into central midfield, onto the wings or into what's known as *the hole* between the opposition defence and their midfield. This 'hole' is difficult to define in practice, but in theory is the part of the pitch where opposition defenders and midfielders are either unsure or unwilling to follow attackers. This gives the deep-lying striker time and space in which to make dangerous passes or take shots on goal.

Total football

In the late 1960s a new approach to football was born in the Netherlands – one which meant that no player (other than the goalkeeper) had a fixed role to play.

The theory was simple: a team would set out with ten outfield players in their respective positions, but after one moved out of position as the game unfolded another in the team would immediately replace him. This would move all along the chain: the player who'd moved into the first player's position would in turn be replaced by another – and so on. The system requires top-quality players throughout the team because each must have the ability to play in several different positions comfortably.

The Dutch national team who reached the 1974 and 1978 World Cup finals practised total football, as did the Ajax side who won three consecutive European Cups in the early 1970s. Johan Cruyff was the star man in both sides.

Hungary's famous 6-3 win over England in 1953 graphically illustrated the benefits of playing in the hole. Seen as a seminal moment in English football – when England realised they'd fallen behind the rest of the world – the game saw Hungarian striker Nándor Hidegkuti dropping between the English defensive line and midfield. With nobody tracking him, he was allowed to run riot.

One of the most effective deep-lying strikers of modern years was Dennis Bergkamp of Arsenal. As well as scoring his fair share of goals, Bergkamp was adept at sitting back, eventually drawing defenders out and passing the ball into space for centre-forwards such as Ian Wright or Thierry Henry, or attacking midfielders like Frederik Ljungberg.

Manchester United's Wayne Rooney often plays a similar role today, although he too can play the more old-fashioned centre-forward role.

Tactics: Linking It All Up

It's all well and good putting 11 players out on the pitch and giving them fancy job titles, but if they don't interact with each other there's little point anyone getting out of bed in the morning.

Dribbling: the first tactic

When organised football began in England during the 1860s the emphasis was firmly on individual play. Most teams sent their players out to *dribble* (run with the ball at their feet) around the field, each player attempting to work themselves into position to shoot at goal. With up to eight forwards on each side – they gave little thought or effort to defence – the game would ebb and flow up and down the field, players taking turns to embark on long, mazy dribbles.

But in the 1870s a new tactic began to evolve in Scotland. Instead of attempting to beat an opponent by dribbling around them, players simply cut them out by passing the ball to a team-mate standing in space elsewhere and then moved on. What seems obvious now was highly controversial at the time – some English sides thought it unsporting – but when the Scottish sides started to repeatedly thrash the English teams it became clear there was no going back: out-thinking your opponents was almost as important as beating them with the ball.

The main styles of play

At the risk of over-simplifying a game most coaches would have you believe is frightfully technical and complex, three basic styles of football exist. These are *possession football*, *counter-attacking football* and the *direct game*.

Possession football

The possession game is the hardest approach to take because it requires – by definition – keeping hold of the ball for lengthy periods of play. You achieve this by a high level of technical skill: impressive close ball control, accurate passing between players and good movement off the ball to give other players passing options.

Possession football isn't necessarily the most physically demanding style of play, because if executed properly the opposition players have to expend more energy chasing around for the ball and making challenges. Providing players from a side playing the possession game keep it simple – playing low-risk passes to team-mates in safe positions – the theory is that eventually a chance to launch an attack will open up because the tiring opposition make mistakes.

Most fans consider this style to be the most attractive to watch. A team playing top-drawer possession football may end up scoring a goal after a sequence of ten or more passes. A famous example of brilliant possession football was the goal scored by Esteban Cambiasso at the 2006 World Cup for Argentina against Serbia and Montenegro. Cambiasso applied the finishing touch to a stunning 24-pass move that made headlines all across the globe.

Counter-attacking football

The counter-attacking game is played by teams with confidence in their defensive abilities and pace in their attack. The idea is to either soak up attacking pressure from the opposition or harry them in midfield. After the opposition has committed players into attack, but has lost the ball, the counter-attacking team spring forward as quickly as possible, exploiting gaps left by the attacking side at the back.

The man who ruined football?

At 3.50pm on 18 March 1950 a former RAF wing commander called Charles Reep took a pencil and pad from the pocket of his overcoat and effectively gave birth to the long-ball game. For it was then – at half-time during a match between Swindon Town and Bristol Rovers – that he decided to undertake a statistical analysis of how goals are scored.

He soon found out that '85 per cent of goals tend to be scored from passing sequences that involve a small number of passes, usually three or less'. He argued that teams should adjust their styles of play accordingly, because this analysis proved that possession football was a waste of time.

Instead, Reep suggested teams should play *reacher passes* – a *reacher* being a 'single pass from the defensive third into the attacking third'. In other words, a long hoof.

Teams used Reep's methods over the years to varying degrees of success. Wolverhampton Wanderers picked them up in the mid-to-late 1950s, winning three titles in six seasons, although no long-ball team has won the English league since. Norway used the long-ball game in the early 1990s and reached two World Cup finals, at one point beating reigning champions Brazil twice in two meetings. Then again, England used a watered-down version of Reep's tactics at the same time, and failed to qualify for the 1994 World Cup finals.

Counter-attacking sides aren't necessarily the prettiest to watch because they spend long periods attempting to break up play. Having said that, when in full flight a counter-attack can be exhilarating to watch as they sweep the ball upfield.

Just because a team takes a counter-attacking approach, it doesn't necessarily mean they'll spend the match hoofing long balls upfield. They're as likely to pass the ball quickly up the pitch as taking a more basic approach. One of the top counter-attacking sides of recent times was Arsenal, who'd use the outrageously skilful Thierry Henry as an outlet to break up the pitch at speed.

The direct, or long-ball, game

Upon winning possession of the ball, teams playing a direct game quickly launch it upfield. Players pump long balls either directly into the opposing penalty box, where they hope the centre-forward will win the ball or cause mayhem, or into the far corners of the pitch, causing opposition defenders to turn and chase the ball, putting them on the back foot as attacking midfielders put the pressure on.

The direct game is based on power rather than technique, and can be tedious to watch. However, those who justify the style argue that it's successful – in the 1980s Graham Taylor took minnows Watford to a second-place finish in the English league, and the method allowed Jack Charlton to lead the Republic of Ireland to their first-ever major finals at Euro 88. Supporters of the direct game also point out that teams of limited skill can implement this style, and that not every team is able to afford the sort of players with the technical ability to execute a possession game.

The long ball game has always been reviled by football's more romantic figures. Brian Clough, the former Derby and Nottingham Forest manager, always tried to implement a pleasing-on-the-eye passing game, famously insisting that 'if God had meant us to play football in the sky, he'd have put grass up there'.

Formations

The term *formation* describes the way a team lines up on the pitch. Formations are usually indicated by a string of numbers giving the number of players in any roughly defined area of the pitch. So a 4-4-2 formation has four defenders, four midfielders and two forwards. The goalkeeper is never included.

1-2-7 (1870s)

This is thought to be the first formation in football history because previously players simply dribbled up and down the pitch in a very haphazard fashion. Three players stayed towards the back – one three-quarter back in the centre, two half-backs either side of him slightly further up the field – although their role wasn't particularly defensive minded because they were charged with firing long balls up the pitch to the front seven.

Those front seven players were divided into three groups – two wingers patrolling each flank with three centre-forwards in the middle. They fired short passes between each other in the hope of creating goal-scoring opportunities. The 1-2-7 formation is shown in Figure 5-1.

2-3-5 (late 1880s)

The better teams were beginning to run up cricket scores thanks to the advent of short passing, so eventually this system, shown in Figure 5-2, was introduced to counter it. Right at the back, two full-backs covered the defensive duties, assisted when required by two half-backs and a centre-back just ahead of them.

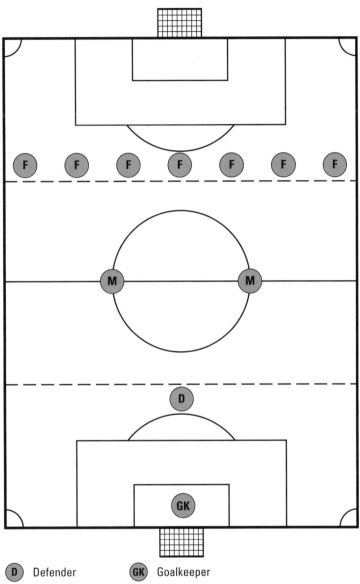

Figure 5-1:
The 1-2-7
formation.

D	Defender	GK	Goalkeeper
F	Forward	M	Midfielder

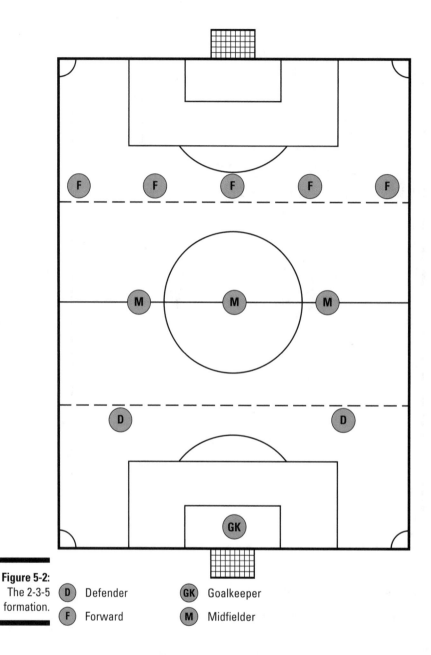

Figure 5-2:
The 2-3-5
formation.

D	Defender	**GK**	Goalkeeper
F	Forward	**M**	Midfielder

Now only five forwards existed – one winger on each flank, two inside-for-wards and one centre-forward – though the half-backs and centre-backs were allowed to move upfield to bolster the attack when required.

M-W (mid-1920s)

In 1925 the offside rule changed, which meant only two defending players had to be between the attacker and the goal, rather than three. This caused an immediate glut of goals, so teams countered by withdrawing more players into defensive positions as seen in Figure 5-3.

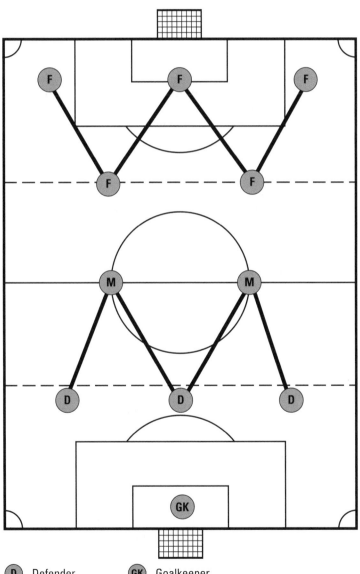

Figure 5-3:
The M-W formation.

D Defender	**GK** Goalkeeper
F Forward	**M** Midfielder

The M-W – so called because of its shape – saw a back line of two full-backs and a centre-back man mark the opposition forward and wingers. Wing-halves patrolled the space directly in front of the full-backs, and the inside-forwards dropped back from the very front line into a more withdrawn position, bolstering the midfield.

Herbert Chapman's Arsenal side in the mid-1920s popularised this tactic, with help from star striker Charles Buchan. Arsenal went on to be the dominant force in English football during the 1930s.

M-U (early 1950s)

The famous Hungarian team of the early 1950s, who won the 1952 Olympics and reached the World Cup final two years later, made a simple, subtle change to the MW. They pulled the centre-forward back into a withdrawn position, causing opposing defences no end of confusion. While the centre-forward pulled the strings from the hole between midfield and attack, the inside-forwards waited to advance into the space left by the withdrawn centre-forward.

Inside-forwards were previously expected to track back to help their defence when required. Now they were ordered to stay upfield, giving the team options to launch speedy counter-attacks. The MU formation is shown in Figure 5-4.

4-2-4 (late 1950s)

The M-U wasn't dominant for long. The flat back four was invented to deal with the spaces created by deep-lying centre-forwards and rampaging inside-forwards. The two central defenders marked the areas the inside-forwards were looking to attack, and were able to track the withdrawn centre-forward along with the help of their two team-mates in central midfield.

Meanwhile both full-backs were able to move up the pitch when required, in order to bolster the midfield and, occasionally, the attack, where four play-ers, two wingers and two centre-forwards plied their trade. This formation can be seen in Figure 5-5.

1-4-3-2 (early 1960s)

The 4-2-4 was an attacking response to the M-U problem, but Italy had found a different solution. *Catenaccio* – literally meaning 'padlock' – reigned for the best part of two decades. A flat back four was assisted by a sweeper, who patrolled just behind them, ready to snuff out any attacks. Three players in midfield were always on hand to drop back and further smother any opposition sortie.

The team was prepared to mobilise quickly in order to launch counter-attacks, but once a lead had been established the padlock snapped shut: 1-0 wins were the norm in Italy for years.

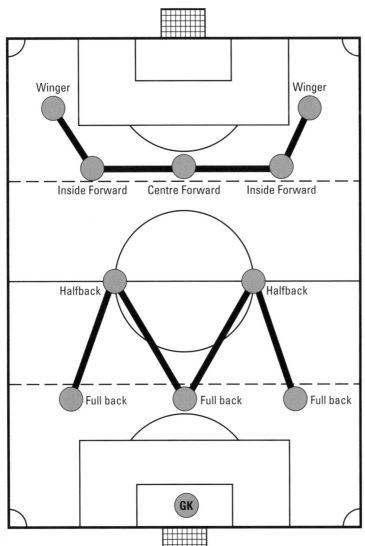

Catenaccio was first developed in Switzerland in the 1930s by the Swiss national coach Karl Rappan, although it was known as *verrou* – literally 'the bolt'. Internazionale coach Helenio Herrera refined the tactic over two decades later, his team winning back-to-back European Cups in 1963 and 1964.

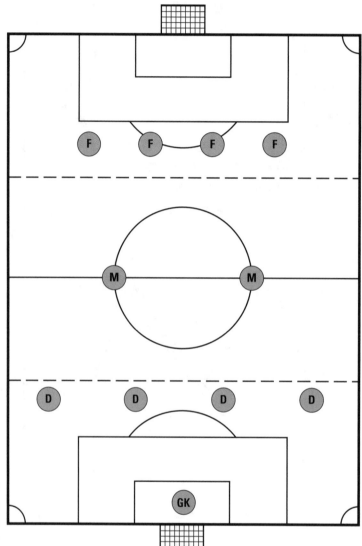

Figure 5-5:
The 4-2-4
formation.

4-4-2 (mid-1960s)

In the 1960s a more defensive mindset was developing and England became the first team to win the World Cup with a safety-first attitude. Alf Ramsey's 'wingless wonders' played four across the back with a defensive midfielder – Nobby Stiles – patrolling in front of them. The left- and right-sided midfielders also worked hard to track back defensively, leaving the attacking to a single offensive central midfielder – Bobby Charlton – and two centre-forwards.

The 4-4-2 (as shown in Figure 5-6) became the classic formation for the next three decades, and despite the current penchant for 4-5-1 (and variations thereof) is still the most widely used tactic today. Its popularity lies in its simplicity and solidity – it's easy for players to understand and execute.

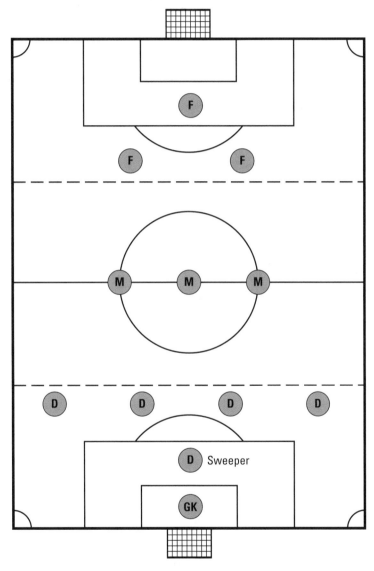

Figure 5-6:
The 4-4-2
formation.

Ⓓ Defender   ⒼⓀ Goalkeeper

Ⓕ Forward   Ⓜ Midfielder

4-4-2 (1980s)

Arrigo Sacchi's Milan side of the late 1980s dominated Europe with a variation on the 4-4-2. The back four operated as a line right across the field, pushing high up the pitch to catch opponents offside. With less space for the opposition attack to unfold in, the rest of the team then played a high-tempo pressing game, hunting down the ball and winning it back while expending as little energy as possible.

3-5-2 (1990s)

The 3-5-2 (as shown in Figure 5-7) was an attacking philosophy that became briefly popular in the 1990s and early 2000s. Teams set out with three central defenders at the back whom, it was hoped, would be able to deal with two forwards of a team playing the predominant defensive 4-4-2.

Should they require help, two attacking wing backs, effectively playing as wingers in a five-man midfield, dropped back to help. A defensive midfielder in the centre, playing just behind two more attack-minded central midfielders, was also on hand.

4-4-1-1 (2000s)

This formation – or variations on its theme – is arguably the most popular formation in use today. Essentially a more flexible version of 4-4-2, it was initially used to position a striker in the hole between defence and a one-man attack.

Increasingly, the player in the hole is an attack-minded goal-scoring midfielder, feeding off the knockdowns from the lone attacker. The 4-4-1-1 formation can be seen in Figure 5-8.

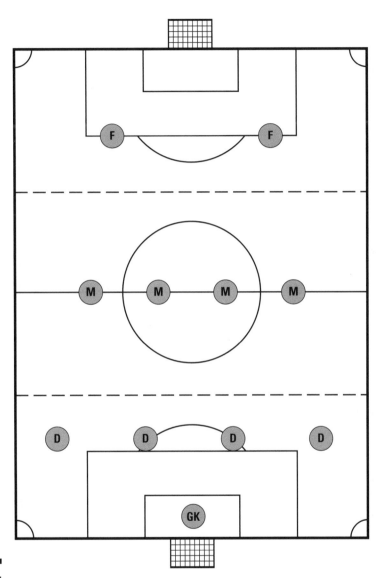

Figure 5-7: The 3-5-2 formation.

(D) Defender (GK) Goalkeeper

(F) Forward (M) Midfielder

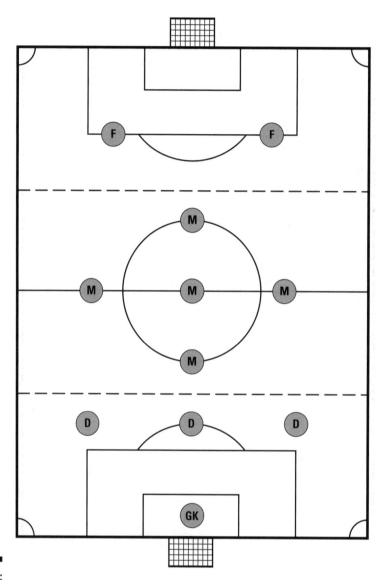

Figure 5-8:
The 4-4-1-1
formation.

D Defender	**GK** Goalkeeper
F Forward	**M** Midfielder

Chapter 6

Honing Your Skills

*F*ootball is the simplest of games to play: just put a ball on the ground, swing your leg at it and you're ready to go. The thing is, like anything else, if you want to be half decent at football you've got to put the hours in, first learning the basics and then embellishing the fundamentals with a few additional techniques. Remember, even Pelé had to spend hours every day practising his art in the street with a ball of scrunched-up newspaper – and if it was good enough for the young Edison Arantes do Nascimento, it's good enough for you.

So in this chapter I take a look at some of the skills you need to become a competent footballer, plus a few extra ones to make you a well-rounded player. I can't promise to turn you into the next Cristiano Ronaldo, or even the next Carlton Palmer, but even if you don't get to the very top you'll be able to enjoy playing the game for fun.

Mastering the Basics

It doesn't take long to acquire the basic football skills of ball handling, passing, receiving the ball, shooting and heading. If you concentrate on building a solid technique for each skill, you'll at the very least be able to join in matches or kickabouts without feeling embarrassed or out of your depth. And when you've gained the confidence to do that, the world's your oyster.

When football was in its infancy back in the mid-1800s there was only one way to play the game – take possession of the ball and dribble with it. Dribbling – another name for ball handling, ball skills or close control – is still the most important skill in football. So where better to start than at the beginning?

Up until 1872, when teams from Scotland worked out that passing the ball around saved a lot of time and energy, players would always dribble with the ball. Some teams fielded up to nine players up front, with only one man defending!

Dribbling

Ball control – the ability to run with the ball at your feet – is one of the most important skills in football.

It's initially a tricky skill to learn. As you'll have found out as a toddler, don't try to run before you can walk! In order to become acquainted with moving along with the ball at your feet, try the skill at walking pace first.

1. **Walk slowly along while bumping the ball forward with your instep – preferably using both feet if you can, one after the other. Keep knocking the ball about 0.3 metres (1 foot) ahead of you each time, roughly the distance of one or two paces.**

2. **When you're comfortable with Step 1, try nudging the ball along with other areas of your feet as well, the insides and outsides.**

3. **When you are happy with Step 2, pick up speed gradually. First walk briskly with the ball at your feet, working your way up to a light jog, then eventually a run. Never attempt to run faster than you can control the ball.**

While you're practising this drill, try to keep your head up. Don't look down at your feet and/or the ball if you can help it. When you dribble in a match you need to keep your head up to look around the pitch for team-mates to pass to, as well as keeping an eye out for opposing defenders.

If you have an open area of the pitch to run into, you can kick the ball farther ahead of you. This allows you to sprint more quickly. Conversely, if any opposing players are approaching you need to keep a closer rein on the ball. The closer an opposing player is, the closer you should keep the ball to your body.

Basic passing skills

Dribbling has never gone out of fashion in football – some of the greatest players in the modern era, from Diego Maradona in the 1980s to Cristiano Ronaldo now, have utilised superlative close skills in order to fox opponents.

But dribbling did quickly go out of fashion as football's premier tactic. In the 1870s teams from Scotland worked out that it was quicker and easier to pass around an opponent with the help of a team-mate than to beat the opponent with a dribble.

Ever since then passing has become the most important basic skill in football. A short, simple pass is required to keep a move going so your team can hold on to possession, and a longer pass is often the one that cracks open an opposing defence, sending a team-mate through on goal. Both are essential skills to learn.

Short pass

The short pass, delivered with the inside of the foot, is the most common technique for delivering a ball to a team-mate. It's also called a push pass because players use a long follow-through as they push the ball, stroking it towards their intended team-mate. You do it like this:

1. **Position the ball between yourself and his intended target.**

2. **Plant your non-kicking foot on the ground, approximately 6 to 15 centimetres (6 inches) to the side of the ball, and pointing towards the intended target. So if you kick with your right foot, plant your left foot down to the left-hand side of the ball, facing the player you're passing to. Make sure you slightly bend the knee: it shouldn't be locked!**

3. **Keep your kicking leg slightly bent. Take a short backswing then make contact with the middle of the ball just below your ankle, along the inside of your foot at the arch.**

4. **Follow through with your leg pointing towards the intended target. The shape of your body naturally ensures that the inside of the foot ends up facing the intended target of the pass.**

Long pass

A longer pass works on the same principles as the short pass, but you use the following steps:

1. **Plant your non-kicking foot slightly behind the ball, as well as to the side.**

2. **Make sure your kicking foot makes contact with the bottom half of the ball. By kicking the underside of the ball, it lifts off the ground, into the air, and travels longer distances.**

It's important to practise the accuracy of your passing, as well as making sure the ball travels the required distance. Players finding the ball missing to either side of the target may find they aren't following through properly but are stopping the kicking manoeuvre upon contact with the ball and 'snatching' at the pass. Imagine a line drawn between you and the target with the ball in the middle – your leg should travel straight along this path. Figure 6-1 shows a short, inside-of-the-foot pass, while Figure 6-2 shows a longer pass.

Figure 6-1:
A short
inside-of-
the-foot
pass.

Figure 6-2:
For longer
passes, kick
the ball with
your instep.

Trapping the ball

It's pointless knowing how to dribble and pass if you're not able to receive the ball and take up possession of it. You can use just about any part of the body to receive – or trap – the ball, apart from the arms and hands.

The idea is to gain control of the ball – whether it's bouncing, rolling or flying through the air, slowly or at speed – and keep it close to your body. The three most useful parts of your body are your feet, your thighs and your chest – but you can also trap the ball with your head.

Great players are able to 'kill the ball dead' – in other words, stop it moving in whatever direction it was heading and take it immediately under their control. Delicacy of touch is the crucial thing here. A good way to conceptualise this is to imagine an egg or a water balloon being thrown at you – and you must keep it from breaking.

Foot

To trap a pass or loose ball using the foot, a player should use the following method:

1. **Position yourself in front of the ball.**

2. **Extend your leg and foot out before the ball arrives, a few inches off the ground (roughly about halfway up the ball when it gets to you).**

3. **Pull your leg back as the ball makes contact with your foot, to 'cushion' it and retain possession. Think of it as 'catching' the ball with the instep, almost as though it's nestling in the inside arch of the foot. Keep your foot relaxed because this can help to control the pass, especially if the ball is travelling at speed.**

The more experienced player can use all parts of the foot to trap the ball, though it's normal – and easier – to concentrate on the inside of the foot.

If the ball takes an unexpected hop, either off a divot on the pitch or as a result of an imperfect trap, the leg helps control the ball providing you've used the inside of the foot (because the ball is being played close to the ankle). Figure 6-3 shows you how to trap a ball with your foot.

Figure 6-3:
Trapping a ball with your foot is an important skill.

Thigh

The thigh is a very effective tool for controlling the ball because it offers a large contact area. A player using his thigh should do the following:

1. **Position yourself in front of the incoming ball.**

2. **Stand on one foot, while raising the other knee and thigh to meet the ball. (It's easier to raise your preferred kicking leg, though good players can trap the ball easily with either.)**

3. **Cushion the impact of the ball as it hits your thigh, lowering the knee until the ball drops down to your feet. You may swivel your hips to pull your thighs slightly backwards as they cushion the ball.**

Keep the thigh as parallel to the ground as possible in order to retain possession of the ball. If you fail to do this, and the leg is at an angle, the ball has a much smaller contact area to hit and may ping away from you. Figure 6-4 shows the right and wrong ways to trap a ball with your thigh.

Chest

The chest is the hardest area of the body to receive the ball with, but once you have a solid technique it can be the most effective, pulling difficult passes and clearances out of the sky. Players must do the following to successfully trap the ball using the chest:

1. **Position yourself in front of, and square to, the approaching ball.**

2. **Puff out your chest just before meeting the ball.**

3. **Pull the ball backwards as it makes contact with your chest, cushioning the blow of impact. The ball should fall to your feet.**

Don't arch your back too much, because the ball could then rear up and bounce over your shoulder or head.

It will initially feel natural to bring your hands in front of your body, either to attempt to catch the ball or as part of an involuntary attempt to shield yourself from being hit by the ball. It's also tempting to use the upper arms to subtly cushion the ball. Both manoeuvres are illegal and will result in the referee awarding a handball foul against you. Figure 6-5 shows you how to trap the ball on your chest.

Figure 6-4:
The right and wrong way to trap the ball with the thigh.

Right   Wrong

Head

If the ball is high in the air, you can bring it down using your head.

1. **Make sure you are on the balls of your feet, able to either jump to meet the ball in flight or rise up on your feet towards it.**

2. **With your arms extended out to keep your balance, hit the ball gently on the hairline of your forehead, almost as though you're cushioning it.**

3. **Lean backwards. The ball should drop to your feet, or onto your chest or thigh, where you can further control it.**

Right   Wrong

Heading the ball

When the ball is high in the air, you need to play it using your head. You can do this in order to retain control, pass to a team-mate, make a defensive clearance or attempt to score.

It's easy to execute a header incorrectly. The last thing you want is for the ball to either skim off the top of your head or smack you straight in the nose. To head the ball properly:

1. **Face the incoming ball.**

2. **Assess the flight of the ball and time your leap into the air so you'll be heading the ball at the highest part of your jump.**

3. **Keep your eyes open and fixed on the ball while keeping your mouth closed. Your eyes should never be closed before the point of impact.**

4. **Head the ball using the hairline of your forehead. Do this while stiffening your neck and chest muscles and thrusting your body forward from the waist up, driving the ball towards the intended target.**

The major principles of heading remain the same whether a player is crashing a header towards goal or cushioning a soft-headed pass to a team-mate. Adjusting the power in your drive forward is the key.

Players attempting to head the ball towards the ground should head through the top half of the ball. Players hoping to make a clearance want to head the ball long and high into the air, so should head below the middle of the ball. Figure 6-6 shows you how to head the ball correctly – and how not to.

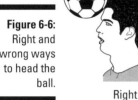

Figure 6-6:
Right and
wrong ways
to head the
ball.

Right   Wrong

Shooting

Shooting is, without doubt, the most enjoyable aspect of playing football. The natural instinct when taking a shot is to hit it as hard as you can – and punt it with your toes. Sadly, the natural instinct isn't always the right one.

The rules of taking a shot using the most basic kick – the instep kick – are much the same as a short pass, and are as follows:

1. **Pick out a target. Decide where in the goal you want the ball to head for.**

2. **Plant the non-kicking foot alongside the ball, pointing at the target.**

3. **Keep your head and eyes over the ball.**

4. **Hit the middle of the ball with the instep of your kicking foot.**

5. **Follow through towards the target.**

Power isn't always important – in certain circumstances good players choose to 'place' their shots with care, sometimes rolling them delicately towards goal – but as a general rule, especially for beginners, some semblance of power is required in the shot.

It's easy for a player to forget two fundamentals that result in the loss of shooting power:

✔ **Keep your non-kicking foot planted right next to the ball.** When you do this you naturally approach the ball from a slight angle, and the resulting hip rotation when you kick, pivoting around your standing leg, generates extra power. If your standing foot is behind the ball you lose much of this power, and may even accidentally toe-punt the ball instead, which also loses shooting accuracy.

> ✔ **Remember to follow through when you've connected with the ball**. If you don't do this, stopping on impact, you've been decelerating before you even kick the ball, thus losing power.

Volleying

You don't take all shots with a stationary ball, or a ball that's rolling along the ground. You can also shoot a ball in the air before it touches the ground – this is called a *volley*, and is the most spectacular way to score.

Volleying is technically an advanced skill, but one that's required so often in a match that you need to master it if at all possible.

1. **Assess the flight and direction of the ball.**

2. **As the ball flies towards you, get the knee of your kicking foot over the ball, with your toes pointing down.**

3. **Take a short, sharp stroke at the ball. (You don't need to swing wildly because the speed of the flying ball supplies the power to the shot.)**

4. **Make contact just above the centre of the ball. Hitting below the ball will cause it to balloon into the air.**

You can also use volleying to pass to your team-mates, but this is an even more advanced technique that you should save for a later stage in your development.

Keeping It Tight at the Back

Defending is ultimately an act of destruction. Football is, when you boil the bones down, about scoring goals, and defenders try to stop that happening. However, you still require top skills to defend properly.

Although defence is less glamorous than attack, it's arguably more crucial. Teams with poor attacks have been known to win cups and titles, but teams with terrible defences almost never do.

Marking

Marking is when a defending player puts himself between the attacking player and his own goal. The object is to guard – or *mark* – an attacker, in order to prevent him from dribbling or passing the ball nearer to the goal, or shooting for goal. If you can't stop the attacker – by dispossessing him or forcing him to run out of play – then you must at least slow his progress.

You have to consider three points when marking an opponent:

- **Stay close.** The closer a defender is to an attacker, the harder it is for the attacker to use the ball constructively, whether he's trying to dribble, pass or take a shot.

- **Be aware of the ball.** It's no use a defender being between an attacker and the goal if he has no idea where the ball is.

- **Notice the attacker's tendencies and foibles.** When you spot an attacker's favoured techniques it's easier to mark them. If he always dribbles with his right foot, for example, a slight adjustment in your positioning may cause him difficulties. If he always plays to one side, you'll find it easier to intercept the ball.

Tackling

Being able to dispossess your opponent is crucial – if your team doesn't have the ball, you're going to find it very hard to avoid defeat.

Block tackle

A defender uses this tackle to dispossess a player who's dribbling the ball towards you. In order to execute a successful block challenge, the defender moves directly towards the player and uses the weight of his entire body to tackle the opponent. The defender blocks the ball by applying steady and even pressure to it with the inside of his leg, the foot staying on the surface of the ball at all times.

Going into a block tackle, the player should plant one foot ahead of the tackling foot and then move in. He should be slightly crouched, enabling the player to react to any sideways movement the attacking dribbler may make. And it's important that the player concentrates on attacking the ball with his foot – ensuring the attacker isn't fouled but can't progress or keep hold of the ball. Figure 6-7 shows you how to execute a block tackle properly.

Shoulder tackle

A defender uses a shoulder tackle when he finds himself running alongside the player in possession. The idea is to use the weight of your shoulder to lean into the other player, easing him off the ball.

Try to get slightly ahead of your opponent when making the challenge. This allows you to ease in front of him with your shoulder, forcing him behind you and off the ball. Figure 6-8 shows you a well-executed shoulder tackle.

Figure 6-7:
The block
tackle.

a   b

Figure 6-8:
A well-
executed
shoulder
tackle.

a   b

Side tackle

Instead of using your shoulder to lever an opponent off the ball, you can also poke the ball away from him while running alongside him. The best time to make a move for the ball is when the attacker is about to pass or shoot, leaving space for the defender to nick the ball away.

After you've dispossessed the attacker, your work isn't necessarily over. If no other players are in the vicinity, make sure you react the quickest, going to fetch the ball you've just poked away. Otherwise the attacker may pick the ball up again himself, wasting the successful tackle.

Sliding

The sliding tackle is the most difficult tackle to execute and one that you usually only use as a last-ditch measure – when the attacker has worked his way into space and is about to either shoot or make a killer pass.

Sliding is a tricky skill to master. Here's a four-step guide:

1. **The approach. When you have been beaten you have to catch up with and approach the attacker from the side. (Tackles from behind are illegal.) You must get up close to the attacker, or the opponent will be able to accelerate off when you begin to execute the slide.**

2. **The sliding leg. Drop your lower body and begin to slide along the ground with your leg closest to the attacker.**

3. **Top leg. As your sliding leg makes contact with the ground it's bent and tucked underneath you and your top leg is extended out.**

4. **The tackle. Using the top leg, knock the ball away from the attacker's feet with as much force as you can possibly generate. This ensures the opponent can't simply pick up the ball again while you are still lying on the ground.**

Figure 6-9 shows you how to get a sliding tackle right.

It's important to execute a sliding tackle correctly. Reckless or overly aggressive tackles will earn a red card and may cause the attacker serious injury.

Key defensive principles

It doesn't matter which defensive tactic the manager chooses, defenders must adhere to some principles at all times:

- ✔ **Don't lunge in.** If you mis-time a tackle or challenge in a state of panic, wily attackers will find it easy to circumvent you and take you out of play.

- ✔ **Help out.** Just because a defender has been given one task to perform, it doesn't mean he has no responsibilities elsewhere. It's vital to assist and cover team-mates who are in trouble. This doesn't just mean making last-ditch challenges to help – you may want to assist in double-marking a dangerous opponent, as a pre-emptive defensive measure.

- ✔ **Protect the 6-yard box.** The area directly in front of the net is where players score most goals. Keeping attacking players – and the ball – out of this zone drastically reduces the opposition's chances of scoring.

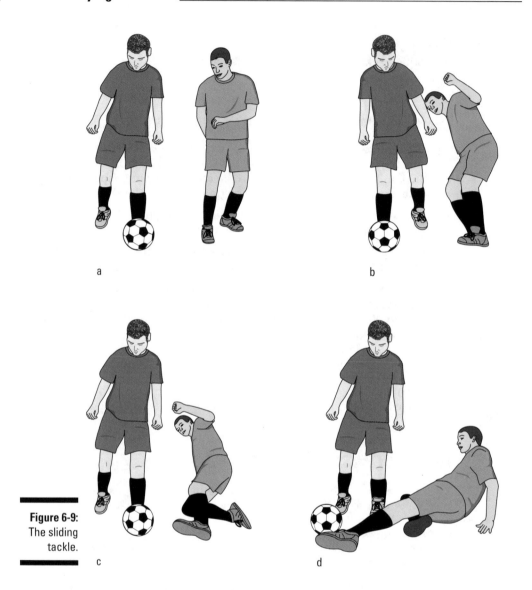

a

b

Figure 6-9:
The sliding
tackle.

c

d

Sharpening Your Skills Up Front

In order to put together dangerous attacks, players must have a variety of
skills to ensure they keep hold of the ball and then confuse the defence into
making mistakes. Here are some of the essential skills.

Shielding the ball

In order to either dribble effectively, or give yourself time to pick out the killer pass, you need to keep hold of the ball under pressure from defensive opponents. You can achieve this by shielding, which involves the attacker keeping his body between himself and the ball.

1. **Keep 'side on'. By turning sideways you create more space between the ball and the defender, allowing you to take full control. It also opens up more of the pitch to you, giving you the options to pass or dribble away.**

2. **Try to avoid turning straight back. As an attacking player it's natural sometimes for you to want to turn around if you see your route ahead blocked by a defender. But unless you know an outlet exists behind you – a team-mate who may be able to quickly 'switch' play to another player in a more advantageous position, for example – it puts you at an immediate disadvantage. The defender will find it easier to tackle you as you turn, and once you've turned around all your team-mates higher up the pitch are out of the game, and the attack is over.**

Chip pass

A highly effective way to beat the last line of defence is to use the chip pass. Chipping over the opposition's defenders can allow a team-mate, timing a run from deep to breach the defensive offside trap, to break free on goal.

1. **Approach the ball from the side and turn to strike it with the inside of your foot.**

2. **Snapping your knee while kicking forward at the ball, you keep your ankle locked at contact, putting backspin on the ball.**

3. **Make contact with the side of your shoelaces (the upper side of the inside foot) just below the centre of the ball. This chips the ball up into the air and sends it spinning back down quickly.**

You should feel like you're clipping the ball into the air. Try to visualise it as a golf shot – a crisp wedge chipped close to the flag, with the flag being your team-mate and the defender a tree or bunker.

Outside of foot pass

Using the outside of your foot as well as the inside gives you added passing options. It allows you to consider other angles without necessarily adjusting the entire shape of your body, sparing you crucial split-seconds in getting your pass away.

1. **Point your kicking foot down towards the ground and slightly inward, with your standing foot planted to the side of the ball and turned slightly away.**

2. **With a locked ankle, deliver the pass with the outside of your foot. When following through, make contact in the centre of the ball with the little toe.**

Back heel

The back heel can look spectacular and tricky, but it's one of the simpler additions to an attacker's armoury.

1. **Simply lift your kicking foot ahead over the front of the ball.**

2. **When your knee and foot are slightly ahead of the ball, snap your heel back onto the front face of the ball, sending it rolling off behind you.**

A deftly executed back heel can instantly wrong-foot a defender, who won't be expecting you to suddenly get rid of the ball – and in a different direction to the one you're facing. If you can direct your back heel immediately to a team-mate, your team will be able to switch play quickly, leaving opponents in disarray.

Bending the ball

Being able to bend it like Beckham puts the attacker at a huge advantage because a whole new range of passing options open up. The ability to bend a ball correctly – a skill also sometimes referred to as a *banana shot* when going for goal – can take defenders totally out of the game.

1. **Approach from the side. When you kick the ball across the front, rather than straight on, you apply spin. Hitting it right to left makes the ball bend to the right (because you're setting the ball bending clockwise on the horizontal axis). Hitting it left to right makes it bend to the left.**

2. **Hit the ball below centre. In order for the ball to curve, it has to fly in the air. You need to make contact with the ball at its bottom half.**

3. **Kick with the inside of the foot. Kick the ball with the inside of the boot, above the big toe. Drive through the ball as hard as you can to impart maximum spin.**

You can apply principles of spin to the ball at all times. For example, you can bend spectacular volleyed passes by stroking across the face of a dropping ball, sending it arcing over long distances through the air. Bending the ball is one of the hardest techniques in the game, however.

Feinting

Feinting is the practice of faking an action in order to convince a defender you're about to do something you're not. It can be a devastatingly effective attacking ploy.

- **Feinting to shoot.** The attacker lifts his shooting foot, pulling the leg back as if to shoot. The defender, buying the *dummy*, goes to block – at which point the attacker can shift the ball round the committed player and into space.

- **Body feint.** Also known as *dropping a shoulder*, this involves leaning to one side in an exaggerated motion, as though the attacker is about to run that way. At the last nanosecond, with the defender ready to commit, the attacker quickly shifts his weight to the other side of their body and moves off in that direction. Caught on the hop, the defender can't shift his weight back in time before the attacker's run off.

Free kicks

Upon being awarded a free kick, it's important to agree with your team-mates who's going to take it. You have three main options:

- **Blast it towards goal.** Whoever has the strongest – and most accurate – shot should hit the ball as hard as he can. A well-struck shot into the top corner of the net can be almost impossible to save if hit at speed.

- **Dink it goalwards with finesse.** A player adept at either chipping or bending the ball may be able to find a route to goal using clever placement. Remember, you may have to get the ball up and over a defensive wall, making a direct blast tricky, and this is a better option.

- **Pass it to a team-mate.** Switching the play to a better-placed player could wrong-foot the opposition. Sometimes teams have worked out complex passing moves before the match on the training ground.

If the free kick is indirect, you should nudge the ball to a team-mate before taking a direct shot. However, if the indirect free kick is at close range, one tactic is to blast the ball direct at goal anyway – if it takes the slightest deflection off any player, attackers or defenders, before going in the net, the goal will be allowed to stand.

Taking penalties

A *penalty* is a free shot at goal from 11 metres (12 yards). In theory it should be an easy skill to execute because the keeper has no time to save a well-struck and well-placed shot. However, nerves play a part because the attacker is expected to convert the chance.

A taker must decide where he's going to place the ball and stick to that decision. Changing his mind as he runs up to take the kick is likely to lead to a scuffed shot, and a missed penalty. A player should simply concentrate on his shooting technique – it will hold up if he blocks out all other thoughts.

Remember to practise penalties before a cup tie because a shootout competition could decide a drawn game. Some teams have failed to do this in the past – infamously England at the 1998 World Cup, when the team were knocked out on penalties against Argentina.

Goalkeeping

The keeper is the last line of defence, the player with the greatest responsibility on the pitch: he has to stop the ball going into the net. The keeper's ultimate aim is to let no goals in during a game – this is called 'keeping a clean sheet'.

It is crucial for a goalkeeper to communicate with his defenders. It is the keeper's job to command the penalty area.

Keepers are the only players on the pitch who are allowed to use their hands to play the ball. Goalies either try to catch the ball or somehow divert it from going into the goal by punching, flicking or parrying it away. The keeper also kicks the ball if necessary – in fact, he uses whatever part of his body it takes to stop a goal going past him.

As a general starting position, a keeper should stand in the centre of the goal with his hands at his side, palms facing the ball. His centre of gravity should be low, and his weight should be on the balls of his feet. He should have his knees slightly bent. This set-up will, in theory, give the keeper the most options when reacting to a shot coming in on his goal.

Catching

If a goalkeeper catches the ball, the opposition is unable to score – simple as that. A good, clean catch immediately puts an end to an opposition attack, and is the perfect way to avert danger. Here are some common methods of catching:

✔ **The chest catch.** If the shot is coming right at the keeper, this is the best option. Getting as much of his body behind the ball as he can, the keeper smothers the ball with his arms when it hits his chest, throwing his arms around it and keeping his elbows close together. The ball should be trapped safely against the chest.

✔ **The diamond, or W, catch.** The simplest catch to take, the keeper plucks the ball from the air when the shot is either wide of him or over his head. The keeper forms a 'diamond' with his thumb and index finger, making a 'W' shape with the fingers on both hands on either side of the ball, just behind its centre. As an insurance policy it's important for a keeper to keep his body behind the ball, because should the shot slip through his hands his body will be in the way to stop it.

✔ **The scoop catch.** The keeper picks up a shot trundling to the goal along the ground with a scoop catch. The keeper bends forward and places his hands on the ground, with palms facing up, gathering the rolling ball into his chest.

After a keeper catches the ball he should bring it close to his chest, so another player can't knock it out. In 1990 Nottingham Forest winger Gary Crosby headed the ball out of the palm of Manchester City keeper Andy Dibble, and rolled it into the empty net. The goal stood, much to Dibble's initial anger and subsequent embarrassment.

Diving

If the ball is heading for one of the far corners, just within range of the keeper's reach, the keeper must first take a stride towards the side of the goal the ball is heading. Then, with arms fully extended – and away from the face so the flight of the ball can clearly be seen – the keeper should dive and attempt to collect the ball using the diamond (or W) catch.

If the keeper is unable to catch the ball he should attempt to tip the ball around the post, averting the immediate danger. This is preferable to parrying the ball back out because the keeper will have dived onto the ground, leaving the goal open for a striker to knock any loose ball back into.

One-on-one

This is the most dangerous save a keeper has to make, but it's the one that offers him the most glory too. The object is to deny an opposition player who has broken clear of the defence – goalkeeper versus attacker, hence the name *one-on-one*.

When a player is advancing towards goal with the ball, the goalkeeper should stay on his feet as long as possible. This forces the striker to make the first decision – does he shoot low or high, attempt to lob the keeper or dribble the ball around him? (Going to ground early helps the player make that decision – it would be easier to dribble around the keeper, or chip the ball over him, for example.)

The keeper should move forward towards the player with his hands low and palms facing the ball. If timed correctly, the keeper can dive towards the ball and smother it, with the striker yet to make his move. Should the striker shoot, the keeper is in position to make a close-range save, parrying the ball away to safety or even smothering the shot and catching it.

Going for crosses

A confident keeper comes off his line in order to claim crosses made by the opposition wingers. Doing this helps relieve pressure on his defence because the central defenders don't have to battle with the attackers for the ball. In theory, a keeper should always have an advantage on every other player in the box because he can extend his arms higher while going up to take the catch.

The goalkeeper's communication is very important when taking the ball. Failing to communicate properly with your defenders could result in a mix-up.

To get the best possible jump, the keeper should leap off one leg and lift his other knee to add to the leap. When leaping in the air your leading leg also offers protection from advancing attackers or defenders. When claiming the ball you should always take off using the leg nearest to the goal to generate lift because this acts as protection. Failing to do so could result in an attacker or defender pushing the goalkeeper in the direction of the goal. Moving forward towards the ball, the keeper should attempt a diamond (or W) catch, before returning to the ground and holding the ball tightly to his chest. Timing of the jump is essential: the keeper should meet the ball at the top of his leap.

If a catch isn't possible, the keeper should attempt to punch the ball away from the goal as far as he can.

It's crucial to hold the ball tightly upon landing, because the ball may otherwise squirm out of the keeper's grasp and back into play.

Goalkeepers often get the benefit of the doubt from referees if they go up for a cross and are knocked over in a challenge by an opposing striker – even if the striker has done nothing wrong! If there's a melee and the ball drops loose, the referee often rules that the keeper was fouled. When you're deciding whether to gamble going for a cross, this knowledge may help you play the percentages in a crowded area.

Punching

If the keeper can't catch the ball, his best option is to punch it clear of danger.

A goalie should punch if he has any doubt over reaching the ball to claim a catch because a missed catch can be quite embarrassing, and often leads to a goal.

The keeper should leap as though he's about to claim the cross, but instead of attempting a catch he should make two fists, hold them together and punch the ball out of harm's way.

The aim of punching is to get the ball clear. Punch the ball just below the middle so that it travels upwards as well as away from goal.

If the keeper is going for a ball at the very outer limit of his reach, he may have to extend one arm out on its own and punch away with one fist.

Parrying and tipping

If the keeper can't catch or punch the ball away from danger, parrying and tipping are two last-resort options.

Tipping the ball away from goal – round the post or over the crossbar – stops the opposition scoring a goal and allows your defence to regroup in order to defend a corner.

Parrying – blocking an effort on goal back into play – is equally effective in the first instance (it stops the opposition scoring a goal) but doesn't do a particularly good job of clearing the danger (because opposing players can pick up the loose ball and have another shot on goal immediately).

Parrying a shot back into play is very much the last resort because you'll be leaving the result to Lady Luck.

Positioning

A goalkeeper can save himself a lot of trouble with good positioning, and make life much harder for the opposition.

One of the most important weapons in a goalkeeper's armoury is 'narrowing the angles'. You do this by moving to the left of the net when the ball is to your left, and the right when it's to your right. This shows the attacker much less of the goal, giving him less space to aim his shot towards.

The near post (the post nearest the ball) is always the goalkeeper's responsibility. Keepers aren't expected to let shots in here. Moving towards the near post forces the attacker to consider shooting to the far side of the goal, a much harder proposition.

Although keepers should spend most of their time on their line, they also need to venture off it in order to claim the ball, close down an angle or put pressure on an onrushing attacker. But it's not a good idea to stray too far from the goal, because chip shots can then beat keepers. These shots are often difficult or impossible to recover; the keeper is left stranded.

Distribution

When a keeper has the ball it's vital that he gives it to a team-mate quickly and efficiently. Goalkeepers are increasingly asked to instigate immediate counter-attacks upon receiving the ball. If distributed quickly and cleverly, the team that had been attacking can suddenly find themselves in danger.

According to the FIFA Laws of the Game, a goalkeeper must release the ball within six seconds of receiving it. Failure to do so will result in the referee awarding an indirect free kick where the keeper was last standing.

The goalkeeper has three options when distributing the ball:

- **Kicking the ball upfield:** By dropping the ball from his grasp and making a long pass up the pitch – this is called a *drop kick* – the keeper looks to find a team-mate (usually one of the strikers) in the middle of the park. The hope is that, with the opposing team having committed players to attack, they will be short of players at the back and vulnerable to a scoring attempt. An accurate kick upfield sets a counter-attacking move in motion very quickly.

- **Throwing or rolling the ball out:** A quick, accurate throw can start the team moving back up the pitch. Keepers usually roll the ball out to one of their defenders, but occasionally try long throws, lancing the ball upfield javelin style if a player is in space in midfield. An accurate long throw can be almost as devastatingly effective as a long drop kick.

- **Dribbling the ball upfield, or passing it out:** This isn't a good idea unless keepers have decent ball skills, though most professionals do since the backpass was outlawed in the early 1990s. A goalkeeper who can pass the ball confidently gives a team more options when looking to start new attacking moves from the back.

Saving penalties

When facing a penalty, a keeper is allowed to move anywhere along his goal line from left to right, but he's not permitted to advance towards the ball before the opposing player has taken his shot.

Goalkeepers are at an obvious disadvantage – though as the striker is expected to score with a free shot from 12 yards (11 metres), the keeper, who isn't expected to save it, has nothing to lose.

 Sometimes the weight of expectation puts the striker under pressure, so use this to your advantage. If there's any way of psyching the penalty-taker out before he takes his kick, do so. (Simply staring at some players increases their nerves!)

Considering a few things may help you save the penalty. Is the taker right- or left-footed? Have you seen him take a penalty before – and if so, where did he put it? Are his eyes giving away where he intends to send the ball?

But, ultimately, it's down to luck. Wait until the very last second before choosing which way to dive – or whether to stand still for a cheeky penalty straight down the middle, the taker expecting you to dive out of the way. A goalkeeper doesn't look stupid if he dives the wrong way – but he appears very clever if he guesses correctly and saves the kick.

Chapter 7

Keeping Fit for Football

. . . .

In This Chapter

▶ How to get warmed up safely – before turning up the heat

▶ Reaching peak physical condition

▶ Eating and drinking well

▶ Injuries: how to prevent them and how to treat them when they do occur

. . . .

*F*ootball hasn't always been the healthiest of sports. Back in the 1950s stars at the top English clubs regularly sat down ahead of a big match and tucked into a large greasy plate of steak and chips. In the 1960s George Best used to turn up to training most days with a stonking hangover. And in 1978 Ossie Ardiles was part of Argentina's World Cup winning squad, despite chugging on an average of 40 cigarettes a day.

These days players simply can't get away with that sort of behaviour. Football is now such a fast, intense and demanding game that players need to commit to an athletic lifestyle – or they'll simply be wasting everyone's time.

It's not just about abstinence off the pitch. Putting the long yards in on the training ground is vital, because even if players live a life so clean and virtuous it would have put Mother Teresa to shame, they'll come off second best if they're not in peak physical condition.

The principle applies to any level of football: you can have all the natural talent in the world, but if the other player is miles fitter, you'll come a cropper. On the other hand, if you've got the talent *and* you've done your training, the sky's the limit.

Keeping Fit

If you aren't 100 per cent fit, it'll show very quickly on the pitch. Even the top professionals have to work hard to reach peak condition and stay there – if they take a week off from training through injury, the rule of thumb is that they'll then require a further two weeks to get back into top shape.

A decent level of aerobic fitness is essential because a player runs on average anything between 6 and 11 kilometres (3.7 and 6.8 miles) in a 90-minute game. They also make several sprints during the match, so speed, power and agility are vital.

Stretching those muscles

First things first: if you want to avoid pulling muscles when exercising, you need to give your legs a good stretch. A stretching session should last between 10 and 15 minutes.

The more stretches you do, the more flexible you become – and the less likely you are to pick up injuries.

Different players have their own personal stretching routines, depending on their physical make-up. A qualified fitness instructor can plan a bespoke programme for you, but there's no need to worry if you can't do that because performing the following stretches should be more than satisfactory.

✔ **Quadriceps:** Stand by a wall. Bend one leg up behind you using one hand to steady yourself against the wall and the other to keep your leg in place by holding onto your foot. To make the stretch gently pull your foot upwards. Figure 7-1 shows this exercise.

Figure 7-1:
Stretching your quadriceps.

✔ **Hamstrings and lower calf:** Sit on the ground. With one foot extended out in front of you, extend your arm towards your foot. While sitting bolt upright, keeping your back straight, run your arm as far down your leg as you can. Figure 7-2 shows this stretch.

Figure 7-2:
Working on your hamstrings and lower calves.

✔ **Groin:** Sit on the ground. Place the soles of both of your feet together, so your knees are bent out to the side of your body. Then, while keeping your back straight, try to press both of your knees as close to the ground as possible. Push your chest out while you do this, as Figure 7-3 shows.

Figure 7-3:
Stretching your groin.

✔ **Lower back:** Lie down on your back. Pull one or both of your knees towards your chest while keeping your shoulders and head on the ground. Figure 7-4 illustrates this stretch.

Figure 7-4:
Stretching
your lower
back.

✔ **Calf muscle and Achilles tendon:** Stand by a wall. Place one leg forward, bending it at the knee. Push forward against the wall, keeping your back foot flat on the ground. The forward leg stretches your Achilles tendon and the back leg stretches the calf muscle. Switch legs and repeat the stretch. Figure 7-5 illustrates this stretch.

Figure 7-5:
Stretching
your calves.

✔ **Hip flexor:** Get on one knee. Bend your rear leg so the knee is near the ground while extending your front leg and your hands towards your toes, as Figure 7-6 shows.

Figure 7-6:
Carrying out
a hip flexor
stretch.

Running

Some footballers run more than others. Former Manchester United midfielder Roy Keane, a *box-to-box player* (one who covers all the ground between the penalty boxes), would run up to 12 or 13 kilometres (7.5 or 8 miles) during a game, covering every blade of grass on the pitch. Equally influential on his team was Jan Molby of Liverpool – though he was invariably overweight and famously rarely left the centre circle, dictating the game with his passing skills rather than energetic drive. Both players were world class. The moral? Running isn't the be all and end all! So don't worry if you're not a natural athlete – providing you have the skills, you can still make it.

Having said that, not being able to run well puts a player at an instant disadvantage in the fast-paced modern game. So it's worth putting in the extra work to get up to speed – literally.

During the close season keep in shape by running regularly. You don't need to do too much: a 45-minute jog each day should suffice. You can break this work up into two separate 20-minute sessions. It's important to keep your heart rate at a healthy level.

During the season you have to ramp it up with both long-distance and short-distance work. Long-distance running builds up your base levels of fitness and your endurance. Hour-long jogs, or several faster-paced laps of the pitch, help you do this.

Shorter sprinting practice is also vital because during games you need that extra burst of pace to explode past an opposing defender. It's much more beneficial to do drills over shorter distances – say between 5 and 20 metres (16.5 and 65.5 feet) – than longer sprints over 100 or 200 metres (328 and 656 feet), distances you're not going to cover in a sprint during a game.

The first few steps in a sprint are vital – a mix of technique and power. Practice helps with technique; weight training with leg weights may help with power (though you don't want to bulk up too much).

Quickness as a player isn't just about sheer physical speed. Mental reactions are vital too. A player who makes sure he keeps concentrating for every second of a match often gets to the ball before a 'faster' opponent simply by being quicker off the mark.

Exercising aerobically

Aerobic exercise is essential if a player is to perform at a good level. Your heart and lungs must be in top condition: after all, the lungs fuel the heart, which pumps more blood to the legs. And legs are a footballer's main tool of work!

Jogging is the simplest and most effective form of aerobic exercise for a football player. Tennis and basketball are also good, because both sports also feature the similar stop-start sudden changes of movement found in football. Swimming is also effective, although you use different muscles.

It's best to double-check with your manager or coach as to what extra exercise you should take. Some managers don't like their players using their 'football' muscles for other pastimes, and so may prefer you to swim. The manager might also not want you to partake in other contact sports such as basketball, where you run added risks of injury.

In modern football, managers hire specialist strength and conditioning coaches to work on their players' health-related components of fitness.

Training with weights

Weight training can be useful to assist in the attainment of general fitness, core strength and improved leg muscles. However, footballers shouldn't be too bulky – mobility, flexibility and agility are the watchwords.

So although you shouldn't neglect your upper body – players often use weights simply to keep their body toned or to recover from a specific injury – it isn't the most vital part of physical training.

If you want to train with weights in order to tone your muscles, repetition is more important than using large weights. Repetition tones; weight adds unwanted bulk.

Sorting out your stomach

Large amounts of running should be enough to keep your abdominal muscles in shape. But if you want to reach peak physical condition, a daily routine of sit-ups or stomach crunches will do no harm.

Cooling down

It's vitally important to cool down properly after practice or matches. If a player has been performing at peak activity but then suddenly stops without cooling down, he runs the risk of cramp because the muscles are fully extended but no longer working.

Jogging slowly for a few minutes is a good way to cool down. You may also want to repeat some – or indeed all – of your pre-match stretches, although you don't need to spend 10 to 15 minutes on them.

By cooling down you not only avoid risking cramp, you will also be much less sore the day after the game or training session. Cooling down exercises help relieve the build-up of lactic acid in the muscles that occurs during strenuous activity.

Professional teams cool down for anything up to 45 minutes. If you hang around in the stadium long after the final whistle you can sometimes see them out on the pitch performing their drills.

Balancing Your Diet

It's important to eat well at all times, but especially so if you're partaking in regular exercise. You're burning more calories and therefore require more energy for practice sessions and matches.

In the know about H$_2$O

Keep properly hydrated before, during and after the match. Here are a few important tips to keeping well watered:

✔ Fluid intake varies per person, but most adults need between 1½ to 3 litres (2.6 to 5.3 pints) of liquid per day. You need more if you're active, so make sure you're fully hydrated before the game. Do this by drinking a glass of water when you wake, and taking regular drinks during the day.

✔ Remember that you only start to feel thirsty after you're already dehydrated, so make sure you take on water before you get thirsty.

✔ Always bring a bottle of water with you to matches and practice. Don't assume water will always be available – sometimes there's none and you need to replenish yourself.

✔ Remember that water has no calories, so drink as much as you like.

✔ As well as water, the body can get fluid from other drinks such as squash, juice, tea and coffee – as well as fruit and vegetables.

A balanced diet is essential. A recommended balance for an active player is:

✔ 60 per cent of your daily calorific intake from carbohydrates

✔ 15 per cent from protein

✔ 25 per cent from fats

Carbohydrates are what keeps you going so you need to take on board a large amount. Foods containing a lot of carbs include pasta, bread, rice, potatoes and cereals.

You find protein in milk, cheese, meat, poultry and fish. Fats are found to varying degrees in most foodstuffs, but especially butter, sweets, carbonated drinks and desserts.

Within one hour after a training session or match try to drink 1 litre (1.8 pints) of fluid and take on board some carbohydrates. This is because the body replaces and stores energy more efficiently after exercise, when the muscles are still active.

Although it's important not to over-eat, if you eat too little you'll be unable to keep up your energy levels during a game.

Investigating Injuries

Football is a physically exerting pastime, and a contact sport to boot. Picking up injuries every now and then, whether big or small, is almost unavoidable, so it's important to know what to do when they occur.

Even so, prevention is better than cure – and it's worth remembering that if you prepare correctly, you significantly limit your chances of picking up many injuries.

Preventing injuries

Follow these tips to decrease your chance of picking up an injury:

- **Check the condition of the pitch:** Adverse conditions can lead to injuries if you don't wear appropriate footwear. The wetter the turf, the longer your studs should be, for example, and a pitch that's full of holes and divots can easily cause injury, especially to the ankle or the knee.

- **Check the weather conditions:** An extremely hot day can lead to players suffering heat stroke. Make sure you have plenty of water handy.

- **Do your pre-match stretches:** As the earlier section 'Stretching those muscles' outlines, a decent stretch of the leg muscles is mandatory. A full and thorough stretching session should last between 10 and 15 minutes, though providing you have at least stretched for a couple of minutes, the likelihood of you pulling a muscle is slim. However, do remember that the longer and more often you stretch, the more flexible you become – and more flexible players are less prone to injuries.

- **Get checked up:** At the start of a season visit the doctor and get yourself a medical. Your doctor can then address any minor health problems there and then, nipping them in the bud. A clean bill of health also gives you peace of mind – and with it added confidence.

- **Make sure your shoes fit:** It may sound obvious, but do your football boots and trainers fit properly? Footwear that's slightly too tight or too big for you causes blisters and other injuries – and could cause long-term damage to your feet. Get your boots and trainers fitted properly by a professional when you buy them, and wear decent cotton socks that won't rub you up the wrong way.

✔ **Remember your shinpads:** You always wear your shinpads for a match, but do you always wear them for practice sessions, five-a-side matches or kickabouts? You wear them in matches for a reason – they protect one of the most sensitive and endangered parts of a footballer's body – so don't be blasé just because you're not playing an official fixture.

✔ **Stay in shape:** If you're out of condition your body can't cope with the rigours of exercise, let alone the trauma of possible heavy contact, as you clank around a football pitch. A fit player decreases his chance of injury. He's also able to bounce back from any knocks more quickly, and return from injury quicker than an unfit player would.

Injury prevention isn't the only benefit of checking the state of the pitch. The 1954 World Cup final was played in wet conditions, but although the highly fancied Hungarian team were forced to wear their heavy-weather boots with long studs, West Germany were able to play in their normal boots – because Adidas had designed their boots with interchangeable screw-on studs. The Germans won 3-2!

Treating injuries

Despite everyone's best efforts at prevention, somebody's bound to pick up an injury at some point. It's important to know how to deal with any injuries should they occur.

Firstly, it's essential that at every match at least one person on the touch lines – *who's not playing and therefore has no chance of picking up an injury himself* – is able to administer simple medical attention to any players who pick up an injury.

I advise that someone on your team's non-playing staff takes a course in first aid. Your local doctor's surgery can tell you where you can take such a course.

Should someone pick up an injury, whether small or serious, they need medical treatment as soon as possible. Players with serious injuries should be taken immediately to hospital.

If you're playing away from home, make sure you know where the nearest hospital is beforehand – don't assume the home side will know, even though realistically they should. Also, keep a mobile phone handy in case you need to call for an ambulance.

It's also preferable that someone pitch-side knows CPR – cardio-pulmonary resuscitation – in the unlikely event a player's heart stops on the pitch.

First-aid kit

The basic essentials in a first-aid kit are as follows:

- ✔ Antiseptic spray or antiseptic wipes: To clean out cuts and grazes.

- ✔ Bandages: Assorted sizes, to cover cuts and wounds.

- ✔ CPR mouth barrier: For the unlikely event of performing mouth-to-mouth resuscitation.

- ✔ Latex gloves: To wear while tending to a bloody cut or wound.

- ✔ Nail clippers: Nails are often torn or ripped by the ball, especially if a keeper isn't wearing any gloves in a practice session.

- ✔ Scissors: For the cutting of bandages and tape.

- ✔ Sterile eyewash and eye pads: For any injuries to the eye – mud, grass and grit often get stuck in players' eyes.

- ✔ Sunscreen: Playing for 90 minutes under strong sun is harmful to the skin – players should wear some form of blocking lotion.

- ✔ Tape: For the application of bandages.

- ✔ Tooth-preserving kit: Thousands of teeth are accidentally knocked out each year on the pitch – this ensures dentists have a good chance of replanting the teeth of an unfortunate player.

- ✔ Tweezers: To remove any debris lodged in a player's skin.

No matter how fit a player appears, it's possible that they have a heart condition. Professional players such as Cameroon's Marc Vivien Foé and Sevilla's Antonio Puerta both collapsed and suffered fatal heart attacks on the pitch.

Treating injuries using R.I.C.E.

Make sure that someone brings a quantity of ice to a game – packed, obviously, in an ice box or cooler. Ice is essential to treat many injuries because you use it to decrease the swelling of a bruise, after pulling or straining a muscle, spraining or sometimes after breaking a bone.

You can remember the way to treat an injury with ice as follows:

1. **R:** Rest. Make sure that the player doesn't move at all.

2. **I:** Ice. To stop or limit blood flow and pain, place crushed ice in a plastic bag, a wet towel or an ice bag, to make an ice pack. Keep the pack on the injury for 15 minutes every waking hour for the first 24 hours to three days, depending on the severity of the injury and how quickly the swelling dies down.

3. **C:** Compress. After the initial pressing of the ice pack, replace it with a tight bandage, preferably an elastic wrap. If you're wrapping a leg or arm, start at the place furthest from the heart, and work towards it in a criss-cross pattern. Expose toes or fingers at the extremities so you can spot any skin discolorations.

4. **E:** Elevate. Raise the injured arm or leg to about the heart level for the first 24 hours to three days.

Figure 7-7 shows the RICE procedure in progress.

Figure 7-7:
The RICE
procedure.

Take a player to the hospital if the injury looks at all serious, if you're in any doubt or if the swelling continues.

Knee injuries

Injured knees are quite common in football and can cause complications, even to the point of ending a player's career. They occur when a player has one leg planted on the ground, only for the leg to be hit hard by a sudden rotation of the body (which could be caused by a collision with another player, or simply by passing or running on his own).

The knee can bend through 150 degrees and is one of the most flexible joints in the body. This flexibility is crucial to a footballer, who needs to change direction quickly. The knee has no muscles, but it does have three bones – the femur, tibia and fibula – which are held together by ligaments.

Although knee injuries can occur in five places – ligaments, cartilage, muscles around the knee, kneecap and tendons – it's the ligaments that are usually troublesome to footballers. The most common injuries occur to the following four ligaments: the anterior cruciate, posterior, medial collateral and lateral collateral.

A tear to the anterior cruciate ligament (ACL) is the worst knee injury. A player can damage their ACL by twisting or turning suddenly, being kicked just below the ligament, over-extending it or slowing down too quickly. A player may hear a sickening loud pop or snap before he feels anything.

If an ACL injury is suspected, you should carry the player off the pitch and immediately apply ice to the knee. Seek medical assistance immediately. Reconstructive surgery could see a player out for at least a year.

Figure 7-8 shows an ACL injury.

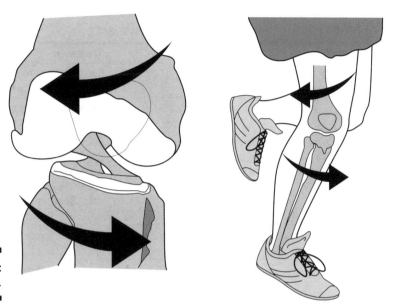

Figure 7-8:
ACL injury.

One of the most famous knee injuries in football was the one suffered by Paul Gascoigne in the 1991 FA Cup final while playing for Tottenham Hotspur. He ruptured his anterior cruciate ligament in a high-speed collision with Nottingham Forest's Gary Charles, and was never considered to be the same player again.

The most common knee injury is the medial cruciate ligament tear. It's the strongest ligament in the knee and injuries to it shouldn't be serious. However, any player suspected of suffering such an injury should be immediately carried off the pitch, with ice applied to the knee. Happily, even severe tears should, with the help of a protective knee brace, see the player back in action within two months.

The degree of a knee injury tells you how much damage has been done. First-degree tears are mild, with only a slight swelling occurring and little loss of movement. A second-degree tear is a moderate tear that causes the player mild pain and requires rest. A third-degree tear is the worst and refers to a complete rupture of the ligament that may require a brace, cast or corrective surgery.

Common injuries

Most injuries in football are, however, not too serious. Although players are known to break legs and arms, dislocate shoulders and suffer head or neck injuries, these are thankfully quite rare – seek immediate medical attention in such an event.

Table 7-1 lists some of the more common ailments, and how to treat them.

Table 7-1	Common Ailments	
Ailment	*Symptoms*	*Treatment*
Abrasion	Loss of skin	Cleanse with antiseptic and apply antibiotic ointment.
Blister	Fluid build-up under skin	Have it drained by a doctor and clean the area with antiseptic.
Concussion	Severe blow to the head that can cause dizziness, dull to severe headache, ringing in ears, disorientation, possible loss of consciousness	Substitute player immediately. Do not allow him to continue under any circumstances, even if he insists he's recovered. Seek medical attention.
Contusion	Bruised muscle or tendon	Treat with ice using R.I.C.E. method.
Cramp	Involuntary and painful muscle contraction	Apply firm pressure on the muscle area, followed by gentle massage. Give the player water to rehydrate him.
Sprain	Injured ligaments	Treat with ice using R.I.C.E. method.
Strain	Torn muscle or tendon	Treat with ice using R.I.C.E. method.

Chapter 8

Coaching, Managing and Leadership

*F*ootball isn't just about the 11 players on the pitch: it's about one particular person standing on the sidelines, watching nervously as the game unfolds. That person is, of course, the team manager – also known in some countries as the coach.

In fact, there's a good case to be made that the manager is by far the most important person involved. Because although the manager can't physically change what happens on the pitch as the game takes place, he's been responsible for picking the players, training them and telling them exactly how to play.

With only a couple of notable exceptions, the personality and footballing beliefs of their manager have shaped and defined all the great teams in history.

A Brief History of the Manager

Although the manager or coach is now the single most important figure of a team and/or club, that hasn't always been the case. The English national team, for example, played their first international in 1872, but didn't have a manager until Walter Winterbottom was installed two years after the Second World War – 75 years later! And even then, Winterbottom was only permitted to train and advise the players. He wasn't allowed to pick the team – that was done by an executive panel of self-appointed Football Association 'experts'.

It was only when Alf Ramsey took over in 1963 that the manager gained full control over the team. Ramsey only agreed to take the England job if he was given the all-reaching powers enjoyed by continental legends like Vittorio Pozzo and Sepp Herberger – the former having won the World Cup with Italy in 1934 and 1938, the latter with West Germany in 1954. Within three years of Ramsey's appointment England had a World Cup of their own too.

Managers like Pozzo, Herberger and Ramsey – along with the innovative Arsenal manager of the 1920s and 1930s, Herbert Chapman, Matt Busby at Manchester United from the late 1940s and Bill Shankly at Liverpool in the 1960s – were some of the first managers who became personalities in their own right. They might not necessarily have been born entertainers, but they imposed themselves and their footballing philosophies on their teams.

Strong-willed managers who run their clubs from top to bottom have ruled the roost ever since, from the era of Brian Clough and Don Revie to the days of Arsène Wenger and Sir Alex Ferguson. Even on the continent, where club owners are notorious for buying big-name players regardless of whether the coach wants them or not, single-minded managers like Fabio Capello and Marcello Lippi have still picked up the lion's share of the big trophies.

It may sound needlessly macho, but history bears it out – nearly all successful managers are determined to do things their way. Few succeed at trying to keep everyone happy or worry about what people think of them.

Coach or Manager (or Boss or Gaffer)?

Historically in England, the person running the team has been known as the manager. That's changed recently, with teams appointing foreign 'coaches' and choosing to keep their job titles.

It's usually a matter of semantics and personal preference – the titles are interchangeable and the difference negligible. However, some clubs – those formerly used to having managers who dealt with the buying and selling of players – now appoint a general manager to deal with transfers and have made a point of changing the old 'manager' job to that of 'head coach'.

Whatever a team decides, the manager or coach nearly always retains the final say-so in who to buy and sell – the general manager is ultimately there to do the paperwork, taking the administrative burden off the person in charge of the team and leaving him to concentrate on purely football matters.

The manager – or coach – may also be known as the boss, the guv'nor or the gaffer.

What the role involves

The manager's role is to ensure a club puts out a team of 11 players – plus however many substitutes are allowed – for every fixture in the season. The manager must pick the most effective 11 players to take on the opposition, and *coach* (advise) them on how best to win the game. The manager's role has much more to it than that, however:

- **Dealing with the media:** At bigger clubs managers must give interviews to television, radio and newspapers in order to maintain a dialogue with the supporters. The more charismatic manager is able to cultivate a relationship with the crowd that may insulate him from criticism when things go wrong.

- **Handling transfers:** The manager has nominal control over a transfer budget in order to build the squad, and must work within that budget. It's the manager's responsibility – along with a general manager and other members of the club hierarchy – not to let the financial affairs of the team spiral out of control. (The board is responsible for overall financial matters.)

- **Managing motivation and morale:** The manager is responsible for the man-management of the entire playing staff. It's his role to keep spirits and confidence high, encourage or criticise players when necessary and ensure the entire team get along with each other and are pulling in the same direction.

- **Picking the team:** The manager selects the team from a squad – a pool of available players he's built, signing and releasing individuals in order to gather together the finest and most adaptable collection he possibly can.

- **Taking charge of games:** The manager reacts to events during games, coaching and supporting his team throughout the 90 minutes. He needs to make tactical changes and substitutions wherever he sees fit.

- **Taking the flak:** When things do go wrong, the manager is expected to shield his players from criticism and take it on the chin himself. The manager is seen as the figurehead of the club, and is ultimately responsible for everything that goes on.

In short, managers are expected to keep a hundred plates spinning at once – and if one smashes to the floor, God help him.

Chess – or all-out war?

There are as many different types of manager as there are different human character traits, but in general two approaches to management exist:

- ✔ **The cerebral approach:** The manager concentrates on tactics, training and meticulous team preparation. He sees football matches like games of chess, intense tactical battles against the opposing manager, and sometimes moves his players around the pitch – and in and out of the team – like pawns on a chess board. Modern managers who take this approach include José Mourinho at Internazionale and Liverpool's Rafael Benitez.

- ✔ **The emotional, passionate approach:** The manager espouses 'pride in the shirt' and tells his team to put everything into every challenge, a blood-and-thunder approach akin to war. The modern manager most famous for this is surely Sir Alex Ferguson at Manchester United.

In practice, though, a truly great manager tries to balance both approaches. He may put more weight on one approach than the other, but he tries to get a mix that works. Ferguson wouldn't have won so many trophies at United without ensuring his teams were properly tactically briefed, while Mourinho famously engendered a close-knit camaraderie at Chelsea that helped the side to hard-fought wins as much as his tight defensive drills did.

Player-managers

It doesn't happen often at the very biggest clubs, but managers are allowed to play for the team as well. Usually this happens when an existing manager has been sacked and a replacement must be found at short notice. In such circumstances clubs occasionally turn to one of their senior players to steady the ship – the idea being that he already knows the inner workings of the club and has the respect of the rest of the team.

Due to the inexperience of player-managers the role is rarely a success. Yet two of the most successful managers in English football began their careers as player-managers: Don Revie at Leeds in the 1960s and Kenny Dalglish at Liverpool in the 1980s. Also Franz Beckenbauer effectively won the 1974 World Cup as player-manager of West Germany, with nominal boss Helmut Schön, depressed with initial results, requiring Beckenbauer to take control midway through the competition.

Get your coaching badges

If you want to become a qualified coach in England, enrol on an FA coaching course. You can register free with the Football Association online (www.thefa.com) as part of their FA Learning scheme. You can access details of all the courses held at sports centres and County Football Associations around the country.

Most applicants start at Level 1, which assumes no knowledge. All you need is the desire to learn more about football and improve your coaching skills. If you've already been coaching for a while, you can start at Level 2.

Building – and Picking – a Team

Selecting a best 11 to send out onto the pitch isn't just a matter of picking names from a hat. First a manager has to pick a squad that gives him plenty of different options. You have plenty to consider.

Building a squad

If you've just taken over as manager of a team or club, you've inherited a squad of players. You're statistically unlikely to rate all of them as players – though you have to utilise some, or perhaps even all, of them at first.

Doing the best you can with the hand you've been dealt is one of the crucial talents a manager requires. If a player is performing poorly, is there a way you can improve his game, perhaps through coaching, teaching him new techniques or simple encouragement?

Perhaps a poorly performing player would benefit from playing in a different position. When Rafael Benitez turned up at Liverpool, Jamie Carragher was an under-performing right back. Benitez converted him into a central defender, a position he excelled at for seasons afterwards.

You need to evaluate each player's skills, strengths and weaknesses.

> ✔ **Is he mobile?** Football is an increasingly athletic game and players who are unfit, lack flexibility or are clumsy are likely to cause problems. Unfit players are also more susceptible to injury and are likely to miss chunks of the season. A fit and mobile runner still needs the ability to play but it's a crucial base upon which to build.

✔ **Does he contribute defensively?** Teams can rarely afford to carry passengers when the other team is attacking. The very best strikers 'defend from the front' by chasing down every ball and pressuring opposing defenders. Does he stand around admiring his own shots and passes? Does he fail to track back? Or will he immediately harry opponents upon losing the ball in an attempt to win it back? Your team may need to battle to win matches, so commitment is important.

✔ **How skilful is he?** Not all players need to be involved with play for the whole 90 minutes. Creative play-makers, wingers and strikers may only need a minute to change a match in your favour – and their talents make them worth their place, even if they're occasionally lax in the tackle.

✔ **What's his spirit like?** A player can have all the talent in the world, but if he lets his mood sour when the team is struggling it can have a detrimental effect on others. A sulking player may go missing, leaving the team effectively playing with ten men – or may even get himself sent off in a fit of frustration, literally leaving the team a man down.

✔ **Does he capitalise on opportunities**? A striker can be hard-working and get himself into good positions, but if he repeatedly misses simple goal-scoring opportunities then he's wasting your team's good work.

✔ **Does he influence the team?** The best players 'take their team along with them', inspiring them to up their game. In an ideal world, a team would have 11 captains, all geeing each other on.

✔ **What's his footballing intelligence like?** Can a player read the game well, spotting the killer pass or making the clever run? Or is he constantly caught offside or finding himself positioned miles away from the play?

Many other factors exist for a manager to consider, but simply by watching a player he will soon make up his mind about that player's strengths and weaknesses – and whether he's the player for the team.

After the manager has identified areas that require improvement, it's time to sign and release players. He moves on the ones he doesn't want, or who are superfluous to the squad, providing he has cover in their positions. He then signs players to replace them, or to bolster other areas in the team that demand fresh blood.

Depending on how many transfers a manager makes, how well he's identified new players and how easily those new players perform on their arrival, his squad will begin to take shape – hopefully at great speed.

Choosing a captain

A manager needs to select one member of his squad to be club captain. That player needs to have a good rapport with the manager, as well as be respected by the rest of the squad. The captain needs to be a good communicator, a player who is likely to start most games – so he can fulfil his captaincy duties on the pitch – and, if he's working at a club of any size, must have a decent relationship with the fan base.

Selecting a first XI

Logic dictates that the manager wants to select the most talented players in each position, but he needs to consider two major factors:

- **Who's in form?** The manager wants to pick the players who are currently on top of their game and delivering the goods.

- **Does the player fit in?** There's no point picking a supremely talented player if he doesn't gel with the rest of the team or if his style of play doesn't work with the tactical system. Sometimes a 'lesser' player may develop understandings with other team-mates that are more beneficial to the overall system and that can't be replicated.

A manager won't necessarily be picking the best 11 players in his squad, but the 11 who work best together as a unit.

Deciding on tactics

A manager doesn't need to decide on one sole tactical approach – in fact, it's beneficial to the team if they learn several different ways of playing. However, chances are the manager in general prefers one particular method of playing and sets his team up accordingly.

Managers might decide on a tactical approach reflecting the abilities of the players in his squad; for example, if the team has several talented attackers, it would be pointless to play an overly defensive game. He may also opt for a certain approach as part of an overall philosophy – a manager may think the team will win a higher percentage of games by playing a long-ball game, and stick with that approach always.

Managers also tweak, or sometimes completely change, their tactics and style of play depending on the opposition. This may even influence a change in starting selection. For example, if a dangerous winger like Cristiano Ronaldo is playing on the right wing, a manager may place an extra defender to nullify the threat. However, managers often decide on an overall tactical philosophy before they make any signings.

Taking Charge Yourself

Unless you've already managed to land yourself a job at a professional league club, chances are you won't be able to appoint a large backroom staff of assistant manager, fitness coach, goalkeeping coach and talent scout. In fact, you may even have to perform the role of physio yourself, not to mention cutting the half-time oranges into segments.

If you're taking sole charge of a team, it's advisable to take a course in basic first aid in case you need to administer any during a game.

But being in sole charge doesn't mean you should isolate yourself. Take advice from trusted friends who come along to watch the games and listen to the players, especially the senior ones, who may have practical and positive suggestions to make.

Preparing the team

When you have your squad of players together, it's time to prepare them for playing. You take them through fitness drills as well as honing their skills on the training pitch. But you also have to make sure they're mentally prepared.

Setting goals

Players know the ultimate goal is to win games, but it pays to be realistic as well. At the start of the season do you expect your team to be challenging for a cup or promotion from their league? If so, set out those parameters at the beginning; that way your players have a target in mind.

If you're a struggling outfit, perhaps the hope of avoiding relegation is all you can ask for. It's better to admit this to yourself, and set your team a goal they can achieve, than aim unrealistically high and watching your players become disillusioned as they fail dismally. Should a team outperform low expectations one season, they could gain confidence to become a better team during the following campaign.

Being realistic in the short term does not necessarily breed pessimism or resignation!

Explaining the tactics

Although you take players through drills in training, you need to hammer home your tactical wishes in a pre-match briefing a day or two before the match. You can use magnetic tactics boards or whiteboards to illustrate tactical situations, but remember to keep it short and sweet. Players get bored if your instructions last too long, and in any case they're likely to forget what you've told them.

Keep it simple. Your players need to recall this information when they're playing the match. Technical jargon will either confuse or be totally forgotten in the heat of battle.

Check out Chapter 5 for the lowdown on the various formations that might suit your team.

Players may find it easier to grasp certain concepts, and how they relate to them, if you show them videos of professional teams in action.

Pre-match motivation

Find out how your players like to prepare for a match. Do they feel more relaxed listening to loud music in the dressing room before the game, for example, or do they prefer silence?

Make sure all players are relaxed and happy. Some may need geeing up; others may prefer a calming arm around their shoulder.

Your players should already be well briefed tactically, so there's no need to go over any plans in detail. If you need to hammer home any reminders, keep them short and simple. All that's left is time for a rousing speech – or a brief 'good luck' if you think that will suffice!

In-game decisions

Just because the referee has blown the whistle to start the game, it doesn't mean it's suddenly all down to the players. You need to keep working with your team as the match progresses – if they start to struggle, they'll be looking to you for help.

Touch-line communication

Don't rant and rave on the touch line, even if a player is having a shocker of a match. If you lose your temper, players on your team are likely to get agitated or panicked, resulting in poor performance. Players specifically targeted by a touch-line tirade from the manager are also likely to deliberately ignore him, looking away from the bench either in anger or embarrassment. You're unable to get any tactical changes or advice across to your players if you act this way. Pass messages and advice to your players calmly, through your captain if possible.

Professional managers and coaches are not allowed to leave the 'technical areas' near the bench. Going walkabout outside of these may result in them being sent away from the bench.

Sir Alf: Motivator extraordinaire

One of the greatest off-the-cuff inspirational speeches of all time was delivered by Alf Ramsey after England let in a last-minute equaliser against West Germany in the 1966 World Cup final. As the team prepared for the rigours of extra time he simply announced, 'Gentlemen, you have already won the World Cup once. Now go and do it again.'

Ramsey also insisted his tired troops stood up during the break in play, despite being totally exhausted. After the game, the West German side – equally spent, with several men lying on the turf being massaged or treated for cramp – admitted to disbelief at seeing England looking so 'fresh'. Psychologically beaten, they lost to a determined England in extra time.

Tactical changes and substitutions

If a mismatch is occurring somewhere on the pitch to the detriment of your side, make efforts to switch things around. If a player for the opposition is running a defender ragged, either detail another player to switch with the defender or get him to double up on the attacker. Alternatively, you may think that your speedy winger will have more joy against a slower defender on the opposite wing to the one they're currently playing on; if so, make the switch immediately, subtly if possible.

Successful managers aren't afraid to make changes to the original battle plan. This isn't an admission that you got it wrong in the first place – just a mature reaction to events unfolding in front of you.

At some point in the match, unless things are going perfectly, you want to make tactical changes to personnel. For example, a fast reserve striker may take advantage of a tiring defence during the latter stages of a game. But be careful not to use all your substitutions for tactical purposes too early: your own players may tire, or pick up injuries, and you don't want to end the game with ten players or less.

Half-time

While the players rest at half-time you need to give them a pep talk. Players may need words of encouragement if they're working hard but getting no reward, praise if they're doing well or some choice critical words if they're playing poorly. It might be time to instigate some tactical changes while you have everyone's ear, or make substitutions. It might also be time for a small rousing speech of encouragement to lift your side before they go out again for the second half.

Full-time

If your team has won, congratulate each member of your side. Making each player feel a crucial part of the victory emboldens him for the following match. Feel free to make any minor technical criticism – happy players are much more likely to take a small nugget of constructive advice on board after a win without taking offence.

If your team has lost, there's no point ranting and raving in the dressing room after the match, unless several of your players have put in an abysmal performance (a lack of effort, perhaps, or needless red cards). It's always better to analyse the match at the next training session, when tempers have cooled down.

If players have been booked or sent off, they may need to pay a fine to the local Football Association. Make sure the players pay up, because failure to do so will result in them receiving further punishment or lengthy bans. You may also choose to additionally discipline the players in-house, although for smaller, more informal clubs this can be counter-productive and cause ill feeling.

Dealing with Kids

All footballers, no matter how old, act like big kids at heart. You may, however, be dealing with real children. Although most of the rules of management still apply, you might like to keep one or two things in mind.

- ✔ **Kids get bored quicker than adults do.** Adults like to hang around at training, chatting between drills, but children want to keep playing. If you keep children waiting, they get tetchy – and the session produces less beneficial results.

- ✔ **Positive feedback is essential.** It's no use shouting at a child who's trying his best to perform a skill in practice or to play well during a match. What gets a good response from an adult doesn't necessarily work with a child.

- ✔ **There's nothing wrong with winning and losing.** Kids love to compete, and think every match is the biggest since the last World Cup final – so if they've lost the game, don't tell them it's okay and that it doesn't matter. Just make sure they keep a sense of perspective and don't slip into a sulk or throw a tantrum. Explaining how they can use their feeling of frustration positively – to train harder and play better next time – will stand them in good stead.

- ✔ **Tell the parents on the touch line to keep calm.** Some mums and dads scream and shout throughout matches, transmitting an aggressive message to the young players. Such an attitude does nobody any favours. Honestly, sometimes parents are worse than the kids.

For the detailed lowdown on coaching children, check out *Coaching Junior Football Teams For Dummies* by Greg Bach and James Heller (Wiley).

The sack – or bittersweet retirement?

They say all political careers are doomed to ultimate failure, and the same is true for football managers. It's a depressing thought but one best faced: whatever level you manage or coach at, you're very unlikely to go out at the very top.

Take a look at what happened to some of the all-time greats. Matt Busby won league titles and the European Cup at Manchester United, yet retired with an ageing and disintegrating team that was eventually relegated. Brian Clough was also a European champion at Nottingham Forest, but stayed too long and suffered relegation in his final season.

Even managers who bow out in a blaze of glory can come a cropper: Bill Shankly built Liverpool into one of the biggest clubs in the world and left in triumph after winning the league, UEFA Cup and FA Cup in two seasons – then spent the rest of his life rueing his decision to retire too soon.

And those are some of the happier endings! The vast majority of managerial careers end in one thing – the sack. But if you do get the boot, take heart: it happens to the best of them. In 1978 St Mirren threw a stunningly unsuccessful young manager on the scrapheap. Whatever happened to Alex Ferguson . . .?

Chapter 9

Getting the Game On

· ·

· ·

Getting a game together takes a little bit of organisational nous; you can't just wander along to the local park and be confident of joining a kickabout. (Unless you're eight years old, that is, but that's not the point right now.) But don't fret: it doesn't take long to find somewhere to play, and someone to play with. It's easy when you know where to look – and plenty of people are available to advise you along the way as well.

You may just want to have a semi-regular kickabout somewhere, or perhaps you'd like to be a bit more serious and play for – or manage – a local side in a local league. It might even be your ambition to start up a team of your own. Whatever your aims, the following advice helps you get your boots on and sends you out on the pitch in time for kick-off.

Midweek leagues exist, but most teams – mindful that people have jobs to do during the week – play their fixtures at the weekend.

Joining an Existing Team

The easiest way of getting a game of football is to join an existing club. Ring your local Football Association (FA) – taking England as an example, each county has its own County FA (affiliated to the main FA) with a list of local teams playing in local leagues. England also boasts the Amateur Football Association, who can advise you on your nearest side or point you in the direction of the best County FA adviser to speak to.

Don't be afraid to contact official football associations – that's exactly why they exist. Many young or inexperienced players assume football associations are busy dealing with professional matters, but someone is always prepared to help.

By all means ring an association, but in the interests of speed and accuracy, the Internet can be your friend here. Many FAs, as well as the Amateur Football Association, have a searchable database of local clubs. Enter your address or postcode and a comprehensive list of teams pops up.

When you've got a list of local clubs, do a bit of research. Many local sides now have websites, so take a look around and see which clubs take your fancy and which club you think you may feel most comfortable at.

Then it's time to take the plunge. Give the club a ring – the website should have a contact number or an FA adviser can give you one – and ask if you can join. (If you're enquiring on the Internet, you can contact the club via the e-mail address or form page on which you can input your personal details.)

The club will ask you a little bit about your footballing history.

- ✔ **Have you played for a club before?** List any teams you've played for, giving dates where possible.

- ✔ **What standard have you played to?** Have you played professionally or semi-professionally? Have you played for a local club's first team? Their second team? Minor levels? Have you never played before?

- ✔ **What age group are you?** Do you fit into the children's category? Youth? Adult? Veteran?

- ✔ **Any relevant information?** It's not a job interview, but if you've won a couple of trophies along the way it may help you get your foot in the door.

Many clubs are *multi-team clubs*, with several sides of varying quality. The first team plays the club's competitive league fixtures, but their other sides play either in lower leagues or friendly fixtures against sides of similar ability. Many clubs try to be as inclusive as possible and will try to help you find your level, so you can still enjoy a competitive game. Don't be afraid to ask!

Clubs may also be looking for players themselves. Keep an eye out for adverts in the local press or notices pinned to boards in local sports centres, sports clubs or civic centres.

If the club aren't looking for new players at the moment, they'll probably have heard of another team who are and will point you in that direction. Similarly, they may recommend a different club if they think from your enquiry that your standard is either too high or too low for their level.

Chances are, though, the club will ask you along for a trial. At the very local levels this will be an informal affair, so don't expect a thoroughly professional workout. If you're of the standard required for one of the club's teams, they'll hopefully ask you to join the club. If you feel comfortable with the people and the surroundings – and remember, at any non-professional level, this pastime is supposed to be fun – shake hands and join!

Thousands of teams exist across the country, from professional level to the rankest of rank amateurs. The FA and the County FAs want everyone to enjoy playing football, regardless of ability, so even if you can't find a team at your level immediately, don't stop trying. There's a competitive match – and hopefully a league – you can play in out there somewhere!

Starting Your Own Club

Perhaps you don't feel like searching for a place in a team by yourself. Or maybe you've already played for other clubs for a while, but now you want to start up your own side. Either way, if you think it's within your powers to get a whole team together and a new club off the ground, you've got work to do.

Building the club from scratch

The first jobs are ones of tedious administration, but it's vital to put the foundations of your club in place.

You should adopt a club constitution, detailing:

- ✔ Accounts
- ✔ Club membership
- ✔ Codes of conduct for players, managers, officials and spectators
- ✔ Dates of Committee meetings and an Annual General Meeting
- ✔ Disciplinary procedures
- ✔ Equality procedures
- ✔ First-aid certification
- ✔ Public liability insurance certification

If you're running a children's team, the constitution should also cover policies regarding child safety.

You can download a model constitution form from the FA website (www.fa.com) that covers these points – but you can adopt your own constitution if you prefer.

The FA, County FAs or other amateur football organisations affiliated to the FA will give you advice if required, or point you in the direction of people who can help.

You need to appoint a chairperson, secretary and treasurer to carry out key duties. These people form the basis of your club's committee. There may be more members on the committee; alternatively, when you're just starting out, you may be forced to take on all these roles yourself!

Chairperson

The chairperson should be a strong leader with an objective outlook on life. That person's role is to chair committee meetings and the AGM, assist the secretary in producing meeting agendas and make decisions for the benefit of the club as a whole.

Secretary

The secretary is the main administrator of the club. The role is to ensure all administrative and organisational duties are carried out efficiently and ensure the club is affiliated to the County FA and the leagues they compete in, and that players are registered with those leagues. The secretary is the main face of the club, attending league meetings, dealing with correspondence and representing the club at outside events.

Treasurer

The treasurer looks after the finances of the club, collecting subscriptions from players and staff, paying any bills and keeping official accounts and receipts.

Affiliation: Counties and leagues

Your club need to affiliate to a County Football Association (FA) and any appropriate local league they wish to compete in. After you decide what league you wish to join, it's up to your Secretary to send off the appropriate fees and paperwork. Fees vary enormously. Check them out with the County FA and the league you're proposing to join.

It's extremely unlikely that you'll be able to join a league in its top division. Your club will join in the bottom division of the league, at the start of the following season. But remember that you'll be able to win promotion – in theory, over time, all the way up the league pyramid to the FA Premier League. However, try not to get ahead of yourself with pipe dreams.

Make sure you get your paperwork in well before the start of the season, or you may find yourself waiting another year before you can get your club playing competitive fixtures.

You may require guidance to ascertain which league is most appropriate for your club's overall level of ability. You'll be able to get guidance from the County FAs or other amateur advisory bodies.

Finding players

If you've decided to start a club from scratch, you no doubt have the backbone of a team of players in mind – probably your friends and acquaintances. But even if you think you have a full squad, it pays to hold at least one trial, in the hope of finding some more talented and willing players to add to the mix.

If you have affiliation with your County FA, you're now on their lists and databases, so players can find and contact you. If you need to be more proactive, advertise for players: stick an ad in the local paper or pin cards up on notice boards at sports centres in your area. You may even find some players at your place of work: everyone involved with the club could post a notice or e-mail a circular at their office.

It's the secretary's job to register the players with the relevant leagues. Clubs should check whether players are already registered with another team, are cup-tied or are suspended for any reason.

Finding a manager

If you require a manager or coach, the FA holds a list of people who've passed their FA Coaching Badges. You may wish to contact one of these qualified coaches, but unless the rules of the league you're competing in stipulate otherwise, you're under no obligation to name a manager with a coaching badge.

Fixtures

The league administers fixtures (or any other competition) your club enters. The league advises you of any upcoming matches. They usually give you a complete list of fixtures at the start of the season. Details of any cup matches are given when the draws are made.

If it's a home match, your secretary must arrange the hire of a pitch and notify your players, opponent and match officials of the kick-off time and venue.

If it's an away game, the secretary must ensure the opposition tells him when and where the match will be played, and he relays that information to everyone involved at your club. He also arranges transport for players.

Cup competitions give you the opportunity to pit your wits against teams from other divisions.

Booking a pitch

Unless you're fortunate enough to have your own ground, or continued access to a ground, you need to find a place to play your home fixtures.

You can go down various routes. Remember that hire charges may vary wildly:

- ✔ **Local authority or parish council:** Most authorities have football pitches or suitable playing fields available for hire. Contact details are usually available on council websites.

- ✔ **Other local teams:** There may be other teams nearby – even semi-professional or professional ones – who'll allow you to rent their ground when they're not using it.

- ✔ **Private land:** Contact the owners of private grounds to see if they'd be willing to let you use a section of their land. Keep an ear to the ground because there may be someone known locally for his willingness to open his land to the community.

- ✔ **Schools, colleges and universities:** Educational establishments often have pitches and playing fields that would otherwise be lying idle and may be available for rent.

If you can agree a deal for an entire season at the same venue, you should be able to negotiate a more favourable hire charge. This also benefits the team, who feel they have a proper 'home' ground and get used to their surroundings.

Match officials

The league, or whatever other competition you enter, will arrange match officials for the game. This doesn't cost the club any money, because the membership fee paid to the league covers the charge.

Insurance

Clubs should have adequate insurance cover for their players, in case of injury or accident while playing or travelling to matches. Clubs should also be covered in the event of an opposing player suing them for an injury caused by one of their players. County FAs can advise on companies offering such policies.

Kit and equipment

You need to purchase suitable equipment for practices and to fulfil fixtures. At a minimum you require sufficient playing kit for the entire squad, goal nets, balls and a first-aid kit.

Chapter 3 gives you the inside track on the sort of gear you need.

Results

Your secretary must remember to pass on the results of all matches to competition regulators. He should also pass on all information to the local paper, which usually runs a results service of every nearby league.

Maintaining a good relationship with the local paper may stand you in good stead if you have serious ambitions for your club. As the club establishes itself, the paper may start reporting on the odd match here and there, and maybe even include the odd news story surrounding your club – all of which may help you attract new players in the future, or even sponsorship.

Disciplinary procedures

The match officials will inform the league of any disciplinary issues arising from your club's fixtures. The player in question should pay any disciplinary fines, which the club secretary processes, in order to ensure the club doesn't get into any trouble with the league. Non-payment of player fines could see the club itself fined, with the ultimate sanction of expulsion from the league.

Fees and funding

Funding is vital to keeping your club going. Initially fees will probably be from player membership and subscriptions alone.

At the start of the season, the secretary should work out the rough costs for the season. This includes:

✔ League membership fees

✔ Pitch hire

✔ Purchase of kit and equipment

✔ Transport to all away games

Realistically, for a new club the subscription fee should be the total cost divided by the amount of players and administrators involved for the season.

Clubs should inform players that they may be asked to top up their subscriptions during the first year because you're making rough estimates of costs. Providing everything is above board and transparent, it's unlikely anyone will object to an honest request for more funds for the club kitty.

Social events

It's important to bring your players and administrators together at social events in order to enhance relationships within the club. You – or a social secretary – need to organise a pre-season event, a Christmas function and an end-of-season celebration at the very least.

Even if your team is the most shambolic in the land, hold an end-of-season awards ceremony. Hand out token awards to as many of your team as you can – including awards for player and goal of the season – all in the name of fun.

You may also want to consider inviting local dignitaries, business people and journalists. It all helps to establish your club within the community, and you may even attract some sponsorship as a result.

Volunteer roles

Perhaps you love football and want to get involved with a local club, but don't want to get involved as a player, manager or even a high-level administrator. You can choose between many other volunteer roles, such as driving players to matches, sorting out half-time food and drinks, washing the kit or even training to become the physiotherapist.

If you're interested in getting involved, keep an eye out in the local press because a club may be advertising for volunteers.

Sometimes those doing seemingly menial roles at the club are rewarded for their service. In 1986, when Oxford United won the League Cup, manager Maurice Evans generously sent the club's 72-year-old physiotherapist, Ken Fish, up the famous Wembley stairs to receive the winner's medal meant for Evans.

Commercial Leagues

Most FA-affiliated leagues play their fixtures at the weekend, but an increasing number of commercially run leagues offer midweek fixtures. These leagues, which you can easily find on the Internet or advertised in the back of local newspapers and football magazines, are relatively hassle-free for teams to enter. For a flat fee the league organises a pitch to play on, opposition to face and a match official.

Commercial leagues aren't as strict on discipline as leagues with the long-established FA disciplinary apparatus behind them. That's not to paint these leagues as lawless free-for-alls, but it's worth remembering this point.

Park Kickabouts

'Any chance of a game?' If you're getting on a bit that might have been something you last asked years ago as a kid, but the question might still lead to a kickabout now.

During the summer months taking a quick wander around the major parks in your town or city may pay dividends. Groups of players often arrange informal matches, dropping a couple of jumpers down for goalposts and getting on with the serious business of having some fun.

Solo players walking by – or even groups – often ask to join in. Unless the game's at a crucial stage, with plenty of players already taking part, the answer's often affirmative. It's a good way to meet other players – you might even end up agreeing to meet again for a regular match. And the players may put you in touch with a regular game with an organised team or club.

Word of mouth is often the best way to find out about possible vacancies in organised teams. It's worth keeping your ear to the ground.

Five-a-side and Futsal

Football isn't just about 11-a-side matches. You also have small-sided games – predominantly five-a-side and six-a-side, as well as the relatively new sport of Futsal – that you play on courts rather than pitches.

You usually play five- and six-a-side matches on hard or artificial courts. A quicker game than 11-a-side, it's more end-to-end, with crisp passing and movement as greater features. (The smaller size of the courts negates the need for long passing. You often play matches with an 'above shoulder height' rule, negating high passes and heading.) No sidelines exist: you can play passes off the walls of the court.

Futsal is a similar five-a-side game, but with a smaller ball that gives less bounce. Ball skills are vital in Futsal; the game was created with developing dribbling in mind. Unlike five-a-side, the ball can go out of play.

It's easy to organise a five-a-side match. Groups of around ten friends usually club together to rent an indoor or outdoor court. Sports and civic centres across the country offer football courts.

Commercially organised five-a-side leagues also exist. As with commercial 11-a-side, the league organises everything for you: pitch, opposition and officials.

Soccer Schools and Training Camps

Most major clubs now operate soccer schools for youngsters. These take the form of either day-attendance events or residential training camps. Trained FA instructors are on hand to offer youngsters different packages of tuition, from the very basic skills to advanced technical training for the more experienced player. A first-team player at some point makes an appearance.

These courses can be quite pricy: a residential package costs over £500 for a week.

Becoming a Referee

If you don't fancy playing but want to take part in the game you have only one other option: become one of the officials. If you want to become a referee you need to fulfil three criteria:

✔ Are you at least 14 years old?

✔ Have you a workable level of fitness?

✔ (Don't laugh at this one.) Is your eyesight okay, with the use of spectacles or contact lenses if necessary?

If you can answer yes to all three questions, you're eligible to register with your local County FA for a basic refereeing course. This consists of several classroom sessions and two examinations as you learn the fundamental rules of the game.

If you pass the exams you're qualified to referee local amateur matches. You're also be allowed to run the line as a referee's assistant.

After a year of refereeing, if you so desire, you can push on and learn the Laws of the Game in greater detail. Check them out in Chapter 4. Along with match-based assessments, you can in theory move up through the leagues via seven levels – seven to one – and then to the FA International List. (However, only ten international referees exist in England at any one time.)

Part III
Exploring the World of Football

'Take me to your football manager.'

In this part . . .

This part explores not only the major football competitions that are played in the British Isles and Europe, but those played at international level. We start the tour of planet football with an explanation of everything you need to know about the World Cup, including its history and format, as well as descriptions of some of the most memorable World Cup moments.

Next, we take you on a comprehensive guided tour of international football and the other major tournaments, such as the European Championships, the Copa America and the Africa Cup of Nations. Away from the international arena, we talk about the major club and tournaments (both leagues and cups), introduce you to some of the great clubs who play in them, and explain, along the way, the whole business of what constitutes a club and the league it plays in.

To round off our voyage through football, we provide you with everything you need to know about the burgeoning world of Women's football.

Chapter 10

The World Cup

. . . .

In This Chapter

▶ The route to the biggest sporting show on earth

▶ What happens when teams get there

▶ The 1930 to 2006 World Cups: eight decades' worth of phenomenon

▶ The 2010 World Cup: the biggest and best yet!

. . . .

The International Olympic Committee would argue otherwise, of course, but football's premier international trophy – officially called the FIFA World Cup, but known to everyone simply as the World Cup – is unquestionably the biggest sporting event on the planet.

The 'event' people refer to as the 'World Cup' is really the World Cup finals, the culmination of a worldwide qualifying process that takes nearly three years to complete. The World Cup finals are held every four years, a month-long festival of football featuring the best players and the greatest teams, culminating in the biggest single one-off sporting occasion in the world of sport: the World Cup final.

This chapter describes everything you need to know about this amazing event: who takes part, how teams get to play in it, how the tournament is organised and what happens during the finals. I also touch upon the most amazing moments in the history of the World Cup, from Diego Maradona's infamous Hand of God goal to Zinedine Zidane's headbutt.

The Biggest Show on Earth

Every single one of FIFA's 207 member countries – from giants like Brazil and Italy, to minnows such as Papua New Guinea and Montserrat – is allowed to enter the World Cup. But only 32 teams are able to participate in the finals tournament, and as the host nation of the finals is automatically allowed entry that means there are only 31 places up for grabs. To determine who reaches the finals the teams play in qualifying tournaments.

The long and winding road begins

FIFA is split into six continental governing bodies, represented by a proper blizzard of acronyms. These are:

- **AFC:** The Asian Football Confederation covers football throughout much of Asia. Russian football, however, comes entirely under the aegis of UEFA, even if a Russian club is, by any other measure, in Asia.

- **CAF:** The Confederation of African Football pretty much does what it says in Africa. Actually, the title is originally French – *Confédération Africaine de Football* – but it amounts to the same thing.

- **CONCACAF:** An abbreviation that doesn't seem to do that much abbreviating. The *Confederation of North, Central American and Caribbean Association Football* is responsible for the game from Alaska down to the Panama Canal, including the islands of the Caribbean.

- **CONMEBOL:** The rather convoluted abbreviation for *Confederación Sudamericana de Fútbol* (if you're a Spanish speaker) or *Confederação Sul-Americana de Futebol* (if you speak Portuguese). Either way, CONMEBOL runs football in South America.

- **OFC:** The Oceania Football Confederation administers the game in the islands of the Pacific, in Polynesia and in New Guinea. It also takes in New Zealand, though not, confusingly, Australia, which has been affiliated to the AFC since 2006.

- **UEFA:** The *Union des Associations Européennes de Football*, to give it its full French title, is the governing body for football in Europe.

FIFA gives each governing body a certain number of World Cup finals berths to fill, and each runs their own qualifying campaign to determine who makes it to the finals.

The relative strength of the teams in each part of the world determines the number of places each continent receives. For example, in qualification for the 2010 World Cup, UEFA – which includes the reigning world champions Italy, three-time winners Germany, France (winners in 1998 and runners-up in 2006) and England – were given 13 berths to fill. By comparison, OFC – who've only ever sent three teams to the World Cup in the tournament's 80-year history; Australia (twice) and New Zealand (once) – received just half a berth! (In practice, this 'half berth' means the Oceania qualification group winners play off for a spot in the finals with the fifth-best team in the Asian qualifiers.)

The shape of things to come

Due to an ever-fluctuating number of countries in the world, the qualification process has taken on many varied shapes since the first qualifiers were held for the 1934 tournament. (For the record, the first-ever World Cup in 1930 was invitation only, but more of that in the nearby sidebar 'The First World Cup'.)

Each continent also prefers their own method to determine who wins through, but the process is always based on some sort of league format. So in South America all ten competing countries play each other, home and away, in one big league. The top four go through and the fifth team goes into a play-off (in 2010, with the fourth-best team in CONCACAF). But in Europe the 13 places on offer are decided by eight groups of six teams and one group of five. The winners of all nine groups go through, and the best eight group runners-up play off against each other for four places.

It's a complicated process, but one that ensures every single nation has – theoretically at least – a chance of making the finals.

The finals countdown

There would be no point putting all that effort into qualifying, only to lose your very first game at the finals and be sent packing straight back home. That's why FIFA have developed a structure that ensures all 32 finalists at the World Cup are guaranteed at least three games – therefore giving everyone at least a second chance of survival.

The structure of the World Cup finals is simple. In the first stage the 32 teams are drawn into eight groups of four. Each group is identified by a letter, A to H. FIFA seed the draw – made roughly seven months before the start of the tournament – in terms of current ranking and historical performance to ensure all the best teams aren't drawn together in the early stages. Each group takes the form of a mini league, the teams all playing each other once. After all the teams have played all the matches the top two teams in the group qualify for the second round.

From the second round onwards it's a straight knockout. In the second round, each first-round group winner plays a runner-up from another group. After that is the quarter-finals, by which time things start getting really hot, then the semis and final. The whole process takes, give or take a couple of days, exactly a month. There are at least two games a day right up until after the quarters, whereupon in order to give the teams still standing a rest – and to make it totally fair – the two semis and the final are spread out over the last week.

The day before the final there's a third-place play-off. But players, managers and fans alike agree: having got so close to the big one, nobody involved really wants to be there at all. Not least because, by now, everyone is on tenterhooks for the final. Always now held on the last Sunday of the tournament, many millions of people worldwide watch the final. Over 260 million watched Italy beat France in the 2006 final, a figure sure to be superceded in 2010. Kick-off is invariably at a time that ensures European viewers (the biggest source of TV advertising revenue) watch the game in daylight hours.

From Montevideo to Johannesburg: Eighty Years of Top-class Drama

With one exception (in 2002, when the finals were staged jointly by Japan and South Korea), one country has hosted each finals tournament. Uruguay were the first in 1930, and have been followed by Italy (1934 and 1990), France (1938 and 1998), Brazil (1950), Switzerland (1954), Sweden (1958), Chile (1962), England (1966), Mexico (1970 and 1986), West Germany (1974), Argentina (1978), Spain (1982), the United States (1994), South Korea and Japan (2002) and Germany (2006). In 2010 South Africa will become the first African nation to host the tournament.

The 1930 tournament in Uruguay featured 13 teams from three continents (North and South America, and Europe), took a mere 18 days to complete and was played in three stadiums in a single city, Montevideo. In 2010 the finals will feature 32 teams from right across the world, take a month to complete and take place in ten stadiums in nine cities. The tournament has come a long way in its 80 years . . .

Uruguay and Italy set the template

Two teams dominated the early years of the World Cup. Uruguay won the inaugural event at home in 1930, before Italy repeated the trick four years later. The Italian success was for ever tainted by rumours that the dictator Mussolini had paid a visit to the referee before the final against Czechoslovakia – and that Uruguay had failed to turn up, annoyed at the reluctance of Europeans to travel to their country in 1930. But the Italian side was undoubtedly one of the greats, powered by the fearsome Luis Monti, and managed by the legendary Vittorio Pozzo, one of football's earliest tactical geniuses.

Italy retained their trophy in 1938, but understandably flopped when the World Cup resumed after the war in 1950. Most of their top players were wiped out in the 1949 Superga air crash, laying to waste the famous Torino team, and the Italian side insisted on travelling to the tournament in Brazil by boat. Exhausted, they bowed out without making an impression. Still, everyone expected hosts Brazil to win – including the country's president, who congratulated his countrymen on their victory in a speech *before* the deciding match against Uruguay. Needing only a draw against Uruguay in the last match of a final-stage pool to win, Brazil conceded twice in the last 19 minutes to lose 2-1. There were suicides in Rio that night.

Figure 10-1:
Brazil won the original Jules Rimet Trophy outright in 1970.

They think it's the World Cup's golden age . . . it is now!

The years between 1954 and 1970 represent the World Cup's classic era. Reigning champions Uruguay lost their first ever World Cup match in 1954, in the semi-final against Hungary. It was hardly a shock, though: the Hungarians reinvented the sport with their clever football, based around the revolutionary deep-lying play-making of Nandor Hidegkuti and silky footwork of Ferenc Puskás. They were reigning Olympic champions and hadn't lost for three years. They were considered shoo-ins for the trophy, especially because they faced West Germany in the final, who they'd beaten 8-3 in the group stage. But despite going 2-0 up in eight minutes, they let West Germany back into the match, eventually losing 3-2.

The next Greatest Team in the World had no problem claiming the big prize: Brazil finally landed their first World Cup in 1958 thanks to the genius of the 17-year-old Pelé (see Figure 10-2) and tricky winger Garrincha. Brazil retained their trophy in 1962, but relinquished it in England four years later, Sir Alf Ramsey leading the three lions to their greatest achievement. People regarded his side at the time as dour and defensive, and they failed to entertain throughout the tournament – until they reached the final against West Germany, that is, when they suddenly burst into goal-scoring life as Geoff Hurst became the first, and as yet only, man to score a hat-trick in a World Cup final. (With a little help from an Azeri linesman – not Russian, despite the legend – who failed to spot his second goal hadn't crossed the line, admittedly, but not even the Germans argued that England had deserved to win on the day.)

Many argue that England were a much better team in the 1970 finals in Mexico. Even though they didn't win this time, they certainly contributed to a tournament considered the greatest in the history of football. Bobby Moore and Pelé embraced after a cat-and-mouse duel between England and Brazil under a psychedelic Guadalajara sun, and West Germany gained revenge for 1966 with a stunning comeback in León in the quarter-finals to put the champions out. England's exit mattered little though: Pelé's Brazil were destined to take their crown anyway, thrashing defensive hardmen Italy 4-1 in the final. Captain Carlos Alberto scored the most iconic goal in the history of the World Cup, ending a pitch-long Brazilian multi-player sashay with a blistering drive into the net. Brazil were awarded the cup permanently, having become the first nation to register a hat-trick of wins.

Germany and Argentina take centre stage

The 1970 tournament was drenched in Mexican sun, but the 1974 version was soaked by German drizzle. Yet once again the World Cup was blessed by a burst of vibrant colour: the 'oranje' of Holland. The Dutch team, built around the twisty-turny talents of Johan Cruyff, lit up the tournament with their Total Football, the idea being that any player on the park could play in any position – defence, midfield, attack – and often did so, interchanging with each other mid-match. Like Hungary 20 years earlier, people considered the side to be miles ahead of all the other opposition, and shoo-ins for the cup. And like Hungary 20 years earlier, they were stymied in the final by a resolute West Germany. Along with the Hungarians, many agree that this Dutch side were the best team never to have won the trophy.

Figure 10-2:
The incomparable Pelé.

Holland felt more pain in 1978, once again losing in the final to the host nation, this time Argentina. The tournament is remembered for the goals of Argentinian striker Mario Kempes, the wonderful ticker-tape celebrations in the stadiums – and the murderous military junta running the country at the time, a sickening backdrop to the tournament.

Four years later in Spain, Italy became the second country to triumph for a third time. They beat West Germany in the final, but the side are chiefly remembered for putting a rampant Brazil to the sword along the way, Paolo Rossi scoring a hat-trick to deny the swashbuckling Zico, Socrates and Falcão. West Germany were back in the final in 1986 and again came up short, as Diego Maradona almost single-handedly dragged an otherwise average

Argentina side to victory. Is the defining memory of that campaign the 'Hand of God' goal palmed in by Maradona against England in the quarter-finals, or the mazy 64-metre (70-yard) run he scored in the same game minutes later? That very much depends on where you're from!

Argentina and West Germany both reached the final again in 1990. This Italian World Cup was a poor tournament, though it's a bittersweet memory in England for Paul Gascoigne's tears in the semi-final, a close match agonisingly lost on penalties to the Germans, who went on to lift the trophy. Maradona also ended his tournament in floods of tears.

Figure 10-3:
Franz Becken-bauer, West Germany's winning captain in 1974.

Figure 10-4:
The gifted
Johan
Cruyff.

Brazil bounce back

On their way to the 1990 final Argentina put out their closest rivals, Brazil, in the second round. It was Brazil's most unsuccessful campaign since failing in the group stage in 1966. The team hadn't reached the final since 1970, so decided from then on to play in a 'European' style – in other words, eschewing the sometimes reckless 'samba' football synonymous with Brazil since the 1950s in favour of a more pragmatic defensive approach. The decision paid immediate dividends. Brazil won the 1994 World Cup in Pasadena, United States – though reaction to the win back home was muted in comparison to previous winning celebrations because many fans felt the team had jettisoned something unique in the pursuit of glory.

Brazil reached the final again in 1998, but their star striker Ronaldo suffered a fit on the morning of the match and was rushed to hospital. In circumstances still unclear to this day, he wasn't even on the bench before the match but with less than an hour to kick-off was back in the team. Ronaldo played as though in a daze, as did the other ten Brazilians. Hosts France, inspired by Zinedine Zidane, coasted to an easy 3-0 win, the largest winning margin in any final.

Figure 10-5:
Zinedine
Zidane's
moment of
madness
in the 2006
final.

Once again, though, Brazil bounced back. The 2002 Korea/Japan tournament was perhaps the poorest of all time in terms of overall quality, with only Brazil standing out. Ronaldo made up for his travails in 1998 by scoring both goals in the final, his team running out 2-0 winners over Germany. Their run of finals couldn't last for ever, though, and in 2006 *Les Bleus* surprisingly made it to the finals and the Zidane-inspired French team beat Brazil.

France could easily have won their second trophy too, proving to be marginally the better side in the final against Italy. But they couldn't press home their advantage after Zidane was sensationally sent off for headbutting Marco Materazzi in the chest and they lost a tense penalty shootout. It was as dramatic a denouement as any final in this grand old competition's history.

And so to 2010 . . .

You can be sure that the 2010 World Cup will add a fantastic new chapter to this already rich narrative. No event on earth offers as much drama; even the tournaments that in retrospect seem less than vintage – 1990 and 2002 spring to mind – were still rollercoaster rides of emotion when they were actually happening.

So which players will stamp their names all over the 2010 World Cup? And which teams have a realistic chance of making the final on 11 July at Soccer City, Johannesburg?

Teams to look out for

Brazil start every World Cup as favourites, and this time will be no different: the reigning Copa America and Confederations Cup champions, managed by 1994 World Cup winning captain Dunga, were in the doldrums for a while but came into good form during 2009. Their main competitors are likely to be Spain, the 2008 European champions, much fancied to reach the final for the first time in their history.

Some other usual suspects line up too. Argentina didn't have a particularly impressive qualifying campaign, under the auspices of the legendary Maradona, but they usually come good. Reigning champions Italy have also hit some recent turbulence, but always do well at the World Cup: since 1978 they've only been knocked out twice by losing a match, an amazing record. (Three of their defeats have been in the lottery of a penalty shootout.) And it's an old cliché, but you can never write off Germany. Again their side looks distinctly average, but they said that in 1954. And 1974.

South Africa are likely to struggle, though they won't want to become the first-ever hosts to be knocked out in the first round. Africa's challenge is likely to be made by either Ghana or Ivory Coast, both teams having gained experience from a decent 2006 tournament and looking stronger as a result. Can either team be the first-ever African nation to become world champions? It's not expected, although Ivory Coast's squad in particular will be packed with stars from Europe's top clubs.

As for England? Under Italian coach Fabio Capello they look more solid than they have done since the glory days of Sir Alf in the late 1960s – though they might have to get over their aversion to penalty shootouts at some point!

Players to watch

Lionel Messi is the latest in a long line of Argentinian players to be lumbered with the description of The New Maradona, but the diminutive Barcelona striker looks like the real deal. He's already scored in a Champions League final, when Barcelona beat Manchester United to land the 2009 trophy, so can he add a World Cup final goal to his tally?

Brazil aren't studded with stars like they have been in the past, but they can still boast the greatest play-maker in the world in Kaka. When the goal-scoring Real Madrid midfielder ticks, so do Brazil. His form could decide the tournament.

Spain will perhaps be the most star-studded team on show. Fernando Torres of Liverpool is one of the greatest strikers in the world at the moment, and has already scored the winning goal in a major international tournament, at Euro 2008. They also boast David Villa up front, while their midfield is teeming with riches, from Arsenal's Cesc Fàbregas to Barcelona's wonderful, bustling Andrés Iniesta.

Figure 10-6:
Lionel Messi
– a star in
2010?

England have some star names in offensive midfielder Steven Gerrard and powerful striker Wayne Rooney, though perhaps their most crucial player will be in goal: will Capello go with the experience of 39-year-old David James or the inexperienced 27-year-old Ben Foster? It's a make-or-break decision.

Chelsea midfielder Michael Essien will hope to power Ghana to glory, but it's Ivory Coast who really catch the eye: Essien's club-mates Didier Drogba and Salomon Kalou star up front, while the excellent Yaya Touré of Barcelona runs their midfield. It would be fitting, though, were the player of the tournament to come from Africa.

And when it's all over . . .

So a month of excitement awaits. And then?

Well, after a 64-year wait Brazil will host its second World Cup in 2014. In December 2010, FIFA will announce the countries to host the 2018 and 2022 events. No one continent can host both tournaments. England and Australia are the favourites to stage a tournament each – although Belgium and Holland, Indonesia, Japan, Qatar, Mexico, Russia, South Korea, Portugal and Spain, and the United States may have something to say about that . . .

Chapter 11

Surveying the International Scene

. . . .

. . . .

The World Cup isn't football's only international tournament. Each continent holds their own international championship too, with rich and varied histories of their own.

Some are older than the World Cup itself – South America had its own championship as far back as 1917 – while others, like the FIFA Confederations Cup, are still in their infancy.

And then, of course, there are friendly matches, where there's nothing at stake. Apart from your country's pride, that is . . .

Friendlies

A friendly is an exhibition game, where there is no competitive prize on offer whatsoever. Until football got itself organised in the early days into knockout cup competitions and leagues – see Chapter 2 for how the game developed – nearly all matches were friendlies.

The very first international match ever played was a friendly. It was contested between Scotland and England in Glasgow on November 30 1872. The Scots wore blue shirts with red hoods, while the English ran about in caps! The game ended 0-0 – the only time the two teams would play out a goal-less match until 1970.

After a while, countries started organising meaningful tournaments. First the home nations – England, Scotland, Wales and a pre-partition Ireland – set up the International Championship (known as the Home Internationals). Later, as we shall see, came the Copa America, the World Cup, the European Championship, the African Cup of Nations and many others – but even so, countries still play friendlies to this day.

The modern friendly international

These days, friendly internationals are mainly staged to help countries prepare for their official tournament matches. England, for example, used to play Scotland every year. But the two teams haven't met since being paired in a qualifying play-off for Euro 2000. (For the record, England won the two-legged tie, but Scotland won the final match, 1-0 at Wembley.)

Nowadays the likes of England and Scotland are more likely to arrange less stressful friendly matches. With much less pride at stake against different opposition, their managers are able to experiment with new, and previously untested, players, formations and tactics. Managers can make up to six substitutions in these games, three more than in official tournament conditions.

But countries still arrange the odd prestige friendly, at which pride is at a premium. Even if there's no cup at stake, England don't want to lose to Argentina, or vice versa!

The European Championships

The UEFA European Football Championship – formerly known as the European Nations Cup – is the international championship of Europe.

The final tournament is held every four years, midway through each four-year World Cup cycle. For example, World Cup finals were held in 1998, 2002 and 2006, while European Championship finals were held in 1996, 2000, 2004 and 2008. The next European Championship will be held in 2012, in Ukraine.

Since 1984, the European Championships have been known colloquially as The Euros, with the year appended. So the 1984 event was called Euro 84, the 1988 staging Euro 88, and so on. Since the turn of the millennium, the full year has been used: Euro 2000, Euro 2004, Euro 2008 and, coming soon, Euro 2012 . . .

How it's organised

Every national side in Europe is eligible to enter, providing they are affiliated to UEFA – the Union of European Football Associations, the governing body of football in Europe.

The tournament is organised along the same principles as the World Cup. There is a qualification tournament, contested by every entrant, followed by a finals tournament, featuring 16 finalists.

The hosts are always exempt from qualifying. In 2012, the tournament will be jointly held by Poland and Ukraine – so that means another 14 finalists have to be found.

Countries are drawn into one of seven seeded qualification groups, with seeding dependent on previous performance in World Cups and European Championships, and the seeds' FIFA World ranking. Countries play home and away against every other team in their group, with the winners and runners-up of the resulting mini-league qualifying for the finals.

Once at the finals, the 16 teams are seeded, then drawn into four groups of four. After playing each other once, the winners and runners-up of those groups go through to the quarter-finals, each group winner being paired with a runner-up from a different group. From then on in it's a straight knockout, through the semis to the final.

It's a simple set-up – though it's a format which has changed often over the years!

The early years

UEFA – the Union of European Football Associations, the governing body of football in Europe – held the first European Championship finals in France in 1960. Only four teams competed – the 'final tournament' was effectively the two semi-finals and final of a cup knockout.

Hosts France were the favourites, but despite being 4-2 up in their semi-final against Yugoslavia with 15 minutes to go, lost 5-4. The final would be won by the Soviet Union, whose star player was goalkeeper Lev Yashin, still said by those who saw him play to be the greatest of all time.

The 1964 tournament was held in Spain, who had defaulted from the 1960 event after their fascist dictator General Franco had refused to allow the communist Soviets into his country for their quarter-final qualifier. This time, with UEFA threatening to take the tournament away from the Spanish, he allowed the defending champions in. Franco would be pleased at the way things panned out, Spain beating the USSR in the final.

The host nation won for the second successive tournament in 1968, Italy defeating Yugoslavia, who had now been runners-up twice in three stagings.

The famous West German team of Franz Beckenbauer, Gerd Muller and Gunther Netzer won the 1972 finals, held in Belgium, but were powerless to retain their trophy in Yugoslavia four years later. In that 1976 final, they were beaten by Czechoslovakia in a penalty shootout, Antonin Panenka scoring the decisive penalty with one of the cheekiest kicks of all time, a dainty chip straight down the middle.

Ever since the 1976 final, a cheeky penalty chipped into the centre of goal, sending the keeper helplessly diving either to the left or right, has been known as a 'Panenka'.

The Euros go large . . . and even larger

The 1976 finals had been extremely popular, so for Europa 80, as it was known, UEFA decided to allow eight teams to compete in the finals. Two mini-leagues of four teams would compete, with the group winners facing each other in the final. West Germany regained the trophy they had lost four years earlier, beating Belgium in the final, but it was a poor tournament that didn't stay long in the memory.

The format was slightly rejigged for the 1984 version in France, with a semi-final stage coming after the opening group phase. If the 1980 tournament was totally forgettable, this one was perhaps the greatest ever, midfielder Michel Platini scoring nine times in five games as hosts France claimed their first trophy, spectacularly beating Portugal 3-2 in a dramatic semi, before beating Spain in the final.

Euro 88, held in West Germany, was another memorable classic. After losing two World Cup finals in the 1970s, Holland finally got their hands on some silverware, beating the USSR 2-0 in the final. The match, and the tournament, will always be remembered for Marco van Basten's sumptuous volley in the final, a dipping cross walloped in from an almost impossible angle to the right of the Russian goal.

Euro 92 in Sweden was less memorable, although the tournament did offer up perhaps the biggest fairytale in the history of the European Championship. Denmark failed to qualify, but were handed a reprieve when Yugoslavia, who had topped their qualification group, descended into civil war and could not compete. The Danes made it all the way to the final, where they beat reigning world champions Germany 2-0.

By now the Euros were becoming almost as popular as the World Cup, so UEFA decreed that Euro 96, held in England, would be competed by 16 teams. The hosts looked as good a bet as anyone, especially after Paul Gascoigne scored a screamer in a 2-0 win against Scotland, and England trounced much-fancied Holland 4-1. But they met Germany in the semi-final, and were knocked out on penalties. Germany beat the Czech Republic in the final, thanks to Oliver Bierhoff, who scored the first golden goal to decide a major tournament.

'*Golden goals*' were introduced in the mid-1990s by FIFA to decide matches in big tournaments which went to extra time. If a goal was scored at any point during extra time, it would automatically win the game. They were not popular, as they gave the losing side no opportunity to come back. They were first replaced by '*silver goals*', which allowed the match to continue to the end of a half in extra time, before the concept was scrapped altogether after Euro 2004.

The Euros in the new millennium

Euro 2000, held jointly by Holland and Belgium, was a huge success, with many high-scoring and dramatic matches. Holland were beaten in the semi-finals by Italy, missing two penalties during normal time. The Italians so nearly won the trophy, leading France 1-0 in the final with seconds to go, but Sylvan Wiltord whipped in a dramatic equaliser, before David Trezeguet scored a spectacular Golden Goal in extra time.

Euro 2004 was a quieter affair. Otto Rehhagel's Greece side was considered dour, not that they'd care: they amazingly won the tournament against all the odds, smothering reigning champions France, the much-fancied Czech Republic and hosts Portugal (twice – in the opening match of the tournament, then in the final).

Euro 2008 was held in Austria and Switzerland, and was most notable for Turkey's efforts to match their rivals Greece's achievement four years earlier. They made it to the semi-finals, thanks to two spectacular comebacks – a 3-2 win from two goals down against the Czech Republic, and a win on penalties against Croatia after plundering a 1-1 draw with the very last kick of the match – but were eventually knocked out by Germany.

The Germans, however, had no answer for Spain, who had been by far the best side in the tournament. They won the final thanks to Fernando Torres's single goal, adding a second European Championship to the one they won back in 1964.

The 2012 tournament will be held jointly by Poland and Ukraine. It will be the last ever staging of the European Championships to feature just 16 teams – UEFA have decided that in 2016, the tournament will be contested by 24 countries!

From its beginnings back in France 56 years previously, when four teams battled it out for the title, the Euros will have come a long way.

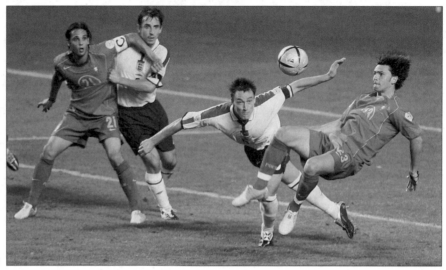

Figure 11-1:
Action from the 2004 European Championship match between England and Portugal.

Copa America

While it took the Europeans until the Swinging Sixties to start up their own international tournament, the South Americans had already been up and running for half a century!

The South American Championship – known since 1975 as the Copa America – is the oldest international football tournament outside of the Olympic Games.

It was first held on an unofficial basis in 1910, then officially in 1916, when it really got going. The championship has been held ever since, though at irregular intervals: sometimes, as in the 1920s, there was one every year, other times there have been breaks of up to eight years (1967 to 1975)!

How it's organised

The Copa America is organised by the ten member countries of the South American governing body CONMEBOL (Confederación Sudamericana de Fútbol, or Confederação Sul-Americana de Futebol): Argentina, Bolivia, Brazil, Chile, Colombia, Ecuador, Paraguay, Peru, Uruguay and Venezuela.

All teams automatically qualify – and are usually joined by two invitees to make the numbers up to a more draw-friendly 12. In 2007, for example, Mexico and the USA were invited. In 2011, the guests will be Mexico and Japan.

The teams will be split into three groups of four, with the top two in each group advancing to the quarter-final knockout stage. The best two third-placed teams will also go through.

The oldest – and the best?

The South American Championship has only recently been decided in the latter stages by knockout ties culminating in a final. Traditionally, the tournament was organised in a group, with the top team in the league winning the trophy.

Argentina won the very first tournament, which they organised themselves in 1910, and only featured themselves, Uruguay and Chile. The real thing started six years later, when Brazil joined the party. Uruguay won that one, and the following championship a year later in 1917.

The championship would be held every year between 1919 and 1927, with Uruguay and Argentina the dominant forces. But soon its staging would become extremely erratic, with several CONMEBOL members showing little interest in the trophy at all, either sending second-string teams or simply not bothering to enter whatsoever.

An erratic history

While all CONMEBOL members enter the competition nowadays, that hasn't always been the case. In fact, it was only in 1975 when every single one of CONMEBOL's ten countries deigned to enter the same tournament.

The 'big three' of Argentina, Brazil and Uruguay entered more often than not. Between the mid-1930s and late 1950s, the championship was held – usually! – every two years. But despite their emergence as kingpins on the world stage, Brazil struggled to win their continental championship: Argentina and Uruguay would become the most successful countries.

The championship nearly ground to a halt in the 1960s and 1970s. Most of the continent's big-name players now plied their trade in Europe, and getting them back to play out a month-long tournament became a major hassle. Only four championships were staged between 1963 and 1983, with the two in the 1970s won by minnows Peru (1975) and Paraguay (1979). It seemed the 'big three' could no longer be bothered, sending teams of players who would get nowhere near a World Cup squad.

Figure 11-2:
Brazilian players hold the Copa America aloft after their 2007 victory.

The Copa's revival

But the status of the tournament slowly grew again. CONMEBOL had rebranded it as the Copa America in 1975, then introduced a World Cup and Euro-style finals tournament in 1993. A group stage followed by knockout games and a final match would generate television revenue and raise the tournament's profile. There would also be guest spots for other countries, such as Mexico and the United States. Suddenly all the CONMEBOL countries were interested again.

Argentina won the first staging of this new format in 1993 – still their last success on the international stage – beating guests Mexico in the final thanks to a late goal from Gabriel Batistuta. Uruguay beat world champions Brazil on penalties in the 1995 final, before Brazil won what was at the time only their fifth title in 1997, triumphing over hosts Bolivia. (By comparison, both Argentina and Uruguay had 14 titles to their name.)

Since then, Brazil have finally become dominant in the Copa America, winning in 1999, 2004 and 2007. Colombia have been the only country to break a run of Brazilian success, becoming surprise winners in 2001.

The Copa America is now held on a regular four-year cycle. The next tournament will be held in Argentina in 2011, while Mexico are pencilled in to become the first non-CONMEBOL team to host the finals in 2015.

Africa Cup of Nations

The Africa Cup of Nations was launched in 1957 by African football's governing body, the Confederation of African Football (CAF). Initially a three-team invitational event, it has grown into the largest competition in Africa.

Behind the World Cup, European Championship and Copa America, it is probably the fourth most prestigious international football tournament on the planet – and one whose influence and popularity is growing rapidly, as world-class African players become a fixture at the world's biggest club sides.

The tournament is often referred to as the African Cup of Nations – but drop the adjectival 'n', because the proper name is the Africa Cup of Nations. Even to this day, many newspapers, television stations and Internet sites get this wrong!

How it's organised

The tournament is held every two years, with 16 teams competing in a finals tournament. The teams are split into four groups of four, with the winners and runners-up moving to a knockout quarter-finals stage.

With 53 countries hoping to make it to the finals, qualification is a long process. A first round, featuring knockout ties between the lowest African nations in the FIFA World Rankings, thins the field out to 48 competitors. Those countries are divvied up into four seeded pots, from which 12 groups are drawn.

The winners of each group, plus the eight best runners up, move forward to a third round. Again, the countries are separated into seeded pots, from which five groups of four are drawn. The top three teams in each group qualify for the Africa Cup of Nations finals.

Because there are so many teams, and so many matches have to be played, the process also often takes in World Cup qualifying. So in 2010, for example, the five group winners in the third round all qualify for the World Cup finals as well.

The ACN: A slow burner

The first tournament, held in Sudan in 1957, wasn't much of an event. South Africa were initially scheduled to play, but refused to field a multi-racial team, citing their apartheid policy, and were forced to withdraw. This meant Ethiopia made the final by default – they refused to countenance a three-team round-robin – but were stuffed 4-0 in the final by Egypt.

Many countries in Africa were too poor to compete – or were still colonised – so it took a while for the competition to grow. The same three teams competed in 1959 – and this time Ethiopia were forced to accept a three-team mini-league – with Egypt again prevailing.

Ghana and Tunisia were the star teams of the 1960s. Ghana's team – known as the Black Stars, or the Brazil of Africa – won in 1963 and 1965, and carried political significance too. Ghana's head of state, Kwame Nkrumah, reckoned a successful football team would show the world an independent African nation could prosper on the big stage. 'It showed we could do things for ourselves and achieve positive results,' said their star striker Joseph Agyeman-Gyau, looking back decades later.

The tournament caught on, and by 1968 15 teams wanted in. By now, too many entrants meant qualification was required for the first time. The CAF decided to hold the ANC every two years, a symbol of its success.

The cup catches fire

After the number of participants increased, so too did the number of winners. Between 1968 and 1980, the Democratic Republic of Congo, Sudan, Republic of Congo, Morocco and Nigeria all won the title for the first time.

Cameroon would be the team of the 1980s, reaching three finals in a row between 1982 and 1986, winning twice. Nigeria were also big players, reaching five finals between 1980 and 1994; they bookended that period with two victories, losing three finals in between.

South Africa would come out of the sporting wilderness in the early 1990s. They failed to qualify in 1994, their first tournament back since the abolition of apartheid, but hosted the event in 1996 – and won their first-ever title.

Since then, Egypt (champions in 1998, 2006 and 2008) and Cameroon (champions in 2000 and 2002) have dominated.

The cup will be held again in 2010 in Angola, but after that the future of the tournament is up in the air. With more African players now playing for top European clubs, there is pressure for the tournament to be moved into the European close season (May to August). This would mean the ANC would have to be held on an odd-numbered year, to avoid clashing with the World Cup and European Championship.

Figure 11-3: Action from an Africa cup of Nations game between Egypt and Cameroon.

Other tournaments

The World, European, South American and African international tournaments might be the biggest on the planet, but they're certainly not the only ones.

The three other confederations – the Asian Football Confederation, the Confederation of North, Central American and Caribbean Association

Football, and the Oceania Football Confederation – stage their own tournaments. FIFA recently launched the Confederations Cup, contested by the champions of each confederation. And, of course, there's the Olympic Games.

Asian Cup

The Asian Cup is the continental football tournament in Asia, contested between members of the Asian Football Confederation. The trophy was held every four years from 1956 until 2004, at which point the four-year cycle jumped back a year in order to avoid clashes with other major tournaments such as the European Championship. The last Asian Cup was held in 2007, with the next one to be held in 2011.

Saudi Arabia, Iran and Japan are the three most successful Asian Cup participants, with three wins apiece. South Korea has won the trophy twice, while Israel, Kuwait and Iraq (the current champions) have each won it once.

Not all the former or current member nations of the AFC are from Asia: 1964 winners Israel, for example, left the confederation in 1974, while Australia, formerly of Oceania, joined in 2006.

Gold Cup

The CONCACAF Gold Cup is run by the Confederation of North, Central American and Caribbean Association Football. The competition was launched in 1991 and has been staged more or less every two years since.

A qualification process ascertains the top five countries from Central America, and the top four teams from the Caribbean zone. These teams join the United States, Mexico and Canada for a 12-team finals tournament, which is nearly always held in the US.

Mexico have won five Gold Cups, the US four and Canada one.

Nations Cup

The Oceania Football Confederation runs the OFC Nations Cup. It has been staged eight times, and won four times apiece by New Zealand and Australia. New Zealand – a minnow on the world stage – are nevertheless the only sizeable nation left in the competition since Australia defected to the Asian Football Confederation in 2006.

Olympic Games

A football tournament at the Olympic Games was first held in 1908 and won by Great Britain. The Brits also won gold in 1912, and after a hiatus for the Great War, were expected to win again in 1920 – but were knocked out by Norway in the first round, Belgium winning instead.

The 1920 Olympic final is the only international final ever to be abandoned. Belgium were 2-0 up when Czechoslovakia walked off the pitch after having a man sent off. They later complained about the ref – who was in his seventies! – but to no avail, Belgium being awarded the gold medals.

Uruguay won in 1924 and 1928, a precursor to their 1930 World Cup win. At this point, with FIFA having launched the World Cup, the Olympic tournament declined in importance.

During the Cold War era, its status as a wholly amateur tournament allowed Communist countries to circumvent regulations using technicalities over employment: all sportsmen were considered amateurs by communist states, though in practice they were full-time athletes, usually employed by the army. As a result, between 1952 and 1980, every single title was won by a nation in the Eastern Bloc.

The tournament was revamped in the early 1990s as an under-23 competition, with each team able to field three overage players. Since then the Olympics have been notable for the first African successes at a major tournament – Nigeria in 1996 and Cameroon in 2000 – followed by Argentinian domination ever since.

All countries affiliated to FIFA and the International Olympic Committee can enter, with qualification usually won through under-21 continental tournaments held by the various FIFA confederations.

One team who has never won the Olympic gold is . . . Brazil! The nation is obsessed with picking up the one major trophy it has never won, but has been unable to do so, despite sending along World Cup winners like Ronaldo, Ronaldinho, Rivaldo and Roberto Carlos.

Confederations Cup

The FIFA Confederations Cup is held a year before every World Cup, in that World Cup's host nation. It is contested by the winners of the European Championship, Copa America, Africa Cup of Nations, Gold Cup, Nations Cup and Asian Cup, plus the reigning World Cup holders and the host nation.

The eight teams are split into two groups of four, with the top two teams in each mini-league playing each other in the semi-finals.

The Confederations Cup started life as an invitational tournament held in Saudi Arabia: the King Fahd Cup. Argentina won the inaugural tournament in 1992, followed by Denmark in 1995, before FIFA took over the running of it and renamed it the Confederations Cup.

Since the relaunch in 1997, Brazil has won the trophy three times, France twice and Mexico once.

All Around the World . . .

From Brazil, Argentina and Spain at the top, all the way down to Brunei Darussalam, Anguilla and St Lucia at the bottom, there are over 200 countries affiliated to FIFA. Some have a richer history than others, of course: The following sections cover some of the most famous nations in the world.

England

England played in the first-ever international match, against Scotland in November 1872. Along with the Scots, they were the best team in the world for the next 20 or 30 years – though that's only because many nations were either yet to take up the game, or arrange international fixtures. England refused to compete in the 1930, 1934 and 1938 World Cups, thinking the competition beneath them – and when they did deign to join in 1950, were humiliated 1-0 by the USA. But England got back up to speed quickly, thanks to the genius of manager Alf Ramsey, and won the World Cup in 1966. England have flattered to deceive ever since, though they did reach the semi-finals of the 1990 World Cup and Euro 96.

England's home shirt is white. They play their home games at Wembley Stadium in London. Famous players (of the past and present) include Stanley Matthews, Tom Finney, Bobby Moore, Kevin Keegan, Bryan Robson, Gary Lineker, Paul Gascoigne, David Beckham and Wayne Rooney.

Scotland

Scotland set the ball rolling with England back in 1872, and their progress was similar for the best part of 80 years: after two or three decades of dominance, they elected not to be a part of the nascent World Cup. Like England, the world passed them by, and when the Scots finally entered the World Cup in 1954 – having sniffily turned down a place in 1950 because they hadn't beaten England that year! – they were humiliated on the big stage, losing 7-0 to reigning champions Uruguay. Sadly for the Scots, unlike England, salvation never came along: despite years of trying, the team has yet to qualify for the second stage of a major tournament.

Scotland's home shirt is dark blue. They play their home games at Hampden Park in Glasgow.

Wales

Wales have only qualified for one major tournament – the 1958 World Cup finals – but they managed to impress when they were there. They reached the quarter-finals, where they met Brazil; without their injured star player John Charles, Wales narrowly lost to a late goal from Pelé. Since then, Wales have had several near misses in qualification, usually involving a total lack of luck with penalties: a handball that never was against Scotland in the 1978 qualifying decider, a late penalty conceded against the same opposition in the 1986 qualifiers and a missed Paul Bodin penalty against Romania in the race for the 1994 finals.

Wales' home shirt is red. They play their home games at the Millennium Stadium in Cardiff.

Northern Ireland

The Northern Irish can boast one of the greatest players in history – George Best – but unfortunately he never played for his country at a World Cup. It was rank bad luck that Best's time at the top fell almost exactly between Northern Ireland's two famous World Cup eras. In 1958 a team including Danny Blanchflower and Peter McParland made the quarter finals before being knocked out by France; in 1982 a side featuring Martin O'Neill and Gerry Armstrong famously beat hosts Spain on their way to an appearance in the second round. Northern Ireland made it to the finals again in 1986, but have yet to play in a World Cup final tournament again.

Northern Ireland's home shirt is green. They play their home games at Windsor Park, Belfast.

Republic of Ireland

The Football Association of Ireland was set up in 1921 following the political division of Ireland. While the Irish Football Association, which ran the former all-Ireland team, continued to run Northern Ireland, the new FAI controlled the team for the Irish Free State. The team was renamed Ireland in 1936, and became the Republic of Ireland in 1953. Ireland became the first foreign team to beat England on English soil in 1949. Despite entering every World Cup apart from the 1930 edition, the Republic failed to reach a finals until 1990, when they famously reached the quarter-finals in Italy under Jack Charlton. The Republic also reached the second round in 1994 and 2002, though the latter campaign was blemished by a pre-tournament row between manager Mick McCarthy and star player Roy Keane, which saw the latter sent home.

The Republic of Ireland's home shirt is green. They play their home games at Lansdowne Road, Dublin (though currently this is being renovated and Gaelic games stadium Croke Park is being used instead).

Brazil

Brazil are the most successful international football team in the world. They are the only nation to have competed in every single World Cup finals tournament. They have lifted the trophy five times (1958, 1962, 1970, 1994 and 2002). Their 1970 team, built around Pelé, is recognised by many as the best in the history of the game. Brazil have also won eight Copa America titles (1919, 1922, 1949, 1969, 1997, 1999, 2004 and 2007) and three Confederations Cups (1997, 2005 and 2009).

Brazil's home shirt is yellow, with green trim. They play the majority of their home matches at the Maracana in Rio de Janeiro.

Italy

Italy are the reigning world champions, and the only European country to have won the World Cup four times (1934 as hosts, 1938, 1982 and 2006). They have also won one European Championship (as hosts in 1968).

Italy's home shirt is blue. They play their home games at stadia all around the country.

Germany

Germany are the most successful European footballing nation, having won three World Cups (1954, 1974 and 1990, all as West Germany) and three European Championships (1972 and 1980 as West Germany, 1996 as

Germany). An independent East Germany team existed between 1952 and 1989, but won nothing – although they did win the only meeting between the two sides, 1-0, during the 1974 World Cup finals!

Germany's home shirt is white, with black trim. They play their home games at stadia all around the country.

France

Pioneers in French football take the credit for the World Cup, the European Championship and the European Cup. It was a while, though, before the national team gained some reward for the country's contribution to world football. In 1984 they won their first title, the European Championship. They would add a second in 2000, but not before winning their first World Cup in 1998 as hosts.

France play in blue, occasionally with red trim. They play their home matches at the Stade de France, Paris.

Spain

Spain won the 1964 European Championship, but for so long were the bridesmaids of the game in Europe. While their clubs were dominant on the continent, the national team struggled. But the Spanish finally won another title in 2008, when they won the European Championship.

Spain play in red with yellow trim. They play their home matches all over the country.

Argentina

Argentina contested the first-ever World Cup final in 1930, but did not win the prize until beating Holland at home in the 1978 final. Thanks to the genius of Diego Maradona, they added a second World Cup crown in Mexico in 1986. They have won the Copa America a joint-record 14 times with Uruguay (1921, 1925, 1927, 1929, 1937, 1941, 1945, 1946, 1947, 1955, 1957, 1959, 1991 and 1993). They have also won one Confederations Cup (1993).

Argentina's home shirt is vertical sky-blue-and-white stripes. They play the majority of their home games at El Monumental in Buenos Aires.

Uruguay

Uruguay won the first World Cup, in 1930, and the second World Cup they entered, in 1950. It wasn't until extra time in the semi-finals of the 1954 tournament that they tasted defeat in the competition. They have also won 14 Copa America titles, the last in 1995.

Uruguay's home shirt is sky blue. They play their home games at the Estadio Centenario, Montevideo.

Chapter 12

The Club Scene

In This Chapter

▶ The make-up of a club, from presidents to players

▶ What clubs play for: leagues and cups explained

▶ The trophies clubs chase, from the Youdan Cup to the Champions League

C lub football is the bread and butter of the game: as the old saying goes, you can change your religion, leave your wife or husband, but you can't get rid of your team.

There are thousands of major football clubs in the world. In this chapter we'll see how clubs started springing up in England during the 1860s, and then all across the world.

Clubbing Together

From multinational concerns like Manchester United and Real Madrid, all the way down to the Sunday League team ran by the drinkers in your local Dog & Duck, a football club is, in the final analysis, a group of people who have 'clubbed together' to play football. The members of that club can then practise with each other, play matches against each other and arrange friendly and competitive fixtures with representative teams from other clubs.

The first clubs

Some form of football has been played in England for centuries, but up until the mid 1800s games were always played by a disorganised rabble. Then university teams, public school teams, works teams and pub teams began to spring up – educational establishments, factories and bars were natural social places for people to get together and arrange proper kickabouts.

But something more concrete needed to be established. Nobody knows exactly when the first bespoke football-only club was set up – universities in London, Edinburgh and Dublin all stake claims to have done so between the 1820s and 1840s – but we do know that in 1857, the first non-university club was set up: Sheffield FC.

And that's when the club scene really began to kick off.

Within three years, Sheffield FC had a local rival – Hallam FC – and regular fixtures between the two were established. Clubs began to spring up all over the country, and within a decade the FA Cup had been set up.

As competitive football became popular, so did the clubs, and vast numbers of spectators would turn up to matches in order to cheer on one team or the other. Football was suddenly big business.

The rise of the super clubs

Economic and social factors mean that some clubs are always going to be bigger than others. Clubs from major cities, for example, can draw on wider support than ones from smaller cities and towns.

(For example, Celtic and Rangers, coming from Glasgow, the third most populous city in the United Kingdom, were always going to be bigger clubs than Caledonian and Clachnacuddin from the small Highland city of Inverness!)

But many of the biggest names in football today also benefitted from being successful at precisely the right times in football's development: the 1950s and 1960s, when televised football and the European Cup caught the public's imagination.

This meant teams such as Manchester United, Real Madrid and AC Milan became huge players in their countries. Other clubs such as Liverpool and Tottenham Hotspur also benefitted in the 1960s, as TV turned football into a glamour sport.

Alongside already established European behemoths like Arsenal, Rangers, Celtic, Juventus and Barcelona, these new clubs slowly began to dominate domestic and international club football – though the balance would not tip totally in their favour until the 1990s.

The name game

What's in a name? Some clubs have the simplest of monikers – the likes of Chelsea, Fulham, Liverpool and Portsmouth do exactly what they say on the tin. But other names offer more than geographical clues.

Some explain how a club was founded back in the midst of time. Sheffield Wednesday were, up until 1929, simply called The Wednesday – after the cricket club from which they sprang up in the 1860s. Wednesday was the day of the week the cricketers played their matches.

Arsenal meanwhile were formed as a works team – of the Royal Arsenal munitions factory in Woolwich.

Common components offer other clues. Teams with United in the title were, more often than not, formed as a result of a merger between two smaller local clubs. In Spain, the prefix Real – meaning Royal – denotes royal patronage, and suggests the club has been favoured, historically at least, by the Establishment. (Real Madrid, the team supported by the dictator General Franco, being an example of this.)

Meanwhile in Italy, many teams were formed by ex-pats from England, and to this day carry English translations of city names: AC Milan (Milano) and Genoa (Genova) are examples of that.

The 'smaller' clubs

Between 1960 and 1990, smaller, provincial clubs still won titles across Europe: Burnley and Derby County won the English league, Kilmarnock and Dundee United became champions of Scotland, and Hellas Verona landed the Italian title. But as the balance of power titled, it became increasingly harder and harder for teams outside of the major clubs to win league titles.

After a while, even major cup competitions were rarely won by smaller clubs. In England, for example, since 1991, only Portsmouth (2008) and Everton (1995) have prised the FA Cup from the grasp of the self-styled Big Four of Arsenal, Chelsea, Liverpool and Manchester United.

It's a shame, and a state of affairs that has caused quite a bit of disillusionment in fans of clubs outside the select few, as trophies are almost impossible to land. However, football fans are nothing if not resourceful, and most have rationalised why they still follow the sport despite the chances of seeing their team lift a cup being slim: it's not really about winning anyway, it's about the fun of belonging.

Figure 12-1:
Not all about the Premier League: A lower-division clash between Northampton and Bournemouth.

Clubs today

These days, many clubs are major multinational organisations, with hundreds of staff members, even at some of the so-called 'smaller' clubs in the lower divisions. But how are they set up, and who works for them?

The players

A football club would be a fairly pointless enterprise without a squad of players! So it goes without saying that all clubs employ them.

Buying, selling and nurturing

Clubs have two methods of finding new players. They either nurture them from a young age, training them in their youth academies and reserve teams, eventually blooding them in the first XI, or buy them from another club.

If they buy them from another club, they usually have to pay a transfer fee. This is to effectively buy out the player's contract with another club. Once a fee has been settled upon, club and player agree a new contract between them.

Sometimes players are given away on a free transfer. This is usually when they are no longer required by the club, and it will be cheaper to write off their contract than to pay them any more wages.

Clubs can also sign players who are out of contract. They do not have to pay the player's former club a fee to do this.

Not all clubs maintain a full-time staff, though. A club in the Scottish Third Division, pulling crowds of 300 spectators per week, will be unable to maintain a full-time squad. So they will field part-time players, paying them a flat match fee for each appearance.

Move up the divisions, however, and clubs become full time, employing a sizable squad of players on increasingly large wages. As a very rough-and-ready rule, an average full-time club will employ around 30 players. The really big clubs, however, sometimes contain upwards of 50 full-time members in their squad, plus assorted reserve and promising youth players on full-time contracts.

The squad of a top-flight English club usually contains at least three players for each position.

The manager

The most important person at any club is the manager. More often than not, he has the final say in the buying and selling of players, who plays in each match, the tactics for each game, and any substitutions and tactical changes during a game.

Different managers take different approaches to the job. Some are highly tactical, insisting their players work within a rigidly defined pre-determined system. Others manage by the force of their personality, either charismatically or through fear and discipline.

Brian Clough, for example, led Nottingham Forest to the 1979 and 1980 European Cups, yet paid no heed to tactical systems whatsoever. Managing on gut instinct, he would either shout and bawl at his players, or put a comforting arm around them, depending on his mood. Occasionally, he would even get them drunk before a game! Idiosyncratic maybe, but it worked.

Suffice to say, the personality of a team – and sometimes an entire club – rests on the personality of its manager. Which goes some way to explaining why, if the team embarks on a losing streak, the manager is usually the first person to be sacked, ushering in a new era.

The manager often goes by the name of coach – this usually means they have less responsibility for buying and selling players, allowing them to concentrate solely on how the team plays.

Backroom staff

A manager will surround himself (or herself) with a team usually referred to as *backroom staff*. The most important backroom role is of assistant manager. Also known as the *number two*, the assistant manager is there to give the manager advice and support.

Often the assistant will be an expert in a particular field – a defensive coach, for example, or a particularly astute spotter of transfer targets.

The manager will also be assisted by fitness coaches, bespoke tactical coaches for defenders, attackers and goalkeepers, and medical staff such as physiotherapists, sports therapists and masseurs.

The club will also appoint scouts, whose job it is to watch other teams in order to find potential new players, as well as assessing how upcoming opponents play tactically.

The chairman, owners and the board

Methods of club ownership vary from country to country. In England, for example, clubs are usually either privately owned by one single investor or company, or they are Public Limited Companies, floated on the Stock Exchange.

The owner usually installs themselves as chairperson of the club, overseeing a board of directors. The chairperson has overall control and ultimate power, though often will take a back seat, empowering one of the directors, a chief executive or managing director with the everyday running of the club.

Transfer windows

Up until comparatively recently – 2003, to be precise – football clubs could transfer players whenever they wanted. This means they could buy players from, and sell them to, other clubs at will.

However now FIFA has decreed that there should be two transfer windows per year. A long transfer window – lasting a maximum of 12 weeks – can be opened roughly between two separate domestic seasons.

A shorter one – lasting a maximum of one calendar month – can be opened at a predetermined point roughly in the middle of a domestic season.

Clubs cannot buy players when their domestic windows are shut, although they can in principle agree deals in advance for players to move during a future window.

In addition, a player from a club whose domestic window is shut can still be sold to a club whose domestic window is open.

The final day of an open window is known as Transfer Deadline Day. These are always big media events, with much expectation of a flurry of last-minute deals, but can often be a complete anti-climax should no big-name moves occur!

This person will oversee the minutiae of day-to-day running of the club, look after budgets and liaise between the board and the manager.

When it comes to the big decisions – namely whether to sack the manager or not! – the chairman/owner has the final say.

Club ownership can often be controversial. Recently major English clubs such as Manchester United and Liverpool have been taken over by investors not trusted by the clubs' fanbases, as they are seen to be putting profit over investment in the team's success.

However other recent buyouts have been more welcome by fans. The Russian billionaire Roman Abramovich's purchase of Chelsea saw major investment in the team, followed by unprecedented levels of success for the club. Manchester City too have recently benefitted from similar money-no-object investment.

It's not just about the amount of money being pumped in, either. Supporters of Aston Villa are, on the whole, positive about their owner, the US businessman Randy Lerner, as they feel he has made the effort to respond to fans' concerns and requests regarding everyday matters from travel arrangements and facilities at the ground, to kit and badge design.

But there are other methods of ownership. Most Spanish clubs – even the giant concerns such as Real Madrid and Barcelona – are owned by their fans. Hundreds of thousands of *socios* pay a membership fee to join the club, and vote to elect presidents, empowering them to spend their budgets as they see fit.

Club Competitions

There are two types of club competition: leagues and cups. All countries run a league over the course of a single season, and most hold at least one cup competition at some point during the same season.

Seasons

This is a fixed period of time during which all domestic club competitions are held. At the opening of a season, no competitions have been started. By the end of it, all the winners of every competition will have been determined.

There is only ever one season every 12 months, though they do not necessarily cover the year January to December. For example, the English football season traditionally starts in August and ends the following May. The season starting in August 2010, therefore, will be known as season 2010/11.

Seasons run at different times across the world, at dates often dictated by local weather systems. To illustrate, while most European leagues run roughly along the aforementioned English timescale, Russian winters are too harsh to play football in, so the leagues there run during the summer months, from March to November.

Each season is preceded by a *pre-season*, which sees clubs play friendlies in order to attain optimum levels of fitness and assimilate new signings into the team.

Every season will have at least one *transfer window*, allowing clubs to sign new players and sell existing ones.

There will also be designated International Weeks during the season. Leagues do not have to break for these, but as FIFA obliges clubs to release players for international matches such as World Cup qualifiers, a *rest week* is usually scheduled.

Leagues

The concept of league football was born in England in 1888, when the Football League was formed. It was the first in the world. Now almost every country which plays organised football operates its own league system.

The first-ever league

The Football League – and the concept of league football – was the brainchild of William McGregor, a Scottish director of Aston Villa in the 1880s.

At the time, the only competition Villa could enter – because it was the only one that existed – was the FA Cup. It was held every year, but if a team was knocked out in the first round, they would only have one competitive game per season. It wasn't much of a money spinner.

McGregor decided to act. Villa were one of the biggest clubs of the day, so he wrote to the chairmen of several other big teams – including Blackburn Rovers, Preston North End, West Bromwich Albion and Bolton Wanderers – proposing a groundbreaking idea.

'Every year it is becoming more and more difficult for football clubs of any standing to meet their friendly engagements and even arrange friendly matches,' he wrote. 'I beg to tender the following suggestion as a means of getting over the difficulty. It is that 10 or 12 of the most prominent clubs combine to arrange home and away fixtures each season.'

Having penned the letter in March 1888, McGregor saw his idea implemented quickly. That September, it was up and running. The world would soon follow.

How leagues work

A league is a round-robin tournament. All entrants play each other – usually twice, home and away – and gain points depending on results. Usually a team is awarded three points for a win, one for a draw, and none for a defeat.

According to results and points awarded, teams are then arranged into a table, placing them in order of points won, top to bottom. After all the matches have been played, the top team is declared the champion.

As a general rule, if teams are level on points after all matches have been played, they are separated on goal difference (the difference between goals scored and conceded). The team with the highest positive goal difference wins. Should goal difference be level, the team with the higher number of goals scored wins. And if the teams are still level after that, the champion may be decided in a play-off match, or even by the toss of a coin!

Goal difference doesn't always decide the order of teams level on points, though. In some major leagues – notably Spain and Italy – the order of teams tied on points at the end of the season are decided on their head-to-head records during the season. So if Barcelona and Real Madrid end up level on 80 points, but Barcelona beat Real Madrid 2-0 at home and drew 1-1 against Real in Madrid, they will win the league.

Divisions, promotion, relegation and pyramids

Of course, because most countries have many teams, they cannot realistically all play each other, home and away, in one huge league. So leagues comprise of a hierarchy of several divisions, between which clubs can move up or down each season depending on results – this is called promotion and relegation.

The overall structure is often called a Pyramid, because of the general shape of the hierarchy: after the top few divisions, there are usually very many more local divisions towards the bottom.

To illustrate, the top of the English league pyramid looks like this:

Level 1: The FA Premier League (20 teams)

Level 2: Football League Championship (24 teams)

Level 3: Football League – League One (24 teams)

Level 4: Football League – League Two (24 teams)

Level 5: Football Conference – National Division (24 teams)

Level 6: Football Conference – Northern Division (22 teams)

Level 6: Football Conference – Southern Division (22 teams)

Every season, the three teams finishing at the bottom of the Premier League will be relegated into the division below – the Championship. In turn, their places in the Premier League will be taken by the teams finishing first and second in the Championship, and the winners of the promotion play-offs.

This principle continues all the way down through the levels (although the number of teams swapping divisions may vary).

The play-offs

A promotion play-off is a mini post-season competition to decide the final team to be promoted after a season.

In the days before the play-offs, the third team in the final table would go up too. But now the teams finishing third, fourth, fifth and sixth in the division go into the play-offs.

The third-placed team will play the sixth-placed team home and away to decide who goes through to the play-off final. Meanwhile the fourth and fifth-placed teams will do the same. Then the winners of a one-off final match will gain promotion.

There are also promotion play-offs in League One, League Two and the Football Conference National Division.

The principle behind the play-offs is to extend interest in the season for a greater number of teams in the leagues. (More teams are likely to be in with a shout of finishing sixth or higher than third or higher.)

Going further down the pyramid . . .

You will notice there are two divisions at Level 6. This is where the pyramid begins to take shape. In this example, four teams from Level 5 – the National Conference – are relegated, to be replaced by two from the Northern Division at Level 6, and two from the Southern Division at the same level.

A similar feeder system works all the way down, to the very local leagues. So, picking up where we left off, let's head down the longest route in English league football . . .

Level 5. Football Conference (24 teams)

Level 6. Football Conference: Southern and Northern Division (22 teams)

Level 7. Southern League: Premier Division (22 teams)

Level 8. Southern League: Midlands Division (22 teams)

Level 8. Southern League: South & West Division (22 teams)

Level 9. Western League: Premier Division (20 teams)

Level 10. Western League: 1st Division (20 teams)

Level 11. Gloucestershire County League: Premier Division (18 teams)

Level 12. Bristol Premier Combination: Premier Division (14 teams)

Level 13. Bristol Premier Combination: Division 1 (14 teams)

Level 14. Bristol & District League: Senior Division (14 teams)

Level 15. Bristol & District League: Division 1 (15 teams)

Level 16. Bristol & District League: Division 2 (13 teams)

Level 17. Bristol & District League: Division 3 (13 teams)

Level 18. Bristol & District League: Division 4 (12 teams)

Level 19. Bristol & District League: Division 5 (13 teams)

Level 20. Bristol & District League: Division 6 (12 teams)

Level 21. Bristol & Avon League: Premier Division (16 teams)

Level 21. Bristol Downs League: Division 1 (14 teams)

Level 22. Bristol Downs League: Division 2 (14 teams

Level 23. Bristol Downs League: Division 3 (14 teams)

Level 24. Bristol Downs League: Division 4 (16 teams)

This means that, in principle, the smallest local club can rise to the very top of the national league system – which in England means all the way from the Bristol Downs League up to the Premier League. Dare to dream: a club need only win 23 promotions!

Apertura and Clausura

In most countries, there is usually only one league championship held per season. However, in most major Latin American countries – such as Argentina, Uruguay and Colombia – the season is split into two separate halves, *Apertura* and *Clausura* (Opening and Closing).

Both sections – *Apertura* and *Clausura* – have their own champions, with no results carrying over to decide the winner. Some countries then stage a final tie between both champions to decide an overall season champion.

Results do carry over to decide relegations, however – if there are any. Movements between divisions in several Latin American countries is often very arbitrary, and not necessarily based purely on results!

Franchises

Some countries eschew the pyramid system, doing away with the concept of promotion and relegation altogether. In the United States of America, for example, Major League Soccer operates a franchise system, where teams play each other in regional leagues – called Conferences – in the hope of qualifying for a final tournament to determine the seasonal champions.

But if teams don't make it through, they don't have to worry about being relegated; they'll still be there next season.

Cups

Nearly all countries hold at least one domestic knockout cup competition. The basic principle is simple: the tournament is divided into rounds, with all teams going into a hat and being randomly drawn to face one other entrant.

The teams play each other in a one-off tie, the winner of each tie going back into the hat for the next round – which now has half the number of clubs as it did before, the losers having been knocked out.

The process continues until there are only two teams left standing. They then play off in a final tie to decide the tournament winner.

Round 1: 32 teams

Round 2: 16 teams

Round 3: 8 teams (this round is known as the 'quarter-final')

Round 4: 4 teams (this round is known as the 'semi-final')

Round 5: 2 teams (this round is known as the 'final')

Some cups are organised so ties are played home and away, the aggregate winners going onto the next round.

Compared to leagues, the winners of cups are less likely to be the 'best' team in the competition, as draws are random and teams have no margin for error in a one-off tie. This means the overall quality of knockout cup competitions are lower, but with the likelihood of shock results and *giant-killing* – when a small team beats a bigger one – greater, they are often more dramatic and exciting.

The Big Leagues

Some leagues are bigger than others. The teams taking part in them have more supporters and more money, and consequently get the best players and the greatest amount of media attention. The section focuses on the leagues you're most likely to hear about.

England: The FA Premier League

The Football League was established in 1888, featuring 12 teams, and quickly expanded. A second division was added four years later, a third in 1920, and a fourth in 1921, whereupon the two lower divisions became regional leagues, the Third Divisions North and South. In 1950, they became national Third and Fourth divisions.

That four-division set-up – with a top flight of 22 teams – was maintained until 1992, when the country's top 22 clubs broke away from the Football League to form an elite division: the FA Premier League. The old Second, Third and Fourth Divisions initially became the First, Second and Third Divisions of a revamped Football League; the divisions are now the Championship, League One and League Two.

Nowadays, the FA Premier League is contested by 20 teams. The winners are crowned champions of England (just as the winners of the Football League were in the years before the formation of the Premier League). Three teams are relegated from the league each year, to be replaced by three from the Championship (the top two teams and the winners of the play-offs).

Teams in the FA Premier League include: Arsenal, Chelsea, Everton, Liverpool, Manchester City, Manchester United and Tottenham Hotspur.

As of 2008/09, Liverpool and Manchester United share the record for the most English titles, having won 18 each. All of Liverpool's titles were won before the advent of the FA Premier League, while United have won 11 FA Premier League titles.

Figure 12-2:
A familiar sight – Manchester United raise the Premier League trophy.

From 1994 to 2007, the FA Premier League was known as the FA Premiership. The two terms are used interchangeably still.

Scotland: The Scottish Premier League

The Scottish Football League is the second-oldest league in the world, after England's Football League. It was formed two years after the English version, in 1890, and rapidly grew, a second division springing up in 1894. A two-division format (of 18 and 19 teams respectively) was maintained for years, until 1975 when the ten-team Scottish Premier Division was formed, two 14-team First and

Second divisions below it. That lasted just over two decades, until Scotland followed England's lead yet again, the top clubs forming a breakaway league in 1998: the Scottish Premier League.

The SPL is contested by 12 teams. The winners are crowned champions of Scotland (just as winners of the Scottish Football League and Scottish Premier Division were before). Only one team is relegated from the SPL each season, to be replaced by the winners of the Scottish League First Division.

The league is dominated by the Glasgow giants, the Old Firm of Celtic and Rangers. Other teams in the league include Edinburgh rivals Hibernian and Heart of Midlothian, and the so-called New Firm of Dundee United and Aberdeen.

Figure 12-3:
Action from an 'Old Firm' clash between Celtic and Rangers.

Rangers have won the Scottish title 52 times, a domestic world record, while Celtic have triumphed 42 times. The disparity between those two clubs and the rest can be illustrated by the fact that the third-placed teams in Scotland's all-time list (Hearts, Hibs and Aberdeen) have only won four titles each.

The SPL splits in half before the final five games of the season. The top six teams then play each other once, while the bottom six do likewise. It is possible for the team finishing seventh to end up with more points than the team finishing sixth – but sides in the bottom half after the split cannot move out of their section.

Wales, Northern Ireland and Republic of Ireland

National leagues elsewhere in the British Isles have historically failed to prosper like the ones in England and Scotland.

In Wales, the largest clubs – Cardiff City, Swansea City and Wrexham – play in the English leagues. In 1992 the Welsh Premier League was founded, a competition which has been dominated by Barry Town.

Northern Ireland's leagues are the third oldest in the world, behind England and Scotland. They were all-Ireland competitions before the partition of 1921, and Northern Irish competitions since. Linfield are the dominant team, with 48 wins ahead of Glentoran's 23. In 2008, the top-flight IFA Premiership was founded, though the competition is still known as it's always been: the Irish League.

The Republic of Ireland's league – the FAI League of Ireland – was founded in 1921. Shamrock Rovers is the most successful club. Both Irish leagues suffer from interest in the SPL, where Celtic and Rangers play.

Italy: Serie A

Italy were one of the first European countries to launch a national championship – the first title was awarded in 1898, in a tournament that involved four teams lasted the grand total of *one* day – but once it got going on a larger scale the champions would be decided in a play-off final between regional champions. It wasn't until 1929 that a national league was established, forming the divisions Serie A and Serie B. The set-up remains the same to this day (although discussions are ongoing to turn Serie A into an independent 'premier' league, albeit with the same name).

Serie A is contested by 18 teams. The winners are crowned champions of Italy, and are awarded the right to wear the scudetto, a tricolour shield, on their shirts the following season. The bottom three teams are relegated to Serie B, to be replaced by the top two teams in Serie B plus either the third-placed team if they are at least ten points ahead of the fourth-placed side, or the winners of a play-off tournament between the teams finishing third to sixth.

Major teams in Serie A include: Milan, Internazionale, Juventus, Roma, Lazio and Fiorentina.

Juventus are the most successful side in Serie A history, with 27 title wins. Internazionale and Milan jointly hold the second-most successful records, with 17 victories apiece.

Teams are allowed to wear a golden star for every ten title wins. Juventus therefore have two on their shirt, Internazionale and Milan one.

Spain: Primera Division

The Spanish operated several regional leagues until 1929, when La Liga was formed, comprising two divisions: the Primera (first) and Segunda (second). Initially the top division only contained ten teams, but the competition swiftly grew: today the Primera has 20 teams, while the Segunda has 22.

The winners of the Primera Division are crowned champions of Spain. The bottom three teams in the division are relegated to Segunda Division, while the top three teams in Segunda win promotion.

Real Madrid and Barcelona are the big players in La Liga; Real have won the title 31 times, Barca 19. Atletico Madrid, Athletic Bilbao and Valencia have nine, eight and six titles between them, while Real Sociedad can boast two. Deportivo la Coruna, Sevilla and Real Betis all have one title apiece – meaning that there have only ever been eight champion clubs in Spain, the lowest number in any of the major footballing nations.

Germany: Bundesliga

Football was played in Germany since the 1870s, but it took nearly 100 years for a professional league to be set up. For much of the 20th century, Germany's national champions were determined by a play-off between winners of regional tournaments. But in 1963 the German FA (DFB) launched the country's first national league: the Fussball-Bundesliga (more commonly referred to simply as the Bundesliga).

It is contested by 18 teams, the winners becoming champions of Germany. The bottom two teams are relegated to 2.Bundesliga, with the third from bottom going into a play-off with the third-placed team in 2.Bundesliga for the right to play in the top flight the following season.

Teams in the Bundesliga include: Bayer Leverkusen, Bayern Munich, Borussia Dortmund, Hamburg, Shalke 04, Werder Bremen and Wolfsburg.

The league was won by seven teams in its first seven seasons, but since has been totally dominated by Bayern Munich, who have won 20 Bundesliga titles. The next most successful Bundesliga side are Bourissia Monchengladbach, who have only won five – the last of which in 1977!

Brazil: Campeonato Brasileiro Serie A

As mentioned earlier, most Latin American countries split their seasons into two halves – Apertura and Clausura (Opening and Closing) – and have a champion for each. Brazil is the only South American country to operate a more traditional single league along European lines. Twenty clubs compete in the league, the winners being crowned champions and the bottom four clubs being relegated to Serie B.

While teams compete in a national league, they also compete in local state leagues. These are historically important – Brazil is such a big country, a national league was only considered viable in 1971 – and the champions of the state leagues are treated with the same reverence as the national title winners.

Argentina: Primera Division

Outside of the United Kingdom, the Argentine league is the world's oldest, formed in 1891. It was a European-style one-league-per-season affair up until 1967, when the championship was divided into two separate stages: Metropolitain and National. A single-league system was reintroduced between 1986 and 1991, but soon replaced with the *Apertura* and *Clausura* system still in place today.

The Primera Division is contested by 20 teams, who play two separate round-robin tournaments. First the *Apertura*, from August to December, then the *Clausura*, from February until June. Each tournament has a champion.

Relegation and promotion is a hornets' nest. Relegation is worked out on a three-year average. At the end of the season, a table is produced. The two bottom teams go down, to be replaced by the two top teams in the Primera B Nacional. The teams in 17th and 18th place in the Primera play off over two legs against the third and fourth teams in Primera B. Winners play in the Primera the following season – but if the tie is drawn, both clubs stay in the division they were in!

Between two and four teams can be promoted and relegated, depending on results.

There are no cup competitions of note in Argentina. Cup football has never been popular in the country, and no such tournament has ever taken off.

USA

Professional football in the United States had two huge false starts. The American Soccer League, created in 1921, only lasted a decade. Then the North American Soccer League, launched in 1967, sputtered out 18 years later, despite at one point coaxing Pelé from retirement to play for the New York Cosmos. However as a condition of landing the 1994 World Cup, FIFA insisted the States gave it another go. And it looks like being third time lucky, with the 1996-launched Major League Soccer currently going from strength to strength.

The league consists of 15 countrywide franchises, divided into two conferences, Eastern and Western. Each team plays 30 matches, playing home and away against every other side, with two additional 'intra-conference' games (usually crowd-pulling fixtures between local or conference rivals).

At the end of the season, the team with the most points wins the Supporters Shield, while the four top teams in each conference proceed to the MLS Cup play-offs. Both play off a home-and-away conference semi-final, then a single-match conference championship final, before advancing to the MLS Cup final, where the two conference winners meet.

MLS will expand to 18 teams by 2011, and plans to add another two franchises by 2012.

Domestic Cups

Most domestic Football Associations organise one or more knock-out cups. While these are usually won by the big clubs who also dominate the league system, there's always the chance of a shock result – if not in the final, then in one of the preceding rounds. This gives cup competitions their drama.

FA Cup

The Football Association Challenge Cup is a knockout cup competition open to all teams in the top ten levels of English league football. Over 700 teams regularly enter the competition.

The draws are totally random, and unseeded. There are six qualifying rounds for the competition proper. In the First Round, the 48 teams from the Football League Leagues One and Two are entered into the draw, along with 32 qualifiers. Teams from the FA Premier League and Football League Championship enter at the Third Round, which signals the point at which there are 64 teams left in the competition. The Sixth Round is the quarter-final stage.

The third round is one of the most glamorous days in the football calendar, as small clubs have a chance to be paired with the Manchester Uniteds and Arsenals of this world. Very occasionally, a small team upsets the odds to cause a giant-killing shock. The last non-league team to beat a top-flight side were Sutton United, who knocked out Coventry City in 1989.

All ties up to this point are played as a single leg, the first team being drawn from the hat playing at home. Should the match be drawn, there will be a replay at the home of the second team drawn from the hat. Should that match be drawn, 30 minutes extra time will be played – and if there is still no result, a penalty shootout will decide who goes through.

Up until the early 1990s, drawn replays would trigger another subsequent replay. Ties would occasionally go to three or four replays: these were invariably described as 'marathons'. Increasingly crowded fixture lists for the top teams eventually put an end to this.

The semi-finals are one-off ties, played at a neutral venue. The final is played at Wembley Stadium, London. Neither semi-finals nor the final now goes to a replay, all matches being decided on the day after extra time and penalties if required.

Manchester United are the most successful club in FA Cup history, with 11 wins as of 2008/09. Arsenal are right on United's heels, with 10 victories. Tottenham have won the Cup eight times, Liverpool and Aston Villa seven apiece.

League Cup

In 1960, the Football League introduced a second cup to the English football calendar. The Football League Cup was a sickly child, and did not come of age for the best part of a decade, most of the biggest clubs in the country refusing to enter. But winners would later be rewarded with a place in Europe, and the big teams soon took an interest.

By the mid-1980s, the trophy was regularly being won by the reigning champions of Europe – Nottingham Forest and Liverpool both lifted the trophy in the same season they won the European Cup. But latterly the competition has fallen out of fashion again, with the larger teams using it as a testing ground for reserve and youth team players.

The tournament is only open to members of the Football League and FA Premier League. The final is played at Wembley.

The League Cup has taken many sponsors' names, and has been known as the Milk Cup, the Littlewoods Cup, the Rumbelows Cup, the Coca-Cola Cup, the Worthington Cup and the Carling Cup.

Scottish Cup

The Scottish Cup is the second oldest national cup competition in the world, after the FA Cup. The knockout format is similar to the FA Cup, although a far smaller number of clubs take part. There are fewer rounds: there is only one preliminary qualification round, and the top-flight teams do not come in until the Fourth Round.

The final is held at Hampden Park, Glasgow.

Predictably, the Old Firm clubs dominate the trophy, Celtic winning 34 cups to Rangers' 33 (as of 2008/09). The next best club is Queen's Park, an amateur outfit whose tenth and final victory was in 1893!

Other famous cups

Nearly every FIFA member country runs its own national knockout cup competition. Notable cup competitions include:

- Spain: Copa del Ray (won most times by Barcelona – 25)
- Germany: DFB-Pokal (Bayern Munich – 14)
- Italy: Coppa Italia (Roma and Juventus – 9)
- France: Coupe de France (Marseille – 10)
- Brazil: Copa do Brasil (Gremio and Cruzeiro – 4)

International Club Competitions

Clubs don't just play football within their own borders, though. They also compete with clubs from other countries, in competitions which are often more prestigious than the domestic leagues and cups.

The European Cup: Born in Paris (and Wolverhampton)

In 1954, the reigning champions of England, Wolverhampton Wanderers, staged some prestigious midweek friendlies against top sides from mainland Europe under their new-fangled floodlights. Some of the biggest clubs in world football – Racing Club, Moscow Dynamo and Spartak Moscow – came to Wolves' Molineux stadium. All were defeated.

But nobody expected Wolves to beat Honved, whose team contained six of the Hungary side that had humiliated England 6-3 and 7-1 during the previous year. Wolves won 3-2, though, prompting the *Daily Mail* to trumpet 'WOLVES: CHAMPIONS OF THE WORLD!' the day after.

Noting this with some disdain, Gabriel Hanot, the editor of French newspaper *L'Equipe*, took the *Mail* to task. 'Before we declare Wolverhampton are invincible, let them go to Moscow and Budapest,' wrote Hanot. 'And there are other internationally renowned clubs: AC Milan and Real Madrid to name but two. A club world championship, or at least a European one.'

Within the year, UEFA had taken Hanot's idea and ran with it, inaugurating the first European Cup in season 1955/56. Wolves eventually qualified for the new tournament in 1959 – and were knocked out in the first round by German side Schalke.

European Cup/UEFA Champions League

The European Cup was launched in 1955, an unseeded knockout cup tournament between the reigning champions of all European leagues. The first five trophies were won by Spain's Real Madrid, before Portugal and Italy shared the spoils in the early 1960s, Benfica, AC Milan and Internazionale adding their name to the roll of honour.

Celtic would become the first club from Britain – and indeed northern Europe – to win the European Cup in 1967, Manchester United following in their wake the year after. By the end of the 1970s, Ajax and Bayern Munich had both completed hat-tricks of wins, Liverpool and Nottingham Forest landing the trophy twice each. Aston Villa became the fourth English team to win the cup in 1982.

The 1980s saw Liverpool win two more trophies before they were embroiled in the Heysel disaster at the 1985 final, which saw English clubs banned from Europe for six seasons. The late 1980s and early 1990s were dominated by Milan, though Eastern Bloc teams finally made their mark too, Romania's Steaua Bucharest (1986) and Red Star Belgrade (1991) winning the trophy.

In 1992/93, the tournament was rebranded the UEFA Champions League, the format changing from unseeded knockout to seeded round-robin groups, guaranteeing competitors a certain number of money-spinning games. In 1998, entrants other than the national champions were allowed to take part.

The new format – up to four teams per country enter – means there is now an established elite, many of the same giant clubs participating year in, year out. Paradoxically, however, no team has retained the trophy in the Champions League era.

The most successful European Cup and Champions League side is Real Madrid, who have won the trophy nine times. Milan have seven wins to their name. Liverpool are the most successful British team, with five victories.

Format

It is up to each individual country to decide how to award their allotted places in the Champions League. All countries, however, choose league position as their qualification criteria.

England, for example, has four places. The FA Premier League champions and second and third placed teams qualify for the group stage of the Champions League automatically. The fourth-placed teams must go through the preliminary rounds.

The group stages involve eight groups of four teams. The draw is seeded, with seedings based on past performances in Europe. After playing each other home and away, the top two teams in each group go through to the knockout stages. (The third placed teams go into the knockout stage of the Europa League.)

The competition is then a straight cup knockout. All rounds are unseeded, and a free draw, apart from the first knockout round: group winners must play group runners-up, and no two teams from the same country can be paired.

The decision to play the 2010 Champions League final, and all subsequent finals, on a Saturday evening – in order to maximize TV audiences – broke with tradition. The game had always previously been played on Wednesday evening.

Although the tournament is now officially called the UEFA Champions League, it is still also referred to as the European Cup. The two terms are interchangeable (although the use of the latter may point usefully to someone's age!).

Europa League and UEFA Cup

In 1955, FIFA launched a strange continent-wide competition called the Fairs Cup, open to teams from cities holding international trade fairs. A London select XI contested the first final – of a tournament that took *three years* to complete – losing to Barcelona. The cup was a right old dog's dinner – but in 1961 three teams from each European country were allowed in, and a meaningful tournament was born.

The unseeded knockout cup – renamed the UEFA Cup in 1971 when the European ruling body took over the running of the tournament – would be won by some of the biggest clubs in football. Over the years, Barcelona, Juventus, Real Madrid, Ajax and Diego Maradona's Napoli all won the cup. English clubs made hay too: Leeds, Liverpool, Ipswich, Arsenal, Newcastle and Tottenham all chalked up victories.

In many respects, the UEFA Cup was harder to win than the European Cup, as it contained more top-quality teams from each country. It's also arguable that the European Cups were contested by teams who were on top form the previous year, while the UEFA Cup often contained up-and-coming teams about to win their domestic leagues.

In recent years, the UEFA Cup has continued to thrill. (In Britain alone, Celtic, Middlesbrough and Rangers all reached finals between 2003 and 2008, while Liverpool won the 2001 trophy with a ludicrous 5-4 final win over Spanish minnows Alaves.) But controversially, UEFA decided to fiddle with the format, adding league stages, finally rebranding the competition as the Europa League in 2009.

Format

There are 12 groups of four teams, who play each other in a round-robin format. The top two teams in each group advance to the knockout stages – where they will be joined by the eight teams who finish third in their Champions League groups. The competition is then a straight cup knockout.

Copa Libertadores

South America staged its first international club championship in 1948, Brazilian club Vasco da Gama winning a tournament staged by the Chilean club Colo Colo. But the event lost thousands of pounds, and the idea was put on the back burner. It was revived in 1960 in the wake of the successful launch of the European Cup, with UEFA offering to stage a World Club Cup between their champions and any South American equivalent.

Penarol of Uruguay were the winners of the first two stagings of the newly minted Copa Libertadores, with Pelé's Santos winning in 1962 and 1963. Independiente of Argentina then matched the feat in 1964 and 1965 – and would become the most successful side in the tournament's history, with seven wins notched up by 1984.

Boca Juniors of Argentina have dominated the tournament since the turn of the millennium, winning the trophy four times between 2000 and 2007.

Format

The format is similar to the UEFA Champions League. After a preliminary round, eight groups of four teams are drawn, the two top teams after a round-robin tournament progressing to the knockout stages.

Other continental tournaments

Africa, Asia, North America and Oceania also hold their own Champions League tournaments. Along with the winners of the European Cup and the Copa Libertadores, all victorious sides qualify for the FIFA World Club Cup.

Intercontinental Cup/FIFA World Club Cup

The Intercontinental Cup or World Club Cup has had a chequered history. Founded as an annual play-off between the champions of Europe and South America in 1960, in order to name a semi-official 'world club champion', the matches often descended into needless violence. Games between Celtic and Racing Club, Manchester United and Estudiantes, Milan and Estudiantes, and Feyenoord and (are you noticing a pattern?) Estudiantes all ended in mass brawls.

During the 1970s, many European champions decided not to take part – Ajax, Bayern Munich, Liverpool and Nottingham Forest all turned down invitations – and the competition suffered as a result.

In 1980, the tournament – previously a two-legged home-and-away affair – moved to Tokyo for a one-off final, where it was regularly contested up until 2004, by which time it had been superceded by the FIFA World Club Cup.

FIFA's new baby was launched in 2005, and is contested annually by the champions of all six continental confederations. The format is straight knock-out, but seeded, with the champions of Europe and South America qualifying automatically for a semi-final spot on either side of the draw.

As of season 2008/09, all four finals have been contested between the two powerhouse confederations of Europe and South America. Two Brazilian sides have won the trophy – São Paulo and Internacional – while two European sides have triumphed – AC Milan and Manchester United.

Chapter 13

Focusing on Famous Clubs

*H*undreds of thousands of football clubs exist on Planet Football, so picking the top few and pleasing everyone is always going to be an impossible task.

I've narrowed it down by going to the most historically important countries in football, and picking the biggest and most successful clubs – and as you see in this chapter, 'biggest' and 'most successful' are nearly always the same thing.

Here follow some very selective histories of the top clubs in the world.

Nearly all of these clubs are at least 100 years old, so it's impossible to mention all their achievements in one book, never mind one chapter. All clubs have potted histories on their official websites, though. And if you're really interested in delving back in time (as all good fans are!) then there's bound to be at least one highly recommended reference book for each club. (Find more on that in Chapter 19.)

England

England was the home of the first-ever football clubs – the oldest, Sheffield FC, formed in 1857, is still going today in the local northern leagues. Sheffield has long been usurped in importance by some other big names, though!

Arsenal

Arsenal hail from North London, though they were formed south of the River Thames in 1886, as an ammunition factory works team in Woolwich. They moved north to Highbury in 1913 and within two decades became one of the most successful clubs in the country: in the 1930s, inspired by influential manager Herbert Chapman, they won five league titles – the first club from the south of England to become champions – and two FA Cups.

Apart from a league and cup double in 1971, Arsenal didn't enjoy sustained success again until relatively recently. They won the league twice under George Graham in 1989 and 1991, then two more league and cup doubles after the arrival of Arsene Wenger in the mid-1990s (1998 and 2002). Once infamous for workmanlike football – the chants '1-0 to the Arsenal' and 'Boring, boring Arsenal' say it all – they've since become a much more attractive side to watch.

They play in red shirts with white sleeves at the Emirates Stadium in London. Their arch rivals are Tottenham Hotspur, though they also have rivalries with other major London clubs such as Chelsea and West Ham United. In addition, they often clash with Manchester United, a result of their title battles in the late 1990s and early 2000s.

Arsenal won perhaps the most dramatic league title of all. In 1989 they needed to win by two clear goals at Liverpool to snatch the championship from the Merseyside club – and did so, Michael Thomas famously making it 2-0 deep into injury time.

Aston Villa

Aston Villa, who come from the city of Birmingham, are most famous for winning the 1982 European Cup. They were founder members of the Football League in 1888, and one of the earliest success stories in English football, becoming the second team (after Preston North End) to win the league and cup double in 1897.

By 1900 Villa had won the league five times and they added a sixth in 1910, though their halcyon days were soon over. They didn't win the title again until 1981, but that unsung team – whose star men were winger Tony Morley and strikers Peter Withe and Gary Shaw – went on to win the European Cup the year after, beating Bayern Munich in the final against all the odds, Withe scoring the only goal of the game.

Villa play in claret shirts with sky blue sleeves at Villa Park stadium. They have won the league seven times, the FA Cup seven times, the League Cup five times and the European Cup once. Their major rivals are Birmingham City.

Herbert Chapman: The visionary who changed football

Herbert Chapman, Arsenal's manager between 1925 and 1934, was always on the lookout for innovative ideas. Among other things, in the early 1930s he:

✔ Advocated that one man should pick the England side (an FA committee was involved until 1963)

✔ Installed floodlights at Highbury (but the club weren't allowed to use them until the 1950s!)

✔ Introduced a stadium clock to inform the crowd how much of the match was left

✔ Got the London Underground to change the name of nearby Gillespie Road tube stadium to Arsenal

✔ Introduced numbers on the back of shirts

Chapman died suddenly of pneumonia while still in office in 1934. The club erected a bust of the great man, which stands in the Emirates Stadium to this day.

By the time Villa's 1981 title-winning side had reached the 1982 European Cup final, manager Ron Saunders had quit. His replacement Tony Barton was so unknown he wasn't listed as manager in the official programme for the game. Instead, the programme named the man who laid out the kits for the players before the game!

Chelsea

For years Chelsea were the Nearly Club of London: always capable of putting on a good show but never quite winning the prize. Up until the 1990s they only had one league title (1955), League Cup (1965), FA Cup (1970) and Cup Winners' Cup (1971) to show for their efforts since forming in West London in 1905. They were more noted for style than substance – their players were more famous for being spotted out on the 1960s 'swinging London' scene than for anything they achieved on the field.

But that began to change from the mid-1990s when the club attracted big-name managers such as Glenn Hoddle, Ruud Gullit and Gianluca Vialli. They won two more FA Cups around the turn of the millennium (in 1997 and 2000), and another Cup Winners' Cup and the League Cup in 1998. Then Russian billionaire Roman Abramovich took over, and they're now one of the most successful sides in the country. Chelsea bought big-name stars with Abramovich's cash, and in 2004 appointed manager José Mourinho, who won back-to-back titles for the club.

Chelsea's strip is all blue. They play at Stamford Bridge. Their historical rivals are Fulham, though they have cross-city rivalries with West Ham United and Arsenal (these are often more intense because up until recently Fulham were usually in the lower leagues).

Up until the 1950s Chelsea's badge had a local icon on it – a Chelsea Pensioner. (*Chelsea Pensioners* are members of a retirement home for former army soldiers.) The club was at the time considered something of a quaint joke, having won nothing, so in 1952 manager Ted Drake ordered the badge to be changed to a rampant lion. Within three years Chelsea had won their first league title!

Everton

The first major team in Liverpool, Everton were founder members of the Football League and have always been one of the biggest clubs in the land. They've only spent four seasons out of the top division of English football, a record no other club can come close to.

The Toffees, as they are known, have enjoyed three distinct periods of success. In the 1920s and 1930s they were regular league and FA Cup winners, thanks to the goal-scoring exploits of two of the game's most famous strikers: first Dixie Dean, then Tommy Lawton. In the 1960s manager Harry Catterick built two great title-winning teams, the first around striker Alex Young – known romantically as The Golden Vision – then the midfield trio of Howard Kendall, Colin Harvey and Alan Ball. Kendall went on to manage the club in the 1980s, winning two league titles, an FA Cup and the Cup Winners' Cup.

Everton play in all-blue at Goodison Park. Their arch-rivals are Liverpool.

Liverpool in the 1980s: Triumph and tragedy

Liverpool were undoubtedly the team of the decade in the 1980s. In that time they won the league title six times, the FA Cup once, four League Cups and three European Cups.

But amid the triumphs came two defining tragedies that shaped the future of English football. In 1985, before Liverpool's European Cup final against Juventus, fans of the two teams clashed at Heysel Stadium in Brussels, Belgium. After throwing missiles at each other, a section of Liverpool's support chased after

Juventus fans, forcing them to flee. A wall collapsed and 39 people were killed. English clubs were banned from European competition until 1991, Liverpool for a further 12 months.

Then, at Liverpool's 1989 FA Cup semi-final against Nottingham Forest at Hillsborough, home of Sheffield Wednesday, 96 fans were crushed to death when mistakes made by police and stadium organisers caused too many supporters into a small fenced pen. The tragedy led to all-seater stadiums in the UK.

No two English rivals are situated closer together than Everton and Liverpool. Goodison Park and Anfield are separated by a five-minute walk across the fields of Stanley Park.

In 1928 Everton striker Dixie Dean scored 60 goals in a season, a record unlikely ever to be beaten. Amazingly, he pipped Middlesbrough striker George Camsell's total of 59, posted only the season before, by scoring a hat-trick on the very last day!

Leeds United

'A rollercoaster ride' is a hoary old football cliché for an up-and-down existence, but if any club deserves to use it, Leeds United do. Leeds were formed in 1919 and achieved little until Don Revie took over as manager in 1961. At the time Leeds were in the second tier, but Revie led the club to promotion and turned them into the team to beat for the next decade. Rivals often did beat them to the prizes – Leeds had a hellish reputation for coming second in leagues and cups – but they did land two league titles, an FA Cup, a League Cup and two Fairs Cup (later UEFA Cup) trophies.

Revie's side had a reputation for ruthlessness and cynicism – they were known to fans of other clubs as Dirty Leeds – and that reputation sticks to this day. But they also played some delightful football, and were unlucky not to win the 1975 European Cup, falling victim to some controversial refereeing decisions in the final against Bayern Munich. Leeds spent most of the 1980s back in the second division, before winning promotion again and landing a third league title in 1992. Since then the rollercoaster has continued. Leeds reached the Champions League semi-finals in 2000, before suffering financial meltdown and dropping to the third division in 2006. If history teaches anything, they'll be back.

Leeds United play in all white at Elland Road stadium. They have no city rivals. Although they have rivalries with other Yorkshire clubs such as Sheffield United, Sheffield Wednesday and Huddersfield Town, the fans reserve most of their bile for cross-Pennine hate figures Manchester United.

Leeds used to play in yellow and blue before Revie decided to change the club colours to all white in homage to Real Madrid.

Liverpool

Liverpool owe their existence to city rivals Everton, who used to play at Anfield but in 1892 left following a dispute with the ground's owner, John Houlding, over rent. Houlding, left with an empty stadium on his hands, decided to form another club – and Liverpool FC were born. They quickly became one of the more successful clubs in the country, winning the league in 1901.

The pivotal moment in Liverpool's fortunes came in 1959, when they appointed maverick manager Bill Shankly, who led the club to three titles and their first-ever FA Cup in 1965. Even more trophies came in the 1970s and 1980s under his successor Bob Paisley, who won three European Cups. Joe Fagan (another European Cup) and Kenny Dalglish continued Liverpool's dominance of the decade on the pitch. Off it, however, Liverpool suffered the twin disasters of Heysel and Hillsborough (see the sidebar 'Liverpool in the 1980s: triumph and tragedy'), and in 1991 Dalglish resigned due to the pressures of the job. Since then Liverpool have yet to win the league again, though in 2005 they won the Champions League in amazing fashion under Rafael Benítez, coming from 3-0 down to beat Milan in the final.

Liverpool play in all red at Anfield. Their city rivalry is with Everton, but although that's intense increased bitterness exists between Liverpool and Manchester United, with both sets of fans (arrogantly, to supporters of other teams) styling their club as the 'greatest' in the land. In terms of trophies won, Liverpool are the most successful in English football, though United are coming up fast on the trail.

Liverpool were the first English club to win a 'treble' of major titles: in 1984, Joe Fagan's first season in charge as manager, they landed the League, League Cup, and European Cup. They were also the first English club to win three cups in one season: in 2001, under Gerard Houllier, they landed the FA Cup, League Cup and UEFA cup.

Manchester City

Despite enjoying levels of success most teams in the country would give their back teeth for – two league titles, four FA Cups and a Cup Winners' Cup – Manchester City have earned themselves a reputation for hapless failure. That's partially down to the ill-fortune of being city rivals with Manchester United, one of world football's biggest powers, and coming a poor second by comparison. But City have also suffered more than their fair share of strange knocks.

In 1937 they won their first league title, only to become the first-ever reigning champions to be relegated the season after. (They were replaced by the team finishing second in the Second Division – who were, naturally, Manchester United.) In 1968 they landed their second league championship, but the feat was overshadowed a fortnight later when Manchester United won the European Cup. And in 1996, threatened with relegation, they thought a draw would be enough in their final match and so played keep-ball until the final whistle to secure the result, only to find they actually needed a win and went down. City fans, though, take a defiant pride in their bittersweet history. And anyway, all that might soon change because, under new Arab ownership, City are now the richest club in the world!

City, who play in sky blue and white at Eastlands Stadium, enjoy a rivalry with Manchester United.

The club's fans will tell you that theirs is the only team in the city of Manchester. Rivals United are technically situated in the neighbouring borough of Salford.

Manchester United

Manchester United are one of the biggest clubs in football, often topping the lists as the world's best supported and most profitable. They were always a big club in England, ever since their formation as Newton Heath in 1878, but after the Second World War, and the appointment of the legendary Matt Busby as manager, the institution grew and grew.

Busby created three great teams. The first won the FA Cup in 1948 and United's first league title for 41 years in 1952. His second – a youthful side known affectionately as The Busby Babes – won back-to-back leagues in the mid-1950s but were tragically cut down in their prime in an air crash at Munich Airport in 1958. See the nearby sidebar 'The Babes perish at Munich' for more information.

The third, starring the triumvirate of Bobby Charlton, George Best and Denis Law, won more titles in the 1960s and the 1968 European Cup. A barren period followed in the 1970s and 1980s, but the appointment of Alex Ferguson as manager saw the club enjoy outstanding success in the Premier League era, the pinnacle of which was the 1999 treble of league, FA Cup and European Cup, a feat unprecedented in English football.

United currently lag behind only Liverpool in terms of major trophies won by an English club, though are by far and away the most successful in the last two decades. They play in red, black and white at Old Trafford. Their city rivals are Manchester City, though they regularly lock horns with (by increasing levels of bile) Arsenal, Leeds United and Liverpool.

United owe their existence to a runaway dog. Club forerunners, Newton Heath, held a fundraising fete in 1901 from which the captain's dog fled. The daughter of a wealthy local businessman found the dog, and wanted to keep it. On tracing the dog, the captain struck a deal with the businessman: his daughter could keep it in exchange for investment – and a deal was done!

The Babes perish at Munich

On 8 February 1958 Matt Busby's young Manchester United side entered the history books in the most tragic way possible. They had hoped to do so in happier circumstances, by winning the European Cup, and had just reached the semi-finals by winning at Red Star Belgrade.

But on the way back, after a refuelling stop at Munich airport, the team's plane crashed while taking off in a blizzard. Seven members of the team were killed on impact; an eighth, the star man Duncan Edwards, died 15 days later in hospital. Red Star asked UEFA to name United as honorary champions of Europe that season, but UEFA insisted the show had to go on. Milan beat a hastily cobbled-together side in the semi-finals. United had to wait until 1968 to lift the European Cup; Busby finally reached his holy grail.

It was the second major plane crash to hit football in a decade: in 1949 Torino had their all-conquering Il Grande Torino side wiped out in a crash at Superga, a hill overlooking Turin.

Nottingham Forest

Nottingham Forest were founded all the way back in 1865. Apart from two FA Cup wins (in 1898 and 1959), until Brian Clough became Forest manager in 1975 the club were probably most famous for playing in the first-ever match to feature goal nets. (For the record, Forest versus Bolton Wanderers, 1890.) Clough's arrival changed all that, though. He took a middling second-tier team and within two-and-a-half seasons had turned them into the champions of England. Within another two seasons they'd won two European Cups.

Forest's achievement is arguably the greatest in the history of European competition: Nottingham is the smallest city to produce a champion of Europe. The team – starring striker Trevor Francis, cigarette-smoking winger John Robertson and goalkeeper Peter Shilton – broke up soon after their European Cup wins, though Forest under Clough won two League Cups at the end of the 1980s. Forest were relegated from the Premier League in Clough's last season as manager, in 1993, and have spent the majority of their time since in the lower divisions, the only former champions of Europe who currently play outside of their top domestic league.

Forest play in red and white at the City Ground. Their city rivals are Notts County, whose Meadow Lane ground is a long goal kick away, just across the River Trent. Forest also have a deep-rooted rivalry with Derby County.

A common mistake is to abbreviate Nottingham Forest as *Notts Forest*, but *Notts* is short for Nottinghamshire and not Nottingham! The correct abbreviation is *Nottm Forest* – unless you want to annoy Forest's fans, that is.

Tottenham Hotspur

Tottenham Hotspur – known to many simply as Spurs – are one of the biggest clubs in England, though their roll of honour doesn't particularly reflect this. Spurs have only won two league titles, yet far less famous clubs such as Portsmouth, Burnley and Preston North End have won the same amount and outfits such as Huddersfield Town and Blackburn Rovers have won more. But Tottenham's fame is guaranteed because they produced one of the most attractive sides of all time in the early 1960s. The team, managed by Bill Nicholson and starring Dave Mackay, John White and (later) Jimmy Greaves became the first team to win the league and FA Cup double in the 20th century – in 1961! – then landed England's first European trophy (the 1963 Cup Winners' Cup).

That Spurs side were committed to playing attractive football, a philosophy summed up by their outspoken captain Danny Blanchflower's famous comment that 'football is about glory, about doing things in style and with a flourish, not waiting for the other lot to die of boredom'. The club have struggled to live up to these lofty ideals since, though they have won the FA Cup eight times, a record bettered only by Manchester United and Arsenal.

Tottenham Hotspur play in white with dark-blue trim. Their home ground is White Hart Lane, London. Their main rivals are Arsenal.

Spurs weren't the first English club to sign players from overseas, but they did lead the way in signing truly top-class stars from abroad. In the summer of 1978, in a transfer still remembered fondly today, they signed midfielders Osvaldo Ardiles and Ricardo Villa, both of whom had just won the World Cup with Argentina.

West Ham United

West Ham United – who hail from the east end of London – have never won the English league. But their supporters will tell you that they've a bigger prize to their name: the 1966 World Cup. That's because the Hammers contributed three players to Alf Ramsey's victorious England team: captain Bobby Moore, midfielder Martin Peters (who scored one of England's goals in the final) and striker Geoff Hurst (who claimed the other three with the only hat-trick ever to be scored in a World Cup final). A statue of the three players outside West Ham's home stadium, the Boleyn Ground, commemorates this feat.

West Ham have won the FA Cup three times, however. The first victory, in 1964, was followed up by triumph in the 1965 European Cup Winners' Cup – making West Ham only the second British side to pick up a continental trophy. They added two further cup wins in 1975 and 1980, notable achievements both: the 1975 team was the last all-English side to win the FA Cup and the 1980 win was the last by a Second Division side.

Rivalries and derbies

There's not a club on the planet that doesn't have a rivalry with another. Ever since Hallam FC were formed in 1860, in order to give Sheffield FC a game, animosities have developed between different clubs. (By way of example, it only took two matches before Sheffield and Hallam started throwing haymakers at each other!)

Rivalries are usually local (though there are exceptions to this rule). More often than not, warring clubs come from the same or neighbouring towns and cities. A match between two rivals is known as a 'derby'.

To illustrate, famous derbies in the UK include Celtic and Rangers; Arsenal and Tottenham Hotspur; Liverpool and Everton; Manchester United and Manchester City; Newcastle United and Sunderland.

But while derbies tend to be local, they don't always involve the closest two teams. Manchester United and Liverpool may be 30 miles apart, but though each has a fierce city rival they concentrate much attention on each other. With both teams enjoying national fan bases, this has less to do with locality than bragging rights at the top end of the English game.

However, some deep-rooted rivalries have little logic: Chelsea and Leeds United simply don't like each other after several ill-tempered matches in the 1960s!

West Ham play in claret and blue shirts. Their home ground is the Boleyn Ground, London, though it is more commonly known as Upton Park. Their main rivals are Chelsea and Millwall, though they also enjoy a less-intense rivalry with near neighbours Leyton Orient.

West Ham played in the first-ever match at Wembley in 1923, losing in the FA Cup final against Bolton. The match is famous because the pitch was over-run by eager spectators before the match and a lone policeman on a horse had to marshal the crowd back into the stands. The game is known as The White Horse Final, though the horse was in fact grey. (The photos at the time had to be over-exposed because it was so overcast!)

Scotland

Organised football in Scotland has been going almost as long as in England. In fact, some say it all began here: although Sheffield FC (1857) is the oldest documented club, recent claims have been made for a 1824 outfit called Foot-Ball Club of Edinburgh!

Today there are 42 league clubs in Scotland, plus hundreds more in regional leagues (the most famous of which is the Highland League) and the junior leagues (which aren't contested, as you'd think from the name, by kids; it's just a lower level of football).

Aberdeen

Aberdeen enjoyed limited success up until the late 1970s, with only one league title, two Scottish Cups and two League Cups to show for their efforts since foundation in 1903. But the 1978 appointment of an up-and-coming young manager changed everything. That manager was Alex Ferguson, and he turned the Dons, as they're known, into Scotland's team of the 1980s.

With players such as defenders Alex McLeish and Willie Miller, winger Gordon Strachan and keeper Jim Leighton, Aberdeen won the title three times in six seasons between 1980 and 1985, and the Scottish Cup four times in five years between 1982 and 1986. But it was in Europe that they cemented their legend, beating Real Madrid and Bayern Munich on the way to landing the 1983 Cup Winners' Cup. Ferguson left for Manchester United in 1986; the club have failed to enjoy such success since.

Aberdeen play in red at Pittodrie. With no near geographical rivals, their supporters' main beef is with Rangers (after a series of particularly foul-heavy matches in the late 1980s and early 1990s).

Aberdeen's success in the 1980s broke the usual hegemony between Scotland's two biggest clubs, the 'Old Firm' of Celtic and Rangers. Dundee United also won their first (and as yet only) league title in 1983, leading Aberdeen and United to be christened the 'New Firm'.

Celtic

Celtic are, along with fellow Glasgow giants Rangers, one half of arguably the biggest rivalry in world football. The club are most famous for their success in the 1960s and 1970s under the legendary manager Jock Stein. The team won nine league titles in a row, winning the 1967 European Cup with a side whose furthest-flung member had been born 30 miles away from Celtic's home stadium. They're still the only Scottish team to have won Europe's premier club competition.

Today, Celtic are regular winners of Scottish football's biggest prizes, and occasionally enjoy good runs in Europe. Under the wily Martin O'Neill, and with the skilful striker Henrik Larsson up front, Celtic reached the 2003 UEFA Cup final, but lost 3-2 to José Mourinho's Porto team.

Celtic play in green and white hoops. Their home ground is Celtic Park, Glasgow, though it is more commonly referred to as Parkhead. Their rivals are Rangers.

Celtic is pronounced 'sell-tik' and not, as you might assume, 'kell-tik'.

Celtic are the best-supported team in Ireland, reflecting their genesis as a sporting club for Irish Catholic ex-pats in the late 1800s.

Rangers

Rangers are the best supported team in Scotland, gaining support from all over the country as well as their Glasgow base. They hold the world record for domestic title wins – they're currently the only side to have won their league title over 50 times – but they've never been able to translate that success internationally, although they did win the 1972 Cup Winners' Cup.

Rangers matched Celtic's nine-in-a-row record in the mid-1990s under the leadership of Walter Smith, who soon left the club to manage Everton and then Scotland. But Smith returned in 2007 to enjoy more glory, leading the club to the 2008 UEFA Cup final, which Rangers lost to Zenit St Petersburg, and then another Scottish league title.

Rangers play in blue shirts, white shorts and black socks. Their home stadium is Ibrox, Glasgow. Their rivals are Celtic.

Rangers are often referred to as *Glasgow Rangers*, but the official name of the club has no reference to their home town: they're simply Rangers Football Club.

Old Firm, old problems

The rivalry between Celtic and Rangers – collectively known as The Old Firm – is one of the most intense in world football.

The two Glasgow clubs are by far and away the largest, best supported and most successful in Scotland, totally dominating all other clubs in terms of trophies won. (No other team, for example, has won the league since Aberdeen in 1985.)

The clubs are infamous for their sometimes sectarian rivalry. Celtic were formed by a Catholic priest and have strong links with the Irish republican community; Rangers are staunchly Protestant, very much the club of the UK establishment.

Up until the late 1980s Rangers had an unwritten rule not to sign Catholic players. Celtic have always been more open-minded in this regard. These days, though, neither club operates such a restrictive policy.

Fans, too, are encouraged not to sing sectarian songs. In the past, Celtic fans would chant pro-IRA songs and Rangers supporters would sing about the Irish famine. This is less a problem than it was, though incidents do still occasionally occur.

Ibrox has been the scene of two of football's biggest disasters. A stand collapsed in 1902, killing 25 fans. Then, in 1971, 66 supporters died in a crush on an exit stairwell. As a result of the 1971 disaster, Ibrox became all-seater, and one of the grandest (and safest) stadiums in the land.

Europe

Although England and Scotland were first out of the blocks, forming football teams from the mid-1800s onwards, the rest of Europe wasn't far behind. It wasn't long before the continent boasted some of the most evocative institutions in sport.

Ajax

Ajax are the largest and most famous of Dutch football's big three – most of the major prizes in Holland have been historically shared out between Ajax, PSV Eindhoven and Feyenoord of Rotterdam.

Ajax's golden period came in the early 1970s with a team starring Johan Cruyff, Ruud Krol and Johan Neeskens. They pioneered Total Football – where every player could interchange positions as the match developed – and won three European Cups in a row between 1971 and 1974. The club discovered the great striker Marco van Basten in the early 1980s, before a youthful side added another European Cup in 1995.

Ajax are from Amsterdam, Netherlands. Their home stadium is the Amsterdam ArenA. They play in white shirts with a thick red stripe down the centre. They've won the European Cup four times, and the UEFA Cup and Cup Winners' Cup once.

Barcelona

Barcelona are one of the two dominant clubs in Spain, the other being Real Madrid. Madrid is seen as the establishment club and a symbol of a unified Spain, and Barcelona represent the region of Catalonia and symbolises that nation's autonomy.

Barca have long been one of the most glamorous teams in world football, attracting the biggest names from around the world – the famous Hungarians Sándor Kocsis and Zoltán Czibor in the 1950s, Johan Cryuff in the 1970s,

Diego Maradona in the 1980s and Lionel Messi today. They had to wait until 1992, however, to win their first European Cup. Since then they've added two more Champions Leagues, in 2006 and 2009.

Barcelona play in blue and red stripes. Their stadium, Camp Nou, is the largest in Europe, seating nearly 100,000 fans. They've won three European Cups, four Cup Winners' Cups and three UEFA Cups.

Bayern Munich

Bayern Munich are Germany's biggest and most successful club, though they didn't become a dominant force in their country until the late 1960s. Since then they've won more titles than any other German club, becoming the most loved – and paradoxically the most hated – club in the country.

Their heyday came in the 1970s, when a team starring defender Franz Beckenbauer, striker Gerd Müller and goalkeeper Sepp Maier – the backbone of West Germany's 1974 World Cup winning team – won three European Cups in a row between 1974 and 1976. Bayern became champions of Europe again in 2001, but they're possibly best remembered for somehow losing 2-1 to Manchester United in the 1999 European Cup final, after going into injury time a goal to the good.

Bayern historically play in all red, though their strip occasionally features large quantities of blue as well. They play at the Allianz Arena, a stadium they share with city rivals 1860 Munich. They have won four European Cups, and one of both UEFA and Cup Winners' Cups.

Bayern are such a dominant force in Germany that it only takes a couple of defeats to spark talk of a crisis at the club. It's for this reason that people often refer to them as FC Hollywood.

Benfica

Benfica are Portugal's most successful and internationally renowned club, even though in recent years they've been forced to play second fiddle to Porto. Benfica's golden era came at the start of the 1960s, when a team built around striker Eusebio won the European Cup in 1961 and 1962. Success abroad has since eluded them, though they did at least reach the European Cup final in 1988 and 1990.

Benfica are from Lisbon, Portugal. They play in red shirts. The name of their home stadium, Estádio da Luz, translates as Stadium of Light, but Luz is in fact a district of Lisbon. Benfica have won the European Cup twice.

Benfica's nickname is The Eagles. Before each game, a trained eagle called Vitoria is released to fly once around the stadium.

Internazionale

Internazionale have always been one of Italian football's powerhouses – they're the only club never to be relegated from Serie A – though their name will always be associated first and foremost with the mid 1960s. That was when manager Helenio Herrera unleashed a defensive style of play called *catenaccio* – Italian for 'padlock' – and led the team to European domination, winning the 1964 and 1965 European Cups.

For many years the club struggled to match their achievements of the 1960s, despite spending more money than any other side in Europe during the 1980s, 1990s and first part of the 2000s. Not even big-name signings such as Brazilian striker Ronaldo could land them big prizes. But recently the club has started winning Serie A titles again, and are looking to finally make their serious mark on Europe for the first time since the Herrera era.

Internazionale are from Milan, Italy. Their strip consists of blue and black vertical stripes. They play at the San Siro, a stadium they share with AC Milan. Inter have won two European Cups and three UEFA Cups.

People often refer to Internazionale as Inter Milan, but this is technically incorrect: it is like saying 'Arsenal London' or 'Everton Liverpool'. If Internazionale seems too much of a mouthful, a simple 'Inter' will suffice.

Internazionale were forced to change their name during Mussolini's fascist era because foreign associations were frowned upon. They were called Ambrosiana, but changed the name back the minute Mussolini had been usurped after the Second World War.

Juventus

Juventus are a strange beast: they're not the best supported team in their home town of Turin (that honour goes to Torino) but they're the best supported in all of Italy! That's partly because the big FIAT car factory in Turin historically attracted workers from all over the country, but mainly because Juve (pronounced 'yoo-vay') are domestically the most successful club in Italian football.

The club – nicknamed The Old Lady – have won a record 27 Serie A titles, though success on the continent has been limited, with only two European Cup wins. Their first win came in 1985, in the wake of the Heysel tragedy (see the earlier sidebar 'Liverpool in the 1980s: triumph and tragedy'); their second in 1996 with a team led by strike duo Gianluca Vialli and Fabrizio Ravanelli. Until 2006 Juve had always played top-flight football, but then they were demoted for their part in a match-fixing scandal.

Juve play in Turin, Italy. They wear black and white striped shirts. Their home stadium is the Stadio delle Alpi, though that's currently being refurbished so they're using the Stadio Olimpico di Torino instead. Juve have won two European Cups, three UEFA Cups and a Cup Winners' Cup.

Juventus have English club Notts County to thank for their strip: a travelling Juve committee member was on holiday in England in 1903 and so liked County's black and white striped shirts that he took a set home for his team to wear!

Marseille

Although the French national team have won World Cups and European Championships, and French bureaucrats were responsible for founding FIFA, the World Cup and the European Cup, French club sides have failed to enjoy much success on the big stage. Reims and St Etienne both reached European Cup finals, but it was only in 1993 that a club from France became champions of Europe.

Olympique de Marseille – known as l'OM in France – had been expected to win the 1991 European Cup final, but a team starring striker Jean-Pierre Papin and English winger Chris Waddle froze on the day, allowing Red Star Belgrade to take the title. But two years later l'OM surprised Milan 1-0 in the first-ever Champions League final. Defender Basile Boli scored the only goal, and midfielder Didier Deschamps lifted the trophy. It was the greatest achievement by any French club – though it was later tainted when Marseille were found to have bribed opponents en route to winning the French league the previous season. Marseille have yet to win a major trophy since the scandal, but remain the biggest club in France.

Marseille play in all white with light-blue trim. They play at the Stade Vélodrome. Marseille have won the European Cup once.

It's often erroneously reported that Marseille were stripped of their 1993 Champions League win as a result of their infamous match-fixing exploits. But they were simply relegated from the French top flight and banned from European football.

Come on you red-blacks!

Wherever you go around the world, football teams are nicknamed according to the colour of their shirts: Manchester United, Liverpool and Arsenal are known as 'the reds', while Everton, Chelsea and Portsmouth would be 'the blues'.

It's not very original – and not particularly romantic in plain old English. However it's all much more lyrical in Italian – and the nicknames are worth learning because people often use them to describe both teams and their fans in English-speaking Serie A reports.

Here are the most frequently used nicknames:

✔ *Viola* (purple): Fiorentina (from Florence)

✔ *Nerazzurri* (black-blues): Internazionale

✔ *Bianconeri* (white-blacks): Juventus

✔ *Biancocelesti* (white and sky-blues): Lazio (of Rome)

✔ *Rossoneri* (red-blacks): Milan

✔ *Giallorossi* (yellow-reds): Roma

✔ *Azzurri* (blues): The Italian national team

Milan

Milan (or AC Milan) have been the most successful club in Europe over the past two decades, winning five European Cups between 1989 and 2007. The club were founder members of the Italian league, but didn't enjoy any sustained success until after the Second World War. In the 1950s their team – built around Swedish trio Gunnar Gren, Gunnar Nordahl and Nils Liedholm, and Uruguay's 1950 World Cup hero Juan Schiaffino – won several titles and reached the 1958 European Cup final, losing to the dominant Real Madrid. Five years later they became the first Italian side to win the European Cup, beating reigning champions Benfica.

Milan won another European Cup in 1969, but went into decline and were relegated for the first time in their history in 1980 as punishment for their part in a betting scandal. They won immediate promotion, but were immediately relegated again, this time simply for being poor. In 1986 media magnate (and future Italian prime minister) Silvio Burlusconi bought the club and injected large sums of money. Within three years a Milan starring Dutch duo Ruud Guillit and Marco van Basten were champions of Europe. The team have been a regular fixture in European Cup finals ever since, the high point being a 4-0 win over Barcelona in 1994, the low an inexplicable loss against Liverpool in 2005 after being 3-0 up at half time.

Milan play in red and black shirts at the San Siro. They've won the European Cup seven times and the Cup Winners' Cup twice.

Milan were founded by English ex-pats, which is why their name doesn't take the Italian form 'Milano'.

Porto

Porto – from Portugal's second city – were for years considered to be the third club in the country, behind the Lisbon giants Benfica and Sporting Lisbon. But in 1987 they won the European Cup, beating Bayern Munich in the final with the aid of a cheeky back-heeled goal from the Egyptian genius Rabah Madjer. And ever since they've been the dominant club in the country.

They enjoyed their grandest years in 2003 and 2004, after little-known coach José Mourinho took over the club and led the team – which contained future Chelsea stars Ricardo Carvalho and Deco – to victory in the UEFA Cup, then the Champions League the following season. Further success in Europe has since eluded them, but domestic domination continues apace.

Porto play in blue and white stripes, at the Estádio do Dragão. They've won the European Cup twice.

The Portuguese league is one of the more predictable in world football. Since it was launched in 1935, either Porto, Benfica or Sporting Lisbon have won it on all but two occasions: Belenenses of Lisbon (1946) and Boavista of Porto (2001).

Real Madrid

Despite the constant claims of others, Real Madrid are without question the biggest club in the world. They've won the European Cup a record nine times, and have over the years fielded many of the game's truly great players in their team. They're also the most successful club domestically in Spain – though detractors will tell you the team earned many of their titles thanks to the influence of fascist dictator (and Real fan) General Franco.

Real's legendary status was sealed in the 1950s, when a side starring Alfredo di Stéfano, Francesco Gento, Raymond Kopa and Ferenc Puskás won the first five European Cups, a run culminating in a famous 7-3 victory over Eintracht Frankfurt in the 1960 final. Although Real added a sixth in 1966, the European trail went cold for 32 years, though a high point in between was five consecutive Spanish titles in the 1980s, strikers Emilio Butragueño and Hugo Sánchez dominating the goal-scoring charts. Then the club won three more European Cups in 1998, 2000 and (spectacularly, thanks to a wonderful volley by Zinedine Zidane) in 2002. The club have since pursued a policy of buying some of the biggest names in world football, such as David Beckham, Cristiano Ronaldo, Kaká and Karim Benzema.

Real Madrid play in all white at the Santiago Bernabéu stadium in central Madrid. They've won nine European Cups and two UEFA Cups.

Real Madrid are the only club to have sacked their manager after winning the European Cup! They got rid of Jupp Heynckes in 1998 because he hadn't won the Spanish league. They also sacked two-time European Cup winning manager Vicente del Bosque in 2003, just after winning the league!

South America

While clubs were springing up all over mainland Europe in the late 1800s and early 1900s, the same thing was happening in South America, thanks to British ex-pats taking the game across the seas. As a result, the continent boasts many of the oldest and most famous clubs in the world.

Boca Juniors

Along with River Plate, Boca are one of the two biggest clubs in Argentina. They play in Buenos Aires and are historically the team of the working class. Even though he didn't play for the club for a particularly long time, Diego Maradona is their most famous player. Boca hadn't won an international trophy until they landed the Copa Libertadores (the south American club championship) in 1977, but now they hold the world record of most international titles (18) with AC Milan.

Boca play in blue shirts with a yellow stripe across the chest. They play at the La Bombonera, Buenos Aires. They've won six Copa Libertadores.

Club representatives decided on Boca's colour scheme as part of a bet, the club agreeing to adopt the flag colours of the next ship to dock at La Boca port. A Swedish vessel sailed in, with the country's blue and yellow flag flapping in the breeze, and so Boca's famous strip was decided.

Flamengo

Flamengo are the biggest club in Brazil, and the representatives of the working classes in Rio de Janeiro. They share a rivalry with their more middle-class rivals Fluminense, from which Flamengo was formed in 1911 by a splinter group. It wasn't until the 1980s that Flamengo made their mark on the world stage, thrashing Liverpool 3-0 in the World Club Cup in 1981 with a team starring Brazilian midfield legend Zico.

Fla play in black and red hoops at both the Maracanã and Gávea stadiums in Rio. They've won the Copa Libertadores once.

Fluminense

Moneyed British ex-pats founded Fluminense in 1902, and to this day they're seen as the team of the Rio chattering classes. Flu are one of the most successful teams in Brazil, though they've had no success on the international scene, a dreadful record for such a big club. Flu were relegated twice during a barren 1990s, but such is their status that political manoeuvring quickly saw them reinstated to the top flight!

Flu play in red and green stripes at both the Maracanã and Laranjeiras stadiums in Rio.

The derbies between Fluminense and Flamengo – known as the Fla-Flu – historically draw huge crowds. In December 1963 a game between the two sides at the Maracanã drew 194,603 spectators. Even the official paying attendance of only 177,656 made it the best-attended club game in world history, a record that stands today. Sure enough, it ended 0-0.

Independiente

Independiente may be the 'third club' in Buenos Aires, losing out in the glamour stakes to city rivals Boca Juniors and River Plate, but they've won more Copa Libertadores than any other team on the continent. However, their achievements are very much in the past – they won their last Copa Libertadores in 1984! The club have struggled to match their illustrious achievements since, yet remain one of Argentinian football's big names.

Independiente play in red. Their home ground is the Estadiuo Libertadores de América. They've won a record seven Copa Libertadores.

Independiente's modern malaise can be illustrated by the fact that their most famous player, to this day, remains Raimundo Orsi, who played for Argentina in the 1930 World Cup final and then scored for Italy as they won the 1934 version!

Millonarios

Millonarios of Bogota, Colombia, haven't won the Colombian championship since 1988 and have never even reached the final of the Copa Libertadores. But they remain without question the most famous name in Colombian football for their money-splashing exploits in the 1950s. That was when they signed football's biggest names, contravening all FIFA transfer protocol when Colombia ran an illegal breakaway league. Alfredo di Stéfano took his first steps to greatness here, eventually leaving the club for Real Madrid. The glory days are now long gone, but the lustre of Millonarios remains.

Millonarios play in all blue at El Campín.

A local journalist gave Millonarios their name. In the 1930s the club – then called Deportivo Municipal – pushed for a professional league in football, so the journalist wrote 'the Municipalistas have become the Millonarios'. The name stuck, and a new identity was born.

Nacional

Nacional of Montevideo are one of the two historically dominant teams in Uruguay. The club supplied most of the players to Uruguay's 1924 and 1928 Olympic champion teams, and their 1930 World Cup winning squad. In 1941 they enjoyed a perfect league season, winning all 20 games in the Uruguayan Primera Division, one of which was a 6-0 win over their arch-rivals Peñarol. This win came in the middle of what is now called Nacional's Quinquenio de Oro: the Golden Five Years. Nacional have won three Copa Libertadores.

Nacional play in white shirts at both Parque Central and Estadio Centenario. They've won three Copa Libertadores.

Nacional claim to be the oldest team in Uruguay, formed in 1899. However, Peñarol insist they're older because they were initially the English ex-pats' Central Uruguay Railway Cricket Club (formed 1891) before becoming totally Uruguayan in 1913. The controversy rages to this day.

Peñarol

Peñarol of Montevideo are Nacional's rivals for the title of 'biggest club in Uruguay'. The club are the most decorated in Uruguay, having won the most domestic titles in the professional era and five Copa Libertadores, two more than Nacional. Along with their rivals they've dominated the Uruguayan game over the decades, though they've not won a league title since 2003. The club famously provided the bulk of Uruguay's victorious 1950 World Cup team, including the two players who scored in the final against Brazil, Juan Schiaffino and Alcide Ghiggia.

Peñarol play in yellow and black stripes at both Estadio Las Acacias and Estadio Centenario. They've won the Copa Libertadores five times.

Since the Uruguayan league turned professional in 1931 Peñarol and Nacional have shared the title for all but ten seasons. All the five other teams to have won titles – Defensor Sporting (4), Danubio (3), Bella Vista (1), Central Español (1) and Progreso (1) – also come from the capital city Montevideo. No other country's league has been totally dominated by a single city like this.

River Plate

River Plate are the 'other' great team in Buenos Aires, Argentina, rivalling the working-class outfit Boca Juniors. River are traditionally the rich relatives of the city, though despite winning many domestic titles they took until 1986 to win their first Copa Libertadores, with Uruguayan midfielder Enzo Francescoli the star of that side. Although rivals Boca can boast Diego Maradona as a star ex-player, River have arguably a more stellar roll call, featuring the likes of future Real Madrid midfielder Alfredo di Stéfano, 1978 World Cup winning striker Mario Kempes and Milan and Chelsea striker Hernán Crespo.

River play in white shirts with a red diagonal sash. They play at El Monumental. They've won two Copa Libertadores.

The derby between River Plate and Boca Juniors – known as the Superclasico – is perhaps the most intense in world football. Nearly 75 per cent of Argentinians are said to either support or strongly express a preference for one team or the other.

Santos

Brazilian club sides have been nowhere near as successful as their international team. There's no better example of this than Santos – who despite winning their two Copa Libertadores all the way back in 1962 and 1963 are still by far the most famous Brazilian club in the world. Why is this? Because they were the club side of Pelé, the most famous footballer ever to have played the game. Pelé was the beating heart of a team that also won the World Club Cup twice, beating two different European champions in Benfica and AC Milan. The club – based in São Paulo – have never enjoyed such success since, but their fame refuses to diminish.

Santos are based in Santos, São Paulo. They wear black and white striped shirts. They play at Vila Belmiro, and have won two Copa Libertadores.

Although Santos remain the most famous Brazilian club, their neighbours Sao Paulo are the most successful. São Paulo have won three Copa Libertadores, more than any other Brazilian team, and more domestic league titles than anyone else.

Some Selected Others

Football took a serious hold in Europe and South America before anywhere else in the world, so it's only natural the majority of famous clubs are from those continents. But that doesn't mean the rest of the world are lacking major institutions of their own.

Of course, there are simply far too many to list, but I've chosen a select few. (Ask me next year and I'd no doubt pick a completely different set of clubs!)

Al-Ahly and Zamalek

Egypt is the most successful African football nation, so it's not surprising the country boasts the fiercest (and most long-lasting) club rivalry. The two Cairo teams Al-Ahly and Zamalek have been at it for a century now – the former began life in 1907, the latter four years later.

Al-Ahly are the dominant partner in the rivalry, having won 34 Egyptian titles and six African Champions League crowns, both records. The feats meant Al-Ahly were titled African Club of the 20th Century by the CAF, the African federation. But although Zamalek have won a mere 11 domestic titles by comparison, they're only one African Champions League behind Al-Ahly, with five wins.

Raja Casablanca

Wydad of Casablanca (WAC) are historically the biggest club in Moroccan football history, but in the last two decades they've been astonishingly superceded by city rivals Raja Casablanca. Raja only won their first domestic title in 1988, but by the end of the century – having won consecutive leagues from 1996 to 2000 and adding three African Champions Leagues in 1989, 1997 and 1999 – they were ranked third in the CAF's African Club of the 20th Century poll!

Asante Kotoko and Hearts of Oak

Asante Kotoko and Hearts of Oak are the two largest clubs in Ghana, one of the most historically successful countries in African football. Asante Kotoko, from Kumasi, have won the African Champions League twice, while Hearts of Oak, from Accra, have won it once. Between them the two sides have won over 40 domestic titles.

Asante's heyday came in the 1970s and 1980s, and Hearts became dominant in the late 1990s. Tragically, Hearts Champions League winning season, in 2000, was overshadowed first by a riot at the Champions League final then a crush at their ground in May 2001, which killed 126 fans. The club have bounced back from tragedy to win all but one Ghanaian championship in the 2000s.

LA Galaxy

The Los Angeles Galaxy are one of the founder members of the Major Soccer League (MSL), and since the league's first season in 1996 have enjoyed a decade of great success, becoming regular-season champions twice and winning the MLS Cup end-of-season play-offs twice. The club's star man over that period was US midfielder Cobi Jones. Galaxy made world headlines in 2007 with the signing of England and Real Madrid midfielder David Beckham, though his time at Galaxy is widely considered to be a failure, with the team struggling and Beckham concentrating on cementing his place in England's squad for the 2010 World Cup.

Galaxy aren't the first soccer team in Los Angeles. Others have included the LA Kickers, the hilariously titled LA Salsa – the side were owned by a restaurateur – and most famously the LA Aztecs, who played in the North American Soccer League (NASL) during the 1970s, signed Johan Cruyff and George Best, and had Elton John as a co-owner.

New York Cosmos

Cosmos are now defunct, having gone out of business in 1985, but their exploits in the 1970s mean their name lives on long in the memory. The New York club were prime movers and shakers in the NASL, which briefly popularised football in the USA during the 1970s and astonished the world by goading Pelé out of retirement in 1975. In 1977, Pelé's final season, the Cosmos boasted a team also starring Brazil's 1970 World Cup winning captain Carlos Alberto, and West Germany's 1974 World Cup winning captain Franz Beckenbauer. Ironically, it wasn't until Pelé left that the Cosmos won Soccer Bowl titles – in 1978, 1980 and 1982 – but the NASL lost momentum and closed along with the Cosmos in 1985.

On 13 June 1985 the Cosmos played a friendly against their striker Giorgio Chinaglia's former club Lazio of Rome. It degenerated into a brawl, forcing the referee to abandon the game. It was the Cosmos's last act on a football pitch.

Ten teams in flight!

Some football clubs are more famous for their wonderful names than anything else. Here are ten of my favourites, some of which are sure to appeal to the inner child:

✔ Prima Ham FC (Japan): Prima Ham were founded by workers at a food company. They've since changed their name to Mito Hollyhock.

✔ Deportivo Moron (Argentina): Moron is a district in Buenos Aires.

✔ Club Destroyers (Bolivia): Having never won a Bolivian title, this second-tier club doesn't do what it says on the tin.

✔ The Strongest (Bolivia): The oldest club in Bolivia. A battle in a 1930s war between Bolivia and Paraguay was named after this club, after several players and staff members took up arms.

✔ Eleven Men in Flight (Swaziland): This Swazi soccer club is surely the most romantically named in the world . . .

✔ Queen of the South (Scotland): . . . although these chaps from Dumfries, southern Scotland, run them close.

✔ Botswana Meat Commission (Botswana): In the mid-1980s, Everton were sponsored by no-frills ham company Hafnia, but even that indignity isn't a patch on the one suffered by this Lobatse team.

✔ Big Bullets (Malawi): As you'd expect, the most successful club in the country are sharp shooters.

✔ Mysterious Dwarfs (Ghana): This first-division club are more commonly known as Ebusua Dwarfs, which isn't as catchy.

✔ Corinthian Casuals (England): Formed following the merger of two famous amateur sides, Corinthians and Casuals. Corinthians were famous in the 1880s and 1890s for their exceptional sporting values, which went as far as a refusal to attempt to save penalties awarded against them. (The feeling was, a foul in the box should be punished by a goal!)

Chapter 14

Women's Football

You can't ignore the elephant in the room: there'll always be football fans, usually male and set in their ways, who argue that women's football isn't a patch on the men's game. Put the England women up against the English men, they argue, and John Terry and the boys would win every time. They'd be too strong, too fast, too skilful.

Well, that's probably right. And yet, this argument totally misses the point – because women's football is *a totally different sport.*

It's simply not relevant to compare the two because the teams would never meet. Does Serena Williams play Roger Federer at tennis? Does Paula Radcliffe compete with Haile Gebrselassie for the marathon? Does Karrie Webb tee it up with Tiger Woods? You get the point, though it's amazing how many lazy thinkers don't!

Still, it's their loss, because women's football is becoming more exciting and more competitive by the day. In 2007 the Women's World Cup broke world-wide viewing records for the sport, and a successful professional league is burgeoning in the United States. Games are usually attractive affairs, with more emphasis on passing than physical contact.

The game's profile is, of course, dwarfed by the men's game, with minuscule media coverage. (In some ways that's to be expected; you can't ignore the weight of over 150 years of history in men's football.) Yet this lower profile will surely change over time because, as we shall see, women's football has overcome bigger obstacles than that to become the successful sport it is today.

From China to Crouch End: How It All Began

Women's football has a history as long as the men's game, with Chinese women from the Han Dynasty (roughly 200BC to 200AD) featuring in pictures playing keepie-uppie with a ball! Sadly, due to a mixture of apathy and oppression the female game was overtaken by the men's when football as you know it today really kicked off during the late 1800s and early 1900s.

While the men were getting their acts together with the formation of the Football Association in 1863, the prevailing mood of Victorian Britain deemed football to be anything but a feminine pastime. Many doctors were also wheeled out to advise that it was medically harmful to the female form, some even suggesting that kicking a ball would render a woman unable to have children.

But in March 1895 the first competitive 'ladies' fixture was held in Crouch End, North London. In truth, it was more a political event than a sporting one: suffragette Nettie Honeyball founded her British Ladies Football Club 'with the fixed resolve of proving to the world that women are not the ornamental and useless creatures men have pictured. I look forward to the time when ladies may sit in Parliament and have a voice in the direction of affairs.' (Women were yet to be given the vote at this point in history.)

The game was considered a success, though, a North London representative XI beating their South London counterparts 7-1. More than 10,000 supporters watched, and newspapers reported that the unreconstructed crowd spent the first ten minutes highly amused at the sight of women playing football but were soon won round by the excitement of the match. 'I imagine that women players may after some further practice develop a style of play which may be both vigorous and graceful,' reported the *Manchester Guardian*'s 'Lady Correspondent'.

A month later Honeyball took the two teams around the country on an exhibition tour. The match they played at the home of Reading FC broke the club's attendance record previously held by a men's game between Reading and Luton Town! Opportunities for the women's game to thrive and prosper definitely existed, and during the First World War its popularity would go through the roof.

Dick, Kerr Ladies get popular . . .

In October 1917, Alfred Frankland, a clerk at the Dick, Kerr & Co. munitions factory in Preston encouraged women working there to set up a team.

(Shown in Figure 14-1.) Frankland had watched the workers attempting to kick a ball through an open window during their lunch hour, and decided that the women were more accurate and skilful than the men.

Figure 14-1: The Dick, Kerr Ladies' team.

Frankland organised a charity event at Deepdale, the home of local club Preston North End, and on Christmas Day that year 10,000 fans – starved of football with many of the men away at war and the Football League suspended – turned up to watch the event. It was a great success: Dick, Kerr beat a women's team from a nearby foundry 4-0, and the match raised £200 for a local hospital.

The men's league restarted in 1919, but the popularity of the women's game – a more skilful, less physical spectacle – continued to grow. A game on Boxing Day in 1920 between Dick, Kerr and St Helens drew 53,000 spectators to Everton's Goodison Park, and an unofficial England–France international (effectively Dick, Kerr versus a French side) attracted 25,000 fans.

During 1921 Dick, Kerr Ladies played 67 matches, drawing over 900,000 paying spectators, all of the money going to hospitals and war charities.

At this point proper competitive women's football was beginning to take root. In the north of England hundreds of clubs sprang up, and in some places people considered these clubs to be equally representative of their villages and towns as the men's teams were. In 1917 a knockout cup competition took place in Workington, followed by two stagings of the snappily titled Tyne Wear & Tees Alfred Wood Munition Girls Cup in 1918 and 1919. People also talked of setting up an English Women's Football Association that would run alongside the existing men's FA, to the benefit of the game as a whole.

. . . and the FA get sexist

Women's football had also become popular in other countries, including the Netherlands and Germany. But with popularity came jealousy, resistance and finally oppression. In 1896 the Dutch FA (KNVB) banned a game between Sparta Rotterdam and an England XI. And worse was to come in England.

In 1919 a women's match at Newcastle United's St James's Park drew 35,000 fans and raised – in today's terms – nearly £250,000 for charity. Two years later the same club banned women from using the ground, because club directors were worried that the sport would eclipse the men's in terms of popularity.

Political concerns also existed. Dick, Kerr had played a series of charity matches to raise money for sacked miners – rubbing up the wrong way the stuffy establishment figures at the FA – and the very fact that these matches raised so much money for charity highlighted to the general public the amount of money football matches raised (and how much was being pocketed by the owners).

The FA launched an attack on the women's game. They orchestrated a smear campaign, accusing Dick, Kerr and other teams of fiddling their expenses and effectively robbing money from the charities. And they wheeled out the doctors again to provide spurious medical evidence that 'violent leg strain' would leave women unable to have children.

In December 1921 the FA used those 'health concerns' and accusations of financial impropriety to ban women from using men's pitches and FA referees. 'The game is unsuitable for females and ought not to be encouraged,' they wrote.

The FA didn't apologise for these slights until 2008, 37 years after they lifted their ban on women's football!

The women fight back

The women responded staunchly: five days after their FA ban in 1921 they formed an English Ladies FA, which kept the flame alight during several dark decades for the sport. Dick, Kerr's continued to play across the country until the 1960s, and a team called Manchester Corinthians prospered in the 1940s and 1950s. Women also attempted to stage meaningful tournaments, such as the English Ladies FA Challenge Cup in 1922 (won by Stoke Ladies FC) and a Championship of Great Britain and the World (Dick, Kerr beat Edinburgh 5-1 in 1937, with the exact score reversed the following year).

But unable to use the country's existing footballing infrastructure, women's teams were effectively banished to the sidelines, able only to play the very occasional exhibition match.

However, the game was gaining popularity across the globe, with thousands of young women taking up football in the United States, China, Germany, Holland and all across Scandinavia. In 1957 women formed a body called the International Ladies Football Association, followed by the Fédération Internationale et Européenne de Football Féminin in 1969. Manchester Corinthians won an unofficial women's European championship. Then in 1970 and 1971 Denmark won unofficial World Cups. The matches didn't generate much media interest, but FAs around the world sat up and took notice.

The FA lift the ban – and FIFA get serious

In 1970 and 1971 several national associations, notably those of France, West Germany and England, lifted their bans on women's football. The move wasn't totally altruistic – the FAs were concerned they didn't have control of the women's game now it was becoming popular – but nevertheless it was a positive step.

In England a Women's FA Cup was set up immediately, Southampton winning the first in 1971 (and going on to dominate the decade, winning another seven FA Cups in the following ten years). The sport in England wasn't organised particularly well, though: there wasn't a league until 1991/92, and despite being historically a major player, England soon fell behind the likes of Germany, Norway, Sweden, China and the United States in terms of ability.

The game began to take off worldwide. In 1975 the first Asian championship was held. In 1984 Europe followed suit, holding their first championships. And during the 1980s more unofficial world tournaments were held – five stagings of the Mundialito in Italy and Japan between 1982 and 1988, a world invitational in Taiwan in 1987 and a FIFA-sponsored jamboree in China in 1988. It was enough to persuade FIFA to launch an official Women's World Cup, and the first was held in China in 1991.

The women's game had finally booked its place at the top table.

The Game Today

Several major women's leagues exist across the world, from dominant nations such as the United States, Germany and China, to smaller countries playing catch-up – like England.

England

The modern women's game in England began in 1971 when the FA lifted its ban on the sport. The Women's FA Cup was launched that year, and seven-time winners Southampton became the team of the decade. The team of the 1980s and early 1990s were the Doncaster Belles, who won six FA Cups between 1983 and 1994. They were in turn usurped at the pinnacle of the English game by the third powerhouse, Arsenal. The Gunners have won ten FA Cups since winning their first in 1993.

A league was only launched in 1991, when the FA Women's Premier League came into existence. Doncaster Belles won the first championship, but the league has since been totally dominated by Arsenal, who've won 11 titles; the next best record is the three titles won by Croydon.

No fully professional women's teams exist in the UK. Arsenal – part of the same club as the famous men's team – are the most professional-minded of all the English sides, with many of their amateur players employed in some capacity elsewhere within the club. Teams like Fulham and Birmingham City have dabbled with professionalism, but with limited success, and are now fully amateur.

Two teams are relegated from the 12-team Premier League each season, with one team coming up from second-level north and south divisions.

The FA plans to re-launch the Women's Premier League as a summer Super League in 2001, taking advantage of the men's off season in the hope of raising the game's profile even further.

Rest of the world

Other leagues across the world are more established, with thriving successful leagues in Germany, Italy, China, Sweden and Norway since the 1970s. The United States' professional league was disbanded in 2003, but in 2009 Women's Professional Soccer (WPS) was launched, initially with seven franchises but with a view to rolling it out to ten by 2010.

WPS has been able to attract some of the biggest names in the game from the smaller leagues – Kelly Smith from England and Marta from Brazil – but as yet few German and Scandinavian players have joined, with their leagues already strong. However, experts predict that WPS will grow and grow, raising the profile of the sport further.

The Women's Champions League

The UEFA Women's Cup was launched in 2001, effectively a European Cup for women. Teams qualified by either winning their national league or cup if no league competition existed.

German teams have dominated the cup, with sides from Germany winning five of the titles between 2002 and 2009. The first winners, in 2001/02, were FFC Frankfurt, who went on to land another two stagings of the competition.

The trophy has headed back to Sweden twice, with Umea winning both times. England can only boast one victory, when Arsenal won the cup in 2007.

As of 2009/10 the tournament was renamed the Women's Champions League. Like the men's version, non-champions are now also permitted into the competition. A one-off final will also take place; all previous finals have been two-legged affairs.

The Women's World Cup

The first – unofficial – women's world championship was held in Italy in 1970. Sponsored by none-more-70s booze firm Martini and Rossi, Denmark won, beating the hosts in a Turin final. The Danes held onto the trophy the year after, again beating the host country – this time Mexico – in the final.

Five more unofficial tournaments, the Mundialito, were held between 1982 and 1988 in Italy and Japan – the Italians winning three and England two – but in 1986 FIFA established a women's committee and the ball was set rolling for a proper World Cup.

Two trial runs took place. In 1987 Chinese Taipei hosted, and won, the Women's World Invitation Tournament. Then in 1988 Norway won the Women's FIFA Invitational Tournament in China. The stage was set for the first FIFA Women's World Cup, to be held a mere 61 years after the men's.

1991: The first World Cup

The first Women's World Cup was held in China. Twelve nations competed, and the tournament was considered a huge success. It was dominated and won by the United States, the country winning their first trophy of any kind.

The winning side boasted a forward line known as the Triple Edged Sword: Michelle Akers, Carin Jennings and April Heinrichs scoring 20 of the 25 goals scored by the United States during the tournament. Akers scored twice in the final as the United States beat Norway 2-1 in Guangzhou.

The tournament comes of age

The United States looked to defend their title four years later in Sweden, but lost their star striker Akers within ten minutes of their very first game of the tournament. They still made the semi-finals but were dispatched by Norway, who went on to win the trophy, beating Germany 2-0 in the final.

The 1999 tournament in the United States was the most successful yet. China looked the most powerful side, with striker Sun Wen scoring seven goals en route to the final and the Chinese walloping defending champions Norway 5-0 in the semis. But China found the host nation to be an immovable object in the final, and the United States won 5-4 on penalties after a goal-less draw.

The attendance of 90,185 for the 1999 final – held at the Rose Bowl, Pasadena, the venue of the 1994 World Cup final – was the largest ever for a women's sporting event. The match is also remembered for Brandi Chastain's celebration upon converting the winning penalty: she removed her shirt to reveal her sports bra.

In 1999 the number of teams involved in the finals increased to 16, a number that's remained ever since. The 2003 and 2007 editions, held in the United States and China respectively, were both won by Germany, who'd by now become the powerhouse nation in women's football, thanks in no small part to the goal-scoring exploits of Birgit Prinz.

The 2011 World Cup

The next Women's World Cup will be held in Germany in June and July 2011. As hosts, Germany have already qualified and are favourites to retain their title. Both the United States and Brazil are expected to give the hosts a good run for their money, and England – after their successful Euro 2009 that saw them reach the final of the tournament, and with a few promising youngsters coming through – are also much fancied to improve on their usual quarter-final thumpings!

Other Major Tournaments

While the men's tournament at the Summer Olympics has been running for over a century, the women's event was only launched at the 1996 Games in Atlanta. The United States have dominated the Games, winning four of the three gold medals on offer in 1996, 2004 and 2008. Only Norway have managed to shove the United States off the top podium, beating them in the 2000 final to claim gold.

The other medals have been divvied up between the usual suspects in the women's game. Brazil have two silvers, China one silver and Germany three bronzes.

Third in the pecking order behind the World Cup and the Olympics is an invitational tournament that nevertheless carries great prestige. The Algarve Cup is held annually in Portugal, with 12 teams invited. The United States have won six Algarve Cups, the best record of any nation.

Like the World Cup, Germany and Scandinavia have dominated the European Championships. The tournament predates the World Cup by seven years, Sweden winning the first event in 1984 and Norway taking their crown two years later. Since then Germany have won seven out of eight European titles (1989, 1991, 1995, 1997, 2001, 2005 and 2009) with only Norway breaking their run in 1993. German superiority doesn't look like slipping any time soon: their 6-2 win over the best-ever England side in the 2009 final was a stunning display of their domination.

The oldest surviving women's international tournament is the Asian Cup, which was first held in 1975. Over the years China have dominated the competition, winning the title eight times. North Korea and Taiwan are next on the roll of honour with three wins apiece.

The determination of the Asian Cup's organisers in the 1970s and early 1980s in the face of political pressure from the stuffy suits at FIFA was an important factor in the world governing body eventually agreeing to stage a women's world championship.

Major International Teams

The women's international game only really took off in the late 1980s, so few teams have been able to claim a place in the pantheon of football as of yet. As the sport develops and creates itself a longer history, that's bound to change. Meanwhile all I can do is note the achievements of some of the sport's major nations.

United States

The United States women's team is the most successful in the world, more often than not to be found at number one in the FIFA world rankings. The United States have won two Women's World Cups (1991 and 1999) and three Olympic golds (in 1996, 2004 and 2008). They've also won six Algarve Cups.

The team played their first match in 1985. Notable players past and present include Kristine Lilly, Mia Hamm, Michelle Akers and Brandi Chastain.

Germany

Germany has won the World Cup twice (in 2003 and 2007) making it the only nation to have won both men's and women's stagings of the tournament. By also finishing runners-up once, they boast the best record of any nation in the World Cup. They've also been the dominant force in European football, winning the UEFA continental championship seven times – an outstanding record when you consider only ten tournaments have taken place.

The team played their first match in 1982. Notable players past and present include Birgit Prinz, Inka Grings, Silvia Neid, Doris Fitschen and Martina Voss.

Norway

Norway boasts one of the strongest women's leagues in the world – the Toppserien – and so it's no surprise that the national team has been one of the most successful, despite the relatively small size of the country. Norway were runners-up in the first-ever World Cup in 1991, losing to the United States in the final, but had their revenge four years later in Sweden. A free-scoring side ripped through the group stage, scoring 17 goals without reply before knocking the defending champions out in the semi-finals. An easy 2-0 win over Germany in the final sealed their finest hour.

The team played their first international in 1978. Their two most recognisable names are Marianne Pettersen and Hege Riise, who scored Norway's goals in the 1995 World Cup final.

England

Despite a long history of international competition – the Dick, Kerr Ladies side represented England against France in the early 1920s – the English national side has always historically lagged behind European neighbours such as Germany, Norway and Sweden. They did, however, win two unofficial world titles in the late 1980s – the invitational Mundialito in Italy in 1985 and 1988. Since then success has been thin on the ground, but a gutsy showing at Euro 2009 – the team unexpectedly reaching the final before being thrashed 6-2 by Germany – bodes well for the future, with several talented youngsters said to be in the pipeline.

The team played their first international in 1972. Notable players past and present include Kelly Smith, Karen Carney, Sue Smith and Hope Powell.

Great Players

The women's game may not get the same media exposure as the men's, but that doesn't mean it's short of stars. In the following sections I look at just a few.

Lily Parr (England)

Alfred Franklin, the manager of the famous Dick, Kerr's Ladies team, discovered Lilian Parr in 1920. Fourteen-year-old Parr was playing for local rivals St Helens as a winger-come-striker. Parr was an instant success, scoring 43 goals in her first season with Dick, Kerr's Ladies. One newspaper of the time reported that there was 'probably no greater football prodigy in the country' than Parr.

In a lengthy career spanning 31 years she scored over 900 goals for Dick, Kerr's Ladies and Preston Ladies. Despite smoking vast quantities of Woodbine cigarettes she was hard-running and powerful, her shot the stuff of legend. Before an exhibition match in the early 1920s a male professional goalkeeper challenged Parr to take some penalties against him. Minutes later he was found rolling around on the floor, having got in the way of one particularly strong wallop. 'Get me to the hospital as soon as you can,' the keeper wailed. 'She's broken my arm!'

Parr was women's football's first star name, arguably the sport's only one until the game really took off in the late 1980s and 1990s. Parr died in 1978, but she was posthumously rewarded for her achievements by becoming the first woman to be inducted into the Hall of Fame at the National Football Museum in Preston.

Kristine Lilly (United States)

Kristine Lilly holds the world record for the number of international appearances in both women's and men's football. At the time of writing she has won over 340 caps for the United States, scoring over 120 goals. She made her debut as a 16-year-old midfielder in 1987, and within four years was part of the United States team that lifted the first-ever Women's World Cup.

She also played in the United States' 1999 World Cup winning side, and was one of the heroes in the final against China, making a goal-line clearance in extra time to avoid almost certain defeat. Lilly also featured in the United States' Olympic gold-winning teams of 1996 and 2004.

Mia Hamm (United States)

The bandy-legged Brazilian legend Garrincha isn't the only World Cup winning footballer to have overcome childhood disability. As a toddler Mia Hamm, (shown in Figure 14-2) had to wear corrective shoes in order to treat a club foot. The condition was rectified and Hamm went on to become a trailblazer in women's football.

Over a 17-year career with the United States national team she won two World Cups (1991 and 1999) and two Olympic gold medals (1996 and 2004), and was named the first-ever FIFA Women's World Player of the Year in 2001, an award she held onto the following year. She retired in 2004 having scored a frankly preposterous 158 goals in 275 matches, more than any player – male or female – in the history of the game.

Hamm was one of only two women to be named in Pelé's FIFA 100 selection, a list collated for FIFA's centenary in 2004 of the 125 greatest-living players in the game.

Figure 14-2:
Mia Hamm
in action.

Michelle Akers (United States)

Along with her former United States team-mate Mia Hamm, Michelle Akers is one of only two women to be named in the FIFA 100, a greatest-living-players list that celebrated the world governing body's centenary in 2004. It was no surprise she was selected: in 153 appearances for her national team between 1985 and 2000 Akers scored a remarkable 105 goals.

Her high point was the 1991 World Cup, when she topped the tournament scoring charts with ten goals. Five of them came in one incredible quarter-final match against Taiwan, and she also scored both goals in the United States' 2-1 victory over Norway in the final. Akers was also a member of the 1999 World Championship winning side.

Sun Wen (China)

A powerful striker, Sun Wen (shown in Figure 14-3) was the top scorer at the 1999 World Cup but was denied a world title when China lost to the United States on penalties in the final. She did, however, gain some personal reward: she became the first-ever woman to be nominated for the Asian Football Confederation player of the year award, and was the first player to be picked in the inaugural draft for the first professional women's league in the United States.

Sun Wen was voted FIFA Women's Player of the Century in 2002, an award she shared with the United States goal-scorer Michelle Akers.

Figure 14-3: Chinese striker Sun Wen.

Kitted out

According to FIFA's Laws of the Game (check out Chapter 4 for more on these), women footballers must play in the same kit as men: shirts, shorts, socks and boots. Predictably, however, women have occasionally attempted to tinker with this basic set-up.

In September 2008 a Dutch women's side called FC de Rakt attracted worldwide publicity when they replaced their shorts with skirts. This was initially thought to be against the rules, but as the players also wore pants underneath their skirts FIFA decided they were technically in compliance. The move didn't do much for the advancement of women's lib – they were also wearing tighter shirts – though it did benefit their website, with hits going through the roof.

Staggeringly, the man in charge of world football, FIFA president Sepp Blatter, has also mooted such ideas. In 2004 Blatter announced that women should 'play in more feminine clothes' to increase the popularity of the game. 'They could, for example, have tighter shorts,' Blatter wondered aloud.

Blatter's unreconstructed views drew widespread criticism. 'As footballers we have to think practically,' responded Norway's Lise Klaveness. 'If the crowd only wants to come and watch models then they should go and buy a copy of *Playboy*.' Blatter, it's worth noting, was during the 1970s president of an organisation called the World Society of the Friends of Suspenders, which aimed to encourage women to keep wearing suspenders rather than tights!

Birgit Prinz (Germany)

Birgit Prinz is a free-scoring striker and the star of the Germany team that's triumphed in the 2003 and 2007 World Cups. She holds the record for the most goals scored in World Cup history with 14. Prinz has also achieved amazing successes at club level, leading her Frankfurt side to a league, cup and European treble in 2008.

In 2003 Italian men's side Perugia offered Prinz a contract, which would have made her the first female player in Serie A. She politely declined the offer.

Kelly Smith (England)

Kelly Smith is widely considered to be the greatest player England has ever had – since the FA ban was lifted in 1971 and the sport entered the modern era, anyway. A skilful, ball-playing striker, Smith has been the star woman in the all-conquering Arsenal side, with a record of more than one goal per game between 2005 and 2009.

Smith really came to national prominence during England's run to the quarter-finals of the 2007 World Cup, during which she scored four goals. She's widely remembered for celebrating one goal by taking off her boot and kissing it. Her feats earned her a lucrative transfer to the new Women's Professional Soccer League – Smith's second stint in the United States, as she was previously the only English player to feature in their former pro league, the now defunct Women's Soccer Association.

Marta (Brazil)

Many consider Marta Vieira da Silva (just Marta for short) to be the most skilful player in the world at present, one of the main reasons the Brazilian team – previously unheralded in the women's game – has become a major force in recent years. She was the top scorer at the 2007 World Cup, leading her team to the final, though they lost to Germany. Marta (shown in Figure 14-4) nevertheless picked up the award for player of the tournament. She has also been honoured by having her footprint pressed in cement at the Maracanã stadium in Rio de Janeiro, the first woman to make the hall of fame at this great stadium.

Marta is often called either 'Cousin of Pelé' or 'Pelé in a Skirt'.

Figure 14-4:
Brazil's
brilliant
Marta.

Part IV
The Fans' Enclosure: Following the Game

'Nothing to do with the price of United's new replica shirt – it's the name of the new Bulgarian signing.'

In this part . . .

This Part is where to come if you want to get seriously into becoming a football fan. Here I tell you everything you need to know in order to get yourself to a game and make the most of the experience. I also cover the media outlets which can improve your knowledge of the game, and how to get the most enjoyment out of watching it being played on television.

I also tell you about the best sources of football information across a range of media such as radio, newspapers, magazines, books, and websites, and I delve into the many different football-related pastimes you can take part in, from collecting to computer games.

Chapter 15

Going to the Match

*T*he sights, the sounds, the smell . . . there's nothing quite like going to the big match. While it's exciting to watch football on television – and watching on TV is how the majority of fans are first exposed to the beautiful game – attending a match in the flesh makes you feel properly involved, in a way you can never be while sitting in front of a screen.

Preparing for the Match

At most major clubs, the days are long gone when you could decide at the last minute to go to the game, turning up at the turnstile gate five minutes before kick-off and paying on the door. While a day out at the football doesn't have to be mapped out with military precision, it does have to be planned in advance – especially at one of the big clubs, where demand for tickets is high.

Season tickets

The best way to make sure of your attendance at a fixture is to purchase a season ticket. These guarantee you the same seat in the stadium for every home league fixture in a season, as well as giving you first refusal on tickets for cup games.

Some smaller clubs with the option of standing, offer tickets for ground admission only at a cheaper rate.

Cup games are usually not included in the season ticket package, as there is no way of knowing how many matches there will be. If your team goes all the way to the final in both competitions, and they were drawn at home in every round, it could prove an expensive season.

As well as guaranteeing you a seat for every home league match, buying a season ticket will be cheaper than purchasing single tickets for every match. It is, however, an expensive initial outlay. Depending on the size of club, and the demand, season tickets can cost anything between £200 and well over £1,000 per season.

It is also possible to buy combined season tickets, so a parent can go along with a child and sit together. A cheaper child's rate will be added to the cost of the ticket.

At bigger clubs, there may be a waiting list for season tickets stretching to several years. The lists at one or two clubs are even rumoured to stretch to decades – over 20 years!

Some clubs have plans to move to new, bigger stadiums, in order to maximise their revenue in season ticket sales. Arsenal's move from Highbury to the Emirates Stadium in 2006 allowed them to allocate thousands of extra season tickets, slashing their waiting list and raising millions of pounds every season.

Season ticket holders earn themselves extra rights, such as first option on purchasing tickets for away games – which will be in limited supply – and the ability to apply for additional tickets for home matches. Should the team reach any major finals, they will get priority booking privileges for those matches too.

Keep an eye out for the dates additional tickets are released for sale. There will be an initial period during which only season ticket holders can apply. After it passes, there may be a further period during which club membership holders can apply. If there are still any tickets remaining, they go on general sale. Dates are usually posted at the ground and on club websites, and can also be found by ringing the ticket office.

Choosing where to sit

Whether you are buying a season ticket, or a single ticket, you may be given several options for where to sit. As a general rule, the nearer you are to the centre circle in one of the stands running the length of the pitch, the more expensive the seat will be. This is because those positions will give you the best view of the pitch.

However, other factors may influence your decision. Sometimes the best vantage point may not be the most famous part of the ground, or the area where the best atmosphere is. Examples of this would be the Stretford End at

Manchester United's Old Trafford stadium, or the Kop at Liverpool's Anfield stadium – both of which are situated at an end behind a goal.

There will also be especially designated singing areas, areas for parents and children, designated areas for wheelchairs, and seats offering audio commentary for partially sighted or blind supporters. If you have any particular requirement, make sure you inform the club when you purchase the ticket – although unfortunately demand may outstrip supply at bigger clubs, lessening the chances of you getting a seat.

Looking into club membership

If you cannot afford a season ticket, or the waiting list is ridiculously long, a way to increase your chances of getting a ticket is to join a club membership scheme. For an annual fee – these vary wildly depending on the club – you can join a supporter's scheme which will give you second option, after the season ticket holders, on tickets for home and away matches.

Buying a single ticket in advance

If you are not a season ticket holder, or part of a club membership scheme, you are at the bottom of the pile when it comes to buying tickets as you must hope the season ticket holders, and the supporter's scheme members, have not bought up any spare tickets.

For the club's biggest fixtures of the year, it is unlikely that any tickets will remain for general sale. You may be luckier with some of the less glamorous fixtures in the calendar – although at the very biggest clubs, your chances may be slim even then.

However, if you know some tickets are going on general sale, make sure to keep a note of the date – and ring the ticket office's credit card hotline the minute it opens. There may also be options to purchase a ticket online.

Buying a single ticket on the day

The scramble for tickets is usually only relevant if you want to take in a game at one of the big clubs. Games at Manchester United, Liverpool, Arsenal, Celtic and Rangers are sold out more often than not. If you are watching at a club where demand is not so consistently huge, chances are you will be able to arrange a ticket in advance with little difficulty.

It is always advisable to purchase your tickets in advance. Many clubs simply do not sell tickets on the day of the match – and even if they do, you are running the risk of tickets selling out before you get there. They may also only sell tickets to home supporters – which will be no good if you want to go in the away end!

However, smaller clubs, especially in the lower leagues, rarely entertain a full house, and will offer a range of tickets on the day of the match. If they do, make sure to arrive at the ticket office in plenty of time, as there may be a large queue.

Except at the very smallest grounds, money is not taken at the turnstiles – the actual entrance to the ground. Buy your ticket at the ticket office, then proceed to the turnstiles.

Away games

If you want to watch your team away from home, tickets can be equally hard to come by – perhaps even more so. Home sides usually only give the away support a small allocation of tickets: stadiums holding 50,000-plus home fans may only offer their opponents a couple of thousand seats!

Tickets are sold through your club. They may be like gold dust – and will probably be snapped up by your club's season ticket holders, or membership card holders.

You can, of course, attempt to purchase tickets directly from the away club, but they will only sell seats in the home areas. If you manage to get a ticket in a stand surrounded by supporters of the other team, you will have to keep very quiet if your side scores – which is very frustrating. And what's even worse, you'll have to pretend to be pleased if your team lets in a goal, then loses! Many fans, desperate to watch their team, have tried this, and come to the conclusion that it is really not worth it.

For matches abroad, your club will probably organise ticket and travel packages, possibly also including accommodation. Some travel agents also organise similar packages, usually in co-operation with the club.

For trips to foreign stadiums outside of the EU, you may require an entry visa. The website of the relevant embassy should furnish you with this information. Find out as soon as possible, as an application may take several days or even weeks.

Executive boxes

As well as standard seating, the majority of big clubs now offer executive entertainment. This usually consists of a seat in an exclusive environment – either a luxury seat in a prime section of the stand, or a seat in an enclosed executive box – dinner in the club restaurant, drinks and a brief introduction to a club legend, usually a former player.

Fans rarely choose to buy a seat in an executive box, considering the atmosphere sterile. (With the game usually viewed behind a glass screen, the atmosphere is a strange mix of being at the ground and watching it on television.) However, bookings are often made for special occasions such as birthday treats or stag parties.

Remember that there are many people in executive boxes who are not huge fans of the game, and are there as business guests of a corporate sponsor who has rented the box. The dinner, the drinks and the chance to chat socially with colleagues may be more important to these match-goers – so don't expect the sort of intense atmosphere you will get in the stand!

Executive hospitality can also be incredibly expensive. For the highest-profile matches in the FA Premier League, a box for ten people could cost anything between £5,000 and £8,000.

International matches

Ticket purchasing for internationals works on a similar principle to buying them for club matches. For home and away games, you should attempt to purchase them through the ticket arm of your country's association.

Many associations operate a fans' membership scheme, which gives you priority ticket booking privileges, as well as the occasional discount.

For major international championships, such as the World Cup and European Championships, the methods of purchasing tickets are more complicated, with worldwide demand far outstretching supply. Fans must register an interest online, then when a "sales window" opens, they can enter a ballot for the matches they wish to attend. Fans are usually obliged to buy tickets for multiple matches.

Making Your Way to the Match

Please remember that some of the following advice is really only relevant if you are travelling away – or if you are paying your first visit to your team's home stadium.

Obtaining your tickets

First things first: don't forget your ticket! You simply won't get into the game otherwise, as clubs don't issue replacements. Also, if you are going to a match overseas, don't forget your passport (or your toothbrush).

Some major tournaments demand that you carry some form of photographic identification to matches, along with your ticket. A passport will usually suffice.

Making travelling arrangements

Make these as far in advance as you can, especially if you live a fair distance from the ground. Some fixtures can be tricky to get to: if you're a Plymouth Argyle fan, and your team are kicking off at 12.45pm at Newcastle United, you'll need to set off in the wee small hours of the morning – or plan to arrive the night before, and get a hotel room.

Some of the newer stadiums have hotels built into the ground.

For away fixtures, clubs and supporters groups usually organise coach services to and from the games. Details for these can be found on club websites and in the home matchday programme.

There are also supporters clubs which will organise travel to home fixtures, especially if they are based far from the home stadium. (There are many London-based supporters groups of teams in the north of England, for example.)

If you're making it to a match under your own steam, first source details of the ground's location. Sometimes grounds are not even in the town the club calls home. For example, Grimsby Town is actually situated in neighbouring Cleethorpes.

If you are taking public transport, it is also worth doing your homework first. If you are travelling to a match at Bolton Wanderers by train, getting off at Bolton will do you no good: you will still be miles from the Reebok Stadium, which is situated in Horwich – part of the metropolitan borough of Bolton, but not the town itself.

Figure 15-1:
A crowd
makes its
way to a
match at
Wembley.

If you are driving, make sure you know the most efficient route, have researched somewhere to park – there are not always facilities at or even near grounds – and have left enough time to get to the stadium.

Football traffic can add another hour to your journey in extreme circumstances, so leave plenty of time. There is no point rushing for kick-off: there have been plenty of tragic accidents involving supporters speeding recklessly to make it in time for the match.

Dressing for the occasion

Sporting fans so often forget that they'll be sitting outside, exposed to the elements for a lengthy period of time, and fail to take account of the weather. Check the forecast, and dress appropriately. If it's going to be sunny, apply sunscreen; if it looks like rain, take a hat and wear a jacket. (Don't take an umbrella, just in case an officious steward decides to confiscate what could be construed as a weapon!)

Even if the weather is decent in the morning, as you leave the house for the stadium, remember that the match won't finish until 5pm. Football is a winter sport in Great Britain – and it might get a lot colder by then.

As well as dressing practically, it's also important to dress tactfully. Many people wear 'club colours' to the game – replica shirts, scarves or other items that make it clear who they support. This in itself shouldn't be a problem, especially if you are playing at home. But if you are travelling to an away fixture, stick with all the other away fans – there is safety in numbers – and stay on the major routes to the ground, where there will be plenty of other people and visible policing.

If you don't go looking for trouble, the risk of getting into any at football is small – providing you are careful and don't take any risks. Straying down local back streets, or into pubs frequented by the home support, may be seen by troublemakers as an inflammatory gesture. Don't give them the opportunity of causing a scene.

Taking a look round the city

If you have given yourself plenty of time by arriving early, or staying in a hotel the night before, take the opportunity to have a look around the town or city you are visiting. So many fans don't bother, especially when visiting towns in their own country, but it's a fine opportunity to take in some sights and places of interest. There's plenty of time to have a few drinks with fellow supporters after the game.

In certain circumstances, you might not be able to do this. At matches between big rivals, or between clubs whose fans have caused trouble in the past, police prefer to shepherd supporters directly from train stations to the ground, and back again after the match, in order to ensure there's no trouble.

Checking out the ground

If you have time, take a wander around the ground and its immediate environs. Unless the police deem the crowds to be volatile, there should be no problem in doing this.

Most grounds have at least one feature worthy of seeking out. Perhaps the ground has a famous façade, like Rangers' Ibrox stadium or the old Arsenal ground at Highbury. There could be a statue worth taking a look at, such as the one of former England captain Billy Wright at Wolverhampton Wanderers' ground Molineux, or West Ham's three 1966 World Cup winners at Upton Park.

There may be a particularly impressive stand – the Holte End at Aston Villa seems impossibly huge – or a pleasant view to take in (the rivers Trent and Thames flow behind stands at Nottingham Forest and Fulham respectively).

You may also want to pay your respects at a memorial: Liverpool's Anfield has an eternal flame for the perished of the 1989 Hillsborough disaster, while at Old Trafford there is a plaque and clock commemorating the Manchester United team killed in the 1958 Munich air crash.

Even if the ground you are visiting seems at face value to be a bit of a ramshackle affair, it's worth having a quick nose about: there's not a stadium on the planet that doesn't have some character, a lot of history and a few redeeming features somewhere.

Some fans make it their life's goal to visit as many stadiums as possible. They may even attempt to visit all the stadiums a league has to offer in a single season, a quest that usually involves military-style planning, the attendance of many midweek matches and a lot of criss-crossing around the country. People who have been to all the league stadiums in England refer to themselves as being members of 'the 92 club' (92 being the number of league teams in the country).

The club shop

It's perhaps not going to be on your checklist if you are visiting a team you don't particularly like, but having a nose around the club shop to see what is on offer can wile away the time before a match. They are, naturally, full of home fans – and can get terribly busy on matchdays.

If you are a home supporter, and live relatively locally, it might be better to come to the ground on a non-matchday. The shops are usually open during normal trading hours.

While it's nice to have the latest official merchandise, don't feel you need to buy any of it to prove yourself a proper fan. Some of the goods on offer can be expensive – and sometimes amazingly overpriced. On the other hand, club shops often stock club-related items which are hard to find elsewhere – from replica strips to books and DVDs.

A pint . . .

If you're old enough to have a drink, a couple of pints in the pub before the match is part of a supporter's time-honoured routine. Arrange to meet a few fellow supporters for a chat and a singsong.

Pubs on matchday fall into two categories: home and away. Usually the pubs closest to the ground will be reserved for home fans, and will be places they have traditionally gathered before a game for decades. However, there is usually at least one pub that will welcome away supporters: the best place to find this sort of information is on the Internet, at sites such as the excellently researched Football Ground Guide (www.footballgroundguide.com).

If there is nowhere near the ground, you should be able to find somewhere to stop in the town centre. Some pubs discourage groups of football fans, though, and may forbid the wearing of club colours.

If you can't get a drink in the pubs around the ground, don't worry: there is usually a licensed bar within the stadium. Real-ale fans are likely to be disappointed, however; the range of beers on offer is usually very limited, and not particularly pleasing to the more discerning palate.

At high-alert matches, between clubs whose support has a turbulent history, there may be a ban on alcohol. This could even stretch to the trains transporting away support to and from the town. Kick-offs at some particularly troublesome fixtures may be held at midday, or even earlier, to discourage drinking at the game.

Some towns, cities and countries will be better than others for getting a pre- or post-match drink in. Anyone visiting a ground in Germany, for example, is unlikely to be disappointed by the quality of lager on sale, even at the ground.

. . . and a pie

Despite football having long links with the food industry – Louis Edwards, for example, the chairman of Manchester United during the glory years of Sir Matt Busby, was a butcher and pie-maker – the sport's cuisine doesn't have a particularly good reputation.

Things have improved from the days when a pie would contain nothing but huge lumps of gristle with a couple of drops of congealed gravy: nowadays it's possible to pick up a decent pie, a burger, or even a baguette of freshly carved roasted meat from one of the many vans you'll pass en route to the ground.

You are unlikely to find a bargain, but prices are not too expensive: expect to buy a pie for between £3 and £5, a decent-sized cheeseburger for roughly the same amount.

Again, making time beforehand is advisable. If you venture further from the ground – perhaps taking a look around the town centre before you head to the stadium – you are sure to find either a passable restaurant, or at least a supermarket selling decent and fairly priced sandwiches.

Some fans even take their own packed lunch – although don't take flasks of tea or coffee, as your flask may well be confiscated by overly conscientious security staff.

The food and drink on offer can vary depending on where you are in the country. A visitor to Plymouth Argyle will spot vans selling Cornish pasties (despite the club being in Devon), while one at a Scottish ground may find himself buying a cup of Bovril at half-time, almost despite himself.

Matchday programmes

On your way to the ground, you will undoubtedly pass several old gentlemen on the street selling official matchday programmes from a cardboard box. Buying a programme is almost a rite of passage – despite there often being absolutely nothing of worth to read in it. Standards in the articles have improved over the years, although they are invariably hopelessly biased towards the home team, to a level that annoys most of the home support as well as the away fans!

While I may not be selling the idea of spending up to £5 on a matchday programme – and at big games, such as cup finals, they could cost anything up to £15! – I would advise you to buy one. A programme is a collectable item, and a reminder of the day you went to the match. Years later, once you have gone to hundreds of games, it would be easy to forget some of the matches you have attended. Find an old programme in the back of your cupboard one day, and all the memories will come flooding back. Worth every penny.

There is also a good short-term practical reason for buying a programme. Unless you have sharp eyesight, and can read every player's name on the back of their shirt, you will be relying on the numbers – and the programme will print a squad list for both sides.

The Game Itself

Before you eventually make your way to your seat, you will have a decision to make: do you go to it in plenty of time, or just before kick-off? Most fans now leave things until the last minute, preferring to enjoy a pint or a cup of tea in the bars beneath the stand, while watching team news coming in should there be a TV screen.

If you enjoy singing with your fellow supporters, though, you may want to arrive a bit earlier to join in, and whip up an atmosphere. You may also want to take in the general ambience before the game, and watch the teams run out – all of which heightens the anticipation.

Don't leave it too late. There is nothing that will annoy your fellow supporters more than making an entire row get up so you can shuffle past towards your seat with the game already in progress. If there's a goal, and you've obstructed someone's view, prepare to receive a few choice words about your timekeeping!

If you're not familiar with the ground, make sure you know which entrance you need to go through in plenty of time. Few things are more frustrating than finding out you are right round the other side of the ground with seconds until kick-off. Also, don't assume just because you are quite near to the entrance, that you will be able to directly walk there. Depending on the stadium geography, there may be something blocking your way – and you could end up having to circumvent almost the entire stadium to get to your destination!

Kick-off

The moments before kick-off are perhaps the sweetest as a football fan: nothing has yet gone wrong, and everything is possible! As the excitement builds, the teams will trot out of the tunnel to cheers.

The stadium announcer will read out the teams over the public address system. He (and it is nearly always a he) will leave a gap between each of the home players' names, allowing the crowd to show its appreciation. The announcer will then run through the away side's team – more often than not at great speed so the away support has no time to cheer for their players. Such are the perks of playing at home.

Often, a club anthem will be played over the PA system either as the teams run out, or just before the match begins. It could be a rousing piece of classical music – Sunderland always run out to Prokofiev's highly dramatic *Dance of the Knights* – while Liverpool and Celtic both belt out a traditional rendition of the Rodgers and Hammerstein showtune *You'll Never Walk Alone*.

Just before kick off, your team may embark on a final pre-match routine, such as a group huddle. In the seconds before the referee blows his whistle to set the ball rolling, there will be a swell of noise. Feel free to scream and shout as loudly as you want – you're not at a library!

Shouting, screaming and other matters of general etiquette

Within the boundaries of human decency, it is pretty much open season on what you can shout out at a football match. The atmosphere is not for the fainthearted, the humour often close to the bone. Industrial language will almost certainly be heard. Take this opportunity to holler abuse at the referee at the top of your voice – you'll be very unlikely to get away with acting like this in any other walk of life!

Singing is also a traditional pastime at the game. There are usually certain parts of the stadium where songs will begin to be sung. Your team's support will have a few traditional numbers they always sing, no matter what happens. Learn the words and join in.

But if you're not the gregarious shouting, screaming and singing type, don't feel pressurised to join in. Many fans inhabit a world of their own as they quietly – and perhaps nervously – watch the match unfold. There isn't any one way to act at the game; if you want to sit quietly minding your own business, that's exactly what you should do. Let others do the shouting for you.

Wireless communication

The match you're at is unlikely to be the only game going on at the time. It's important to keep track of scores in other matches, too – especially if they affect your team's standing in the league. Taking a small transistor radio with an earpiece allows you to keep in touch with events around the country. Even in the days of text messaging and mobile Internet technology, this is still the most popular way of getting such information – as you can listen to what's happening elsewhere without taking your eyes off the match.

Half-time

At half-time, the PA announcer will read out the latest scores from around the country. Meanwhile, you have 15 minutes to go and get a drink and a pie, and visit the lavatory.

Stewards, police and PA announcements

The PA announcer may relay some messages during the match. Usually these are requests to move cars parked in illegal spots, or messages for family members or friends who have somehow lost each other on their way to the game. Sometimes a request will be made for a fan to go and meet a friend at the entrance – to give them their ticket so they can get in!

Towards the end of a game, an announcement is usually made to away fans. Sometimes they will be asked to remain in their seats for a few minutes, while the home crowd disperses. They may also be given important travel information – especially at away matches in foreign lands.

Keeping out of trouble

Football hooliganism was a big problem in the 1970s and 1980s, but is generally under control these days. There is rarely, if ever, large-scale fighting within a ground now; closed-circuit cameras pointing into every corner of the stadium, making identification and subsequent prosecution of troublemakers much easier, has seen to that.

You are more likely to walk into trouble outside of the ground. Keep to the main thoroughfares on your way to and from the stadium, whether you are going back to your car, a coach or the local train station. With thousands of other fans around you, there is rarely any bother. Only when you stray off the beaten track are you likely to get into any trouble.

In any case, police presence is usually large at any fixtures with a history of crowd trouble, with sets of fans well segregated, as they are forced to take very different routes to and from the stadium.

Some fighting does still occur sporadically, with rival *firms* of hooligans arranging meet-ups for gang brawls. But these are often staged well away from the stadium – and its attendant police presence. It should also be remembered that such gangs are usually more interested in beating each other's idiotic heads in, than involve any random passers-by.

Chapter 16

Compulsive Viewing: Football on Screen

*P*eople have been catching football on camera ever since the early days of moving pictures: plenty of grainy old black and white footage is in existence from the early 1900s that shows men in long shorts chasing around after a ball. Cinema newsreels soon featured clips of big matches, television got in on the act in the 1930s, films were made and videotapes and DVDs released for posterity.

Nowadays football viewing is a multi-billion-pound industry, with something for everyone to watch. It's never been a better time to be an armchair fan, and in this chapter I search out all the places you can find the game on a screen. Settle back, there's a lot on . . .

Television

Football has been a fixture on British television screens since 1937, with the rest of the world following soon after. For many years there wasn't a whole lot to watch – in England up until the mid-1950s the only matches transmitted live on the BBC were the annual FA Cup final and England–Scotland internationals.

The advent of Britain's third channel in 1955 – Independent Television (ITV) – saw things shaken up, albeit slowly. First ITV transmitted midweek live matches from the new European Cup. Then in 1960 ITV attempted to show live Football League fixtures, though they aborted this experiment within a month because clubs were unwilling to risk an effect on attendance. It galvanised the BBC into action – in 1964, they launched *Match of the Day*, England's first Football League highlights programme.

But for the next two decades there were still precious few live games on television. You could watch a scattering of extra England internationals, but apart from the FA Cup final, little else.

League clubs were against the showing of live football on TV because they thought televised games would adversely affect attendances at other matches. Disputes about payments also existed – the TV stations only wanted to show the big teams but the smaller clubs in the league wanted an equal share of the proceeds.

That was until 1983, when the Football League allowed the two broadcasters to show several games per season on a Sunday afternoon. The matches proved very popular, with viewing figures for the BBC and ITV high. Eventually the clubs cottoned onto the fact that TV companies were paying peanuts for the rights to show live football – the BBC and ITV were acting as a duopoly, keeping the price down. But when the government legalised satellite television in the UK, the playing field was (literally) altered for ever.

The Football League initially managed to get more money (£44 million) from ITV in 1988, but all 92 clubs were still splitting the proceeds: Liverpool and Manchester United, on the box every other week, were only getting the same cash as Rochdale, who were never on it. The top clubs decided to break away from the league, a decision that led to the formation of the FA Premier League – and a massive £304 million deal with Sky in 1992.

With hundreds of live games now on television every season, and millions of pounds sloshing around, football would never be the same again.

TV's first-ever live game

The very first live football match on TV wasn't much of a spectacle. A trial run by the BBC at Arsenal's Highbury stadium on 16 September 1937, the game was a training run-out between Arsenal and their reserve team!

'Three cameras will be used, one being on the stands to give a comprehensive view of the ground,' previewed the *Manchester Guardian* on the morning of the big event. 'Two others near the goalmouth will give close-ups of the play and players. No film will be used, transmission being by radio direct to Alexandra Palace which can actually be seen from the ground.'

In the event the BBC only showed 15 minutes of the game live, but the experiment was considered so successful that the Beeb transmitted the first full game the following April – the England–Scotland international at Wembley.

Terrestrial

Although satellite channels have shown the majority of live football since the early 1990s, free-to-air terrestrial television has still always had at least some live matches to show. Several events are protected by government legislation: by law they can't be shown in the UK on subscription channels alone. These events are the World Cup finals, the European Championships, the FA Cup final and the Scottish Cup final (in Scotland).

Terrestrial channels show highlights packages of domestic league football, such as the BBC's *Match of the Day* (which features the FA Premier League) and *The Football League Show*, and coverage of all rounds of the FA Cup (currently under contract to ITV).

ITV shows live Champions League games, though the broadcaster shares the rights with satellite station Sky.

Either the BBC or ITV show World Cup and European Championship finals matches. The broadcasters divvy the games up at the start of the tournament, although both show the really big matches towards the end of the finals.

The BBC currently have a contract to show several live Football League games per season. ITV are the current holders of the contract to show live home England internationals.

Keep an eye on the late-night listings of terrestrial broadcasters such as Channel 4 and Five. They occasionally snap up the rights to show foreign leagues, such as the Italian, Dutch, German, Argentinian and Brazilian leagues. However, increasingly these matches are being lost to pay-to-view channels.

Satellite and cable

Nowadays you find nearly all live football on satellite networks. The two main players in the UK are Sky Sports (owned by Rupert Murdoch) and the relative newcomer ESPN (owned by Disney). Sky show hundreds of live FA Premier League and Football League games every season. ESPN also show at least one live Premier League game every week.

Sky show live internationals featuring all the Home Nations plus the Republic of Ireland. They also transmit many internationals featuring the big names in world football, including Argentina, Brazil, France and Italy.

Both Sky and ESPN have the rights to various leagues around the world and also feature major tournaments such as the Copa America.

With a proliferation of satellite channels there's always a fair chance that a big game you want to watch will be screened live. Go to www.livesportontv.com to find out.

Sky Sports also feature many highlights programmes in their schedules. Sky Sports News is a 24-hour rolling sports news channel, concentrating mainly on the FA Premier League. ESPN Classic shows famous old matches and sporting documentaries, a treasure trove for anyone with an interest in football history.

Sky Sports and ESPN are subscription channels. To find out how to subscribe to them go to www.skysports.com and www.espn.co.uk.

Official club channels

Major UK clubs like Manchester United, Liverpool, Arsenal, Chelsea, Celtic and Rangers all have their own official TV channels. Programming ranges from live reserve and youth team matches – they never have live first-team games, save the occasional pre-season friendly – to player interviews, news and classic old-school action.

These club channels have a reputation – as you would expect – of being heavily biased in favour of the club, although one or two transmit discussion programmes that are *occasionally* critical of the current team. If you're a fan of another club you should avoid such channels, as there'll be little of interest for you.

Apart from the Real Madrid channel – which features discussion programmes with a surprisingly wide-ranging all-Spanish remit, albeit ultimately from a Madrid viewpoint – foreign clubs aren't represented by their own channels in the UK.

Some services are subscription based, free with certain subscription packages or free to air. Check your TV service provider to find out.

Essential shows and channels

If you're going to hold your own at the water cooler on a Monday morning, you'll need to know your way round televised football in the UK. The following sections cover everything from the essential Saturday tea-time results round-ups to trips into the footballing archives.

Match of the Day (BBC One)

Match of the Day was launched in 1964 and was an instant hit. Initially, it only showed highlights from one game – hence the programme's title – but now it covers every single FA Premier League game played on Saturday. (It's transmitted on Saturday evening.) The programme gives each match at least a few minutes, with the best games of the day afforded lengthy coverage. Two former professional players analyse each game, with extensive replays, and there are post-match interviews with managers and players.

The Football League Show (BBC One)

A newcomer to the schedules, the BBC's *Football League Show* is a highlights package of all the games in the Football League Championship and Leagues One and Two. It's shown on Saturday evenings (or, more accurately, the early hours of Sunday morning) directly after *Match of the Day*. The show features one or two matches in each division, the goals from every other game and news from one match by the programme's roving reporter.

Football Focus (BBC One)

A staple in the schedules since the late 1960s, *Football Focus* is transmitted at Saturday lunchtime and previews the weekend action. Concentrating heavily on the FA Premier League, it usually previews one or two of the upcoming big games in depth. There's also usually a report of the big talking point of last week, whether on the pitch or in the news.

Soccer AM (Sky One and Sky Sports 1)

A light-hearted three-hour marathon every Saturday morning, this show fuses together last week's action, previews, celebrity interviews and comedy sketches. An acquired taste, because it has a youthful and laddish flavour, but essential cult viewing for many fans.

Soccer Saturday (Sky Sports 1)

Perhaps the most popular football show on British television – and certainly the strangest. *Soccer Saturday* is a latest-score service that begins at lunchtime with a couple of hours of previews and analysis then segues into the live action – of four ex-professionals watching matches on screens. The viewer can't see the games themselves, only the reactions of those watching as they scream in excitement and report on what's happening. A rolling ticker at the bottom of the screen records every goal in the country. Its success is down to the easy-going charm of the host, Jeff Stelling, who chairs proceedings with light-hearted assurance. After all the games have finished a classified pools check takes place.

Legendary commentary

Over the years the utterances of commentators have become almost as big a part of football culture as the action on the pitch itself.

The most famous example in the UK is the reaction of BBC commentator Kenneth Wolstenholme to Geoff Hurst's hat-trick goal in the 1966 World Cup final. With fans encroaching the playing area at the end of extra time, and Hurst bearing down on goal, Wolstenholme cried, 'Some people on the pitch . . . they think it's all over . . . it is now!'

German radio has its own Wolstenholme in the form of Herbert Zimmermann, a radio commentator who reacted to West Germany's unexpected winning goal in the 1954 World Cup final with eight seconds of silence, followed by an impassioned scream of 'Germany lead 3-2! Call me mad! Call me crazy!'

While Wolstenholme and Zimmermann will always be remembered for specific commentaries, others have gone down in history as a result of their styles. The BBC's John Motson is synonymous with his sheepskin coat and in-depth knowledge of minute statistics, while his predecessor David Coleman is fondly remembered for his trademark scream, upon a player scoring an opening goal, of 'One-nil!' Simple, but effective.

The classified pools check runs through every final score in every league, division by division. As well as informing the viewer of the final scores it allows entrants in the football pools to check their coupon. Flick to Chapter 18 for more on the pools.

Final Score (BBC One)

The BBC's version of *Soccer Saturday* isn't half as good, but it does boast the eccentric reporting of former Spurs striker Garth Crooks, who often gets into hilarious arguments with fellow ex-pros over incidents that have occurred during the afternoon's action. *Final Score* is a decent enough substitute for those with only terrestrial channels. As on *Soccer Saturday*, when all the games have finished there's a classified pools check.

Champions League Weekly (ITV1)

Transmitted late on a Monday evening, *Champions League Weekly* is a round-up of the previous action in Europe's premier club competition, plus a preview of upcoming matches. The show usually includes interviews with big-name players and managers from across Europe. Made under the auspices of UEFA, it isn't a critical programme but still offers thoughtful coverage of the Champions League.

Sky Sports News

This is a 24-hour rolling news channel, specialising in the latest from the FA Premier League. It can occasionally descend into farce, when bored presenters attempt to jazz up the most minor stories on slow news days, but when big stories break there's nothing better than watching them unfold here. The channel has a good record of breaking big football stories first.

ESPN Classic

For anyone with an interest in football history, this is the best channel in the UK. A treasure trove of classic matches, old highlights programmes and in-depth documentaries, *ESPN Classic* showcases an eclectic mix of football through the ages. (It also covers other sports.) The output is occasionally themed to coincide with major events, so expect much classic World Cup action during the summer of 2010.

The Internet

There's now an almost unlimited supply of football to watch thanks to the advent of the Internet, from live matches to video of classic action.

Live streaming

Most worldwide television channels now have live streaming facilities on their websites, for those without a television. Live matches and highlights programmes are either streamed as they go out on the respective television channel, and/or you can access them through an iPlayer for a limited period of time.

Territory rights are a thorny issue, however. For example, those outside the UK can't view the BBC's *Match of the Day* package, because broadcasters from other countries have separate rights to screen FA Premier League highlights.

Even if you don't own a television you may have to pay a subscription or licence fee. In the UK you must have a TV licence to view over the Internet.

Some official club websites stream live action of games not covered by major television contracts – for example, overseas friendlies, reserve-team fixtures and youth fixtures. They also transmit live audio commentary of all games.

The Internet also offers options that are legally dubious to say the least: live streaming through third-party sites. Judicious searches on Google unearths feeds, not that I'd recommend them: as well as technically breaking the law, they're usually of extremely poor quality and the action seizes up at inopportune moments. Even when the feeds work they often fall at least a couple of minutes behind real time.

Recent action

Many video-sharing sites such as YouTube feature up-to-the-minute action or crucial clips from recent matches. Remember, though, that these clips are often put up in strict violation of broadcasting rights, although some smaller TV channels and leagues have a laissez-faire policy because popular clips act as effective free advertising.

You can usually find clips of goals of the day from all leagues easily somewhere on the Internet. Clips of particularly good goals, vicious fights or outrageous fouls often become widely disseminated online.

Classic clips

Video-sharing sites can be a treasure trove of classic football action, with fans worldwide posting snippets of their favourite video cassettes and DVDs up on the Internet. Again, much of the content posted has technically violated someone's rights somewhere down the line, yet thousands of hours of classic action have been left up on sites with no one taking action.

It's worth searching around because hours of old matches, clips of famous players from the past and long-forgotten programmes are now floating around somewhere in the ether.

Exploring Radio

Technically not 'on screen', of course, but while I'm discussing broadcasting it's only right that I should touch upon one of the oldest – and still one of the greatest – ways to keep up with the very latest football action.

The two main national sport stations – the state-run BBC Radio Five Live and the independent Talksport – offer live commentary of FA Premier League matches, Champions League games and other European ties. You can find Football League, FA Cup, League Cup, Scottish Premier League and Scottish Cup matches on Five Live alone. Both stations offer an up-to-the-minute breaking news service and report latest scores in all matches being played at any given time.

Independent local stations across the country concentrate mainly on regional teams. If you support a small club routinely ignored by the mainstream national media then it's best to search out news and commentaries on these stations, where local sides get increased coverage.

Nearly all local radio stations, like their national counterparts, now stream live online so you no longer have to live in a certain part of the country to pick up a signal. That's worth remembering if you support a team that only benefits from local media coverage but you've moved away from the region.

Live commentaries

Because the medium lacks a visual aspect, radio commentators are more descriptive and voluble than their TV counterparts. They're certainly more opinionated; listening to a commentary on radio can sometimes be as entertaining as watching the action yourself on TV.

While radio commentaries concentrate on the game in hand they often break off for reports at other matches, especially on Saturday afternoons when there's a full fixture list. The commentator usually mentions every goal scored soon after it's scored.

As a result, radio shows are perfect for keeping up with scores around the country when you're actually at the match – for decades fans have taken small personal transistor radios to the game in order to keep in touch with the latest action.

Round-ups

Radio stations also provide a post-match results service, required listening to catch up on all the scores. A classified pools check, announcing all the scores in every division, is followed by round-the-ground reports from all the major matches.

BBC Radio Five Live's round-up programme, broadcast at 5pm on a Saturday afternoon after the main 3pm football fixtures finish, is the legendary *Sports Report*. It's not uncommon to hear this blazing from the radio of every car as traffic filters slowly away from grounds across the country.

Listener phone-ins

Over the last couple of decades, listener phone-in shows, such as *6-0-6* on Radio Five Live, have become very popular. A soapbox for fans to have their say on the latest issues, the show inevitably degenerates into a litany of rants from moaning fans as they make their way home from their team's latest defeat.

Some listeners argue that this misses the point of the initial phone-ins, from when the genre took off back in the early 1990s. Then the shows were designed as a forum for fans to discuss the day's matches, but also to laugh and joke about the lighter and quirkier side of the game. Over the years, though, this approach has made way for the more vituperative ranting of today, although the shows are unquestionably more popular than ever.

Podcasts

You can download many football shows on the radio – mainly previews, magazine shows and phone-ins – as podcasts from station websites, or by subscribing on iTunes. Major newspaper websites such as the *Guardian* and *The Times* also offer excellent weekly or bi-weekly podcasts, as do specialist blogs. Many of these podcasts offer something more cerebral and informed than the offerings of the major radio networks, which have to cater for a more mainstream audience.

Focusing on Football Films

On the whole, football has been badly served by the silver screen. Nobody seems to know exactly why sports such as baseball, golf and *even rugby league* have cinematic classics to their name but football doesn't have a single flick worthy of legendary status.

The reasons for this have long been debated. The main argument is that football generates such unbelievable dramatic tension in real life, it simply doesn't wash when re-enacted in a work of fiction.

Still, there have been some decent efforts though, as you will see, some of the very best are only about the sport in the loosest sense.

Escape to Victory

This is the most famous football movie of all time. Michael Caine and Sylvester Stallone star in a prisoner of war caper, which sees an Allied team take on a side made up of Nazis in a propaganda match, and make like the title. There's a star-studded cast of footballing extras, including Pelé, Bobby Moore, Ossie Ardiles and, er, former Ipswich man Russell Osman. A schmaltzy tale, but good fun.

The plot of *Escape to Victory* isn't as ridiculous as it may seem. It's loosely based on games between Russian PoWs and Nazi soldiers in 1942. The PoWs, formerly professionals with FC Start, repeatedly thrashed the German sides despite being warned of severe repercussions should they win. Unlike the film, there was no Hollywood ending: several members of the Russian side were eventually tortured for their insolence, and then shot.

Zidane: A 21st-Century Portrait

Simple and atmospheric, *Zidane* tracks – guess who? – Zinedine Zidane as the Real Madrid midfielder plays in a league game against Villarreal in 2005. Seventeen cameras track his every movement on the pitch, which are shown in real time. Scottish art-rockers Mogwai provide the soundtrack for the film.

Towards the end of the match Zidane is involved in a brawl and sent off, a serendipitous climax to the film.

The Damned United

David Peace's superb novel *The Damned Utd* fictionalised the story of Brian Clough's doomed 44-day reign as manager of Leeds United in 1974. This film, starring Michael Sheen as Clough, isn't quite as hard-hitting as the book – it's at times an almost comedic take on events – but it's still an evocative snapshot of life in 1970s England: preposterously muddy pitches, cigarette smoke, brown wallpaper and all. Oh, and Sheen's impersonation of Clough is *priceless*.

The Firm (1988 TV movie)

Hooligan films are very popular, though most have an unfortunate – some would say unpleasant – tendency to glamorise fighting between 'firms'. Critics condemned this made-for-BBC-TV movie, starring Gary Oldman, for its graphic violence, though the inexorable descent of a respectable estate agent into the grim world of football hooliganism gives the film a solid moral core. It was remade in 2009 by the makers of *The Football Factory* – ironically, one of the latter-day movies criticised for glamorising violence.

The Arsenal Stadium Mystery

This British crime thriller, made in 1939, is set at Highbury, the home at the time of Arsenal. The plot involves Arsenal taking on a fictitious team called The Trojans, one of whom is poisoned during the game. Suspicion then falls on the players of The Trojans. Several Arsenal stars of the time feature, as do players from Brentford as members of the Trojans side, although the only speaking part goes to the Arsenal manager George Allison.

Allison was used to speaking publicly, having once been a commentator for BBC Radio!

Although Arsenal's stadium was known as Highbury, its official title was Arsenal Stadium – hence the name of the film.

Gregory's Girl

A gentle romantic school comedy, *Gregory's Girl* tells the story of a goal-keeper in a terrible school team who falls in love with the side's new striker and star player – a blonde girl called Dorothy. Considered one of the best British films of the past 30 years, it admittedly has a tenuous link with the sport, but the film did earn the actor who played Gregory, John Gordon Sinclair, the chance to sing lead on the 1982 Scotland World Cup squad's top-ten single 'We Have a Dream'.

Looking for Eric

Looking for Eric, a 2009 film by the British director Ken Loach, is the only feature film to star a former world-class professional footballer in one of the lead roles. The former Manchester United and France striker Eric Cantona plays himself, offering philosophical advice to a troubled postman. Cantona also had a cameo role in the 1998 film Elizabeth alongside Cate Blanchett.

Cantona isn't the only player to cross over into acting. The former Rangers striker Ally McCoist starred alongside Robert Duvall in the 2001 flick *A Shot at Glory*, and Graeme Souness, then playing for Liverpool, took a cameo role in the acclaimed 1980s BBC drama *Boys from the Black Stuff*. Midfield enforcer Vinnie Jones, too, has become as well known for his portrayals of hard men off the pitch as for his role as one on it.

Discovering DVDs

Ever since ownership of video cassette machines became widespread in the early 1980s, the market has been flooded with football titles – first on VHS video, later on the DVD format (and now Blu-Ray). The quality has always varied widely with, I should warn, an awful lot of opportunistic rubbish being released over the years, but plenty of quality productions exist too.

Season reviews

During the late 1980s and early 1990s the Football League released an end-of-year season review called *Race for the Championship*. Featuring all the big and pivotal matches of the campaign, the film told the story of the season from a totally neutral point of view. But they also released club-specific videos, recording every single goal scored during the campaign by each team. These were hugely successful and so eventually the FA dropped the divisional reviews in favour of club-specific ones.

Today these annual DVDs are constant best-sellers and shift huge amounts should a club win a major trophy that year. The DVDs, as a rule, contain every goal scored by the club that season in all competitions, extended highlights of major matches and notable victories, and interviews with top players, the manager and sometimes notable backroom staff and fans.

Production quality varies, with the bigger clubs having bigger budgets to spend, but one thing remains constant: the backing music is always – *always* – ear-bleedingly appalling!

Most league clubs produce an end-of-season review. Some smaller clubs won't be able to secure deals to sell them in high street shops, but they're likely to be at least available online and in the club shop. This applies to any club-specific DVDs. (Major club shops also often stock back copies of older DVD titles that are no longer stocked on the high street.)

Club histories

Most clubs have released an 'official history' at some point over the last few seasons. They're usually pretty comprehensive DVDs, detailing the club's progress from its earliest days using as much old footage as exists. Most discs are inevitably skewed towards more recent times, where more television footage is available, but nevertheless the discs are usually scrupulously compiled, produced with knowledgeable fans in mind.

These discs are often good starting points for young or new fans, helping them get up to speed with the history and the culture of the club. They also represent good value for money because they're often priced reasonably (having been on sale for some time) and also boast long running times – sometimes up to three hours on a disc.

Other club titles

Major clubs, such as Manchester United and Liverpool, are able to package their histories in many different ways. For example, both clubs have comprehensive DVD packages of their European exploits, having enjoyed such success on the continent that the subject can fill a disc on its own.

There are also series, such as *Match of the 70s*, that take in several of the bigger clubs.

Clubs often release DVDs containing famous matches – nearly always victories – in their entirety. (A warning for non-fans: they may not necessarily be 'classics' that would please a neutral.)

Clubs also have a questionable habit of releasing DVDs to cash in on the popularity of a certain player, usually padded with tedious interviews and containing little action. They also release regular video 'magazines', which although often containing unintentionally hilarious segments – 'Cooking with Brian McClair', anyone? – aren't so funny on the whole if you've shelled out the price of a DVD on nonsense filler. Fans appear to have got wise to the practice because few clubs now persist with such titles. If you do come across one, you're best avoiding it.

Country histories

Just as clubs release histories, so too do countries. England, for example, boasts many different DVDs: an overall history, great goals, great players, great matches. The 1966 World Cup final is obviously a big seller, and worth watching in its entirety to see how different football was back then and to appreciate what a sudden shock West Germany's last-minute equaliser would have been at the time – as was England's famous 5-1 win in Germany in 2001.

As ever, the Brazilians are the big draw here, with a superb DVD called *The Boys from Brazil* charting the team's history. A BBC production, it's been out for the best part of two decades – it was first released on video – and only goes up to 1986, but it's very cheap as a result and a real bargain. The football is *fantastic*.

Player histories

These are often a mixed bag, with quality varying wildly. DVDs about a specific player often disappoint, with too much emphasis placed on interviews and clips of the player going about his everyday business, in lieu of proper action. Choose wisely.

It's by no means a guarantee of quality but a general rule of thumb is: the longer a player has retired, the better the player history will be. Put another way, if the player is 23 years old, the chances of an hour-long DVD being captivating all the way through are very slim indeed, no matter how many trophies they've already won.

Tournament histories

All the major tournaments now have superb retrospectives: namely the World Cup, the European Championship and the Champions League. Each disc has every goal from the tournament, plus extended highlights of major matches and incidents.

As well as 'all the goals in the tournament' retrospectives, each World Cup has an official FIFA film – the 1966 film, *Goal!*, is widely considered to be one of the most evocative of its time – but nearly all of them are currently unavailable.

Classic matches

Thousands of classic matches in their entirety are on general release, ranging from obvious money-spinners featuring the big clubs to 'classic' games from years gone by. For example, the BBC have released a choice selection of the best FA Cup finals from 1950 to 1990.

Novelty titles

Every Christmas sees a slew of new 'novelty' football titles. These are usually humorous clip compilations fronted by a comedian or popular celebrity. There's often a general theme – goals, fights, bloopers – and some of the action can be very entertaining. But make sure you're a fan of the presenter because if you can't stand him or her then the DVD will be winging its way out of the window well before the end, no matter how good the clips are.

Classic television programmes

Some classic television series over the years have seen their way into box sets – the greatest highlights from *Match of the Day* between the 1960s and the 1980s have been collated, for example – but much remains unreleased. The BBC's excellent *Match of the Sixties, Seventies and Eighties* gathers dust in the vaults (although it was released on VHS in the 1990s).

You can find full programmes on YouTube or as downloadable torrents, but beware because they're almost certainly not legal copies.

You and your friends, or members of your club's support, could contact TV companies to request a specific match, tournament or programme you remember. It's unlikely to guarantee a release but in the past some DVD distributors have released comedies and dramas as a result of viewer demand. So if there's enough of you asking, and the DVD company can see a way to make money, you never know!

Chapter 17

Read All About It!

*P*ut all the other sports in the world together, and still they wouldn't have as many words written about them as football. From up-to-the-minute websites and newspapers containing the latest breaking news to huge tomes full of statistics of every match played by every team under the sun since the late 1800s, everything is covered somewhere. You just have to know where to look . . .

Knowing the Newspapers

Ever since the first-ever club fixture was played in 1860 between Sheffield FC and Hallam newspapers have been interested in covering what occurs on the football pitch. As the world's most popular sport, papers are duty bound to cover it – and in any case, it makes for great copy.

What newspapers offer

To this day newspapers – whether in good old-fashioned paper form or on the Internet – still offer the football fan the most comprehensive coverage of the sport. A football section is usually included in the main part of the paper (–historically at the back) –or in a completely separate pull-out sport or football section. Here's what to expect from them.

Match reports

This is a description of how the match unfolded. Match reports are usually – whatever fans believe – written from as neutral a perspective as possible.

They describe all the major incidents, offer mild opinion on them – whether a red card was justified or not, for example – and add some post-match reaction from players and managers.

All top-flight matches, major cup games, European fixtures featuring teams from the UK and internationals have their own separate match report. Games from the lower divisions or abroad usually get less coverage than the top flight. They either appear in small bite-sized reports or are simply mentioned as part of a divisional round-up.

Reports in the local press, especially if the paper covers an area containing only one team, are usually weighted with the local favourites in mind.

Latest news

This is a selection of the latest stories from the world of football. In lieu of big stories – such as a manager getting sacked, a player being banned for bad behaviour or a 'war of words' between two stars, managers or club officials – these concern player injuries, upcoming team selection decisions and choice quotes made by players and managers.

Transfer gossip

One of the biggest drivers of sales in newspapers is transfer gossip. Every day papers contain a sprinkling of news stories linking clubs with high-profile players. A lot of the gossip is genuine, even if the transfers don't always end up happening. However, sometimes the gossip is clearly totally made up in order to fill space in the paper, or generate some excitement on a slow news day.

Fans are aware of the idiosyncratic nature of transfer gossip and take it all with a pinch of salt. Most consider weighing up the chances of a story being true or not to be one of the simple pleasures of football fandom.

Opinion pieces

Every newspaper has at least a couple of big-name columnists whose job it is to opine about the latest action and news. Often these columnists simply look for a controversial angle on events – but right or wrong, most fans agree that columns are rarely boring.

Opinion pieces in the tabloid press usually take a 'man on the street' (populist) angle, and the middlebrow and broadsheet papers attempt a more considered response.

Often newspapers generate 'controversy' for its own sake, spinning a quote into a controversial 'top line' or dragging out an incident from a match – perhaps a bad foul or a dive – for as long as possible. Keep this in mind because although there'll be thousands of news stories and opinion pieces over the season people will probably only remember one or two for much longer than a week!

The nationals

All the daily national newspapers give exhaustive coverage to football, with several having separate Sport sections which tend to be dominated by the game. However, the style of coverage varies widely.

Tabloids

The biggest-selling paper in the UK is the red-top tabloid the _Sun._ (_Tabloid_ is the name given to the size of the page.) Tabloids pursue a brash, populist agenda, attempting to generate controversy with every story. Rational analysis isn't always to be found – especially during World Cups, when a one-eyed pro-England agenda can lead to players and referees being turned into national pariahs.

The red-tops are often the best papers for transfer gossip: the _Sun_ and _Mirror_ break more big stories than all the other UK papers together.

Broadsheets

The _broadsheets_ (the collective term for the likes of _The Times_, the _Guardian_ and the _Daily Telegraph_, even though they're all very different shapes these days) take a more considered approach. They pride themselves on longer match reports, less reactionary comment, and less jingoistic reporting during major tournaments.

Mid-market

By definition, middlebrow papers such as the _Daily Mail_ and _Daily Express_ sit somewhere between the tabloid agenda and the broadsheet mentality. It's far from a hard and fast rule but in general their news gathering is more in tune with the hard-nosed tabloid variety, and opinion columns and analysis pieces display a more broadsheet sensibility.

The locals

Local papers are suffering in the modern media age, with many making severe cutbacks or closing down altogether. Those still battling on provide a crucial service to local clubs. Indeed, for supporters of teams outside the big leagues, they're a lifeline for those who need to keep in touch with what's going on at their club.

Local papers, by definition, have a more parochial flavour. The news and match reports sometimes have a non-critical and non-questioning tone – local journalists can scarcely afford to queer their own patch by causing trouble at the club.

Employing the Internet

Traditionalists may not like it but the most popular medium for football news, views and journalism today is the Internet. Many football-only websites exist that carry the latest news, views and scores, although the most popular are run by existing newspaper, television and radio companies.

What the Internet can do for you

As well as many – if not all – of the features offered by newspapers, the Internet offers additional services and features.

Breaking news

Sports news is now a 24-hour business and all the top sites offer the latest breaking news on rolling tickers. Some sites are faster than others to put up fully written-up stories – both the BBC and Sky Sports use their extensive journalistic network to break big news quickly – but there is usually more in-depth coverage on the newspaper websites (although you may have to wait an hour or two for comprehensive analysis).

Live scores

Most major news and sport sites offer a live score service. Some sites, such as the BBC, provide up-to-the-minute details of latest scores, scorers, bookings, sendings off, injuries and attendances from the FA Premier League right the way down to non-league divisions.

Live minute-by-minute reports

One of the newest and most popular methods of following games online is the live minute-by-minute text report. These are running text commentaries that describe events as they unfold, adding some colour and description to bare statistical analysis. These reports often editorialise, adding comment, opinion or humour to the basic description of events. Many also encourage reader participation via email, message board or poll voting.

Breaking opinion

In the old days considered opinion on noteworthy events in football often didn't appear in newspapers until a couple of days after the events had occurred. Nowadays the turnaround is much quicker, with discussion points often identified within minutes of the final whistle and brief opinion pieces published not long after. These are usually put up as 'blogs', with readers invited to respond and generate debate 'below the line'.

The mainstream media

The major Internet sites in the UK – indeed around the world – are run by the usual media companies: in the main, television and radio stations and newspaper companies.

In the UK the market leader is the BBC (www.bbc.co.uk/football), which offers an up-to-the-minute breaking news service, live scores, minute-by-minute text reports and clips of action from the FA Premier League, the Football League, the Scottish Premier League and other competitions.

Several newspapers have major sites offering in-depth coverage from their papers plus live, bespoke online reports. The *Guardian*'s site (www.guardian. co.uk) has been the biggest and most successful of recent years, though *The Times* (www.timesonline.co.uk), the *Daily Telegraph* (www.telegraph. co.uk) and the *Daily Mail* (www.dailymail.co.uk) all now offer similar services. The tabloid papers still concentrate more on big stories than live action, though they too now offer minute-by-minute services.

Many standalone football or sports news sites also exist, such as Football 365 (www.football365.co.uk), Teamtalk (www.teamtalk.com), ESPN Soccernet (www.soccernet.co.uk) and Sporting Life (www.sporting life.co.uk). All offer news, transfer gossip, live reports, chat, features and humour.

Blogs and other websites

Although the mainstream media covers top-level football in depth it doesn't touch upon many aspects of the game. But thanks to the Internet, experts in specific fields are able to maintain sites and blogs on subjects widely ignored by the usual media outlets.

Subject matter can vary widely, from latest news and opinion about clubs, leagues or countries that get scant coverage in the media to idiosyncratic topics such as football programme collecting, the history of football crests or the best pubs near football grounds.

Usually run on a shoestring, these sites have a habit of either closing down or moving from one address to another, so there'd be little point in listing them here. But it's worth using search engines to hunt for subjects you're interested in, no matter how niche you think they might be – because chances are someone has set up a site or blog to cover those specialist subjects you love.

Making the Most of Magazines

Football hasn't always been well-served by magazine publishers, though in recent years this has changed, with the advent of several well-written and thoughtful publications. Previous to the advent of titles such as *When Saturday Comes*, *FourFourTwo* and *Champions*, the market consisted mainly of comics for young children and the occasional staid world football digest.

Most magazines have some presence on the Internet, posting a taster selection of their articles online. Some magazines are considering putting up their entire back catalogue for perusal, either free or via subscription.

FourFourTwo

The biggest monthly football magazine in the UK, *FourFourTwo* includes big-name interviews, extended features on the pressing issues of the day, historical pieces about old players and teams and a world football round-up. Popular regular features include 'More than a game', on famous rivalries, and 'Sing when you're winning' in which a celebrity talks of their love for football. *FourFourTwo* is editorially mainstream, offering something for every type of fan.

Champions

This is the official magazine of the UEFA Champions League. It contains interviews with players and managers featuring in the current Champions League, plus statistics, photographs and reports from the competition. However, it also features a superb range of historical articles, about players and clubs who have made their mark on the European Cup in 1955. A must read for anyone with an interest in the sport's history and who wants to learn more about the game on foreign shores.

When Saturday Comes

Launched in the mid 1980s, *When Saturday Comes* started off as a non-club-specific fanzine and quickly grew into one of the biggest and best football magazines in the UK. Giving a voice to fans of clubs across the country – not all of the writers in the mag are professional journalists – *WSC* is the most eclectic magazine out there, offering a mix of politics, humour and considered opinion.

World Soccer

As its name suggests, _World Soccer_ is a digest of the game around the world. It's part of a federation called European Sports Magazines, which includes other famous football publications from across the continent, including _La Gazzetta dello Sport_ (Italy), _Kicker_ (Germany), _Don Balon_ (Spain) and _Voetbal International_ (Netherlands).

France Football

This mag is widely available in the UK, although that's not much good to you unless you speak French. However, I mention it because it's without doubt the most famous magazine in world football. As well as its in-depth take on the sport, it's also noted for the Ballon d'Or, its prestigious annual award to the best player in the world.

The Official Club View

All clubs, from the very top of the league pyramid to the very bottom, publish some sort of literature, even if it's just their match day programme. The bigger clubs publish glossy magazines that go on sale nationwide. And nearly all clubs now have an official website.

Matchday programmes

Ever since the late 1880s and the advent of regular league football in England, clubs have produced a match day programme. Initially just a team sheet printed on a piece of paper or card, the programme grew in size over the years into the mini-magazines we see today.

In truth, the programme is usually not an in-depth reading experience. An average programme contains a message to supporters from the club manager – usually a rallying cry, plus a welcome to the opposition team – and another message from the club captain. It features the squad numbers of both sides and sometimes an approximate guess at each side's starting line-up. There are profiles of players from the visiting side, along with a piece about their recent form and matches. And the programme includes an in-depth round-up of the home team's latest game.

The editorial tone of a magazine is invariably heavily biased towards the home side – who are producing the programme after all – but nods are made to the visiting team. The tone is always be respectful and polite, as befits an official publication.

Some of the larger clubs have scaled up their programme operations and style their offering as a 'match day magazine'. There are usually more features in these, though they're often more expensive too.

Programmes can cost anything from £2 up to £10 at major matches such as cup finals or internationals. It's questionable whether they offer value for money, although some programmes over time become sought after by collectors, and their value soars.

Although programmes for average league fixtures are unlikely to rise in value, other than in exceptional circumstances – the more famous (or infamous) a match becomes, the more likely it is that the price of the programme will soar – a complete season's collection is some worth to collectors.

Hundreds of vendors exist who trade in old programmes. They often trade near football grounds, in shops or from street stalls, and also have an online presence.

Official club magazines

The bigger clubs in the country produce glossy magazines, usually published each month, which you can find in major newsagents all across the country. These contain big-name interviews with star players, features and interviews about the club and their current players, nostalgia pieces usually reminiscing about famous old matches or ex-players and opinion pieces from in-house writers.

There's nothing too controversial in these magazines: the editorial team toe the club line. Often these magazines can be slightly bland as a result, although they remain very popular and are especially so with children and younger fans.

Official websites

All clubs, no matter how small, now have a presence on the Internet. Club sites at least contain information about upcoming fixtures, as well as details ranging from player profiles to contact details for the club such as the ticket office, club reception and club shop.

Larger clubs offer rolling news services, allowing fans to keep in touch with the latest from the club. This is inevitably the official club line, so should your club or one of its players be embroiled in a controversy of some sort, don't expect any reference to it on the official site!

You may also find magazine style features and interviews, usually with current players and staff, occasionally with famous names from the past. Many bigger league clubs also offer video clips of action, live audio commentary of matches and live televised streaming of reserve or youth team games plus the occasional friendly.

Clubs now use social networking sites, such as Facebook and Twitter, in order to transmit the club's latest news.

The Fans' View

Almost since club football began back in the late 1800s it was argued that neither professional journalists nor club employees reported on the sport from the viewpoint of the paying spectator. It was a rational argument – writers on club publications were hardly going to bite the hand that feeds, and journalists from newspapers, either regional or local, had to maintain relationships with managers and players if they wanted continued access and a steady flow of quotes and insider stories.

In the 1980s, though, supporters began to get their act together. Working on the 'do-it-yourself' principles of the self-published fanzines that sprang up in the wake of punk music in the 1970s – when the major music papers were slow to report the new music – supporters began to write their own reports on what was going on at the club.

Fanzines

Since the 1980s fans of hundreds of clubs from the top divisions in England down to the non-leagues have produced fanzines. They vary widely in quality – some are little more than a pamphlet and others are professionally produced colour magazines – but all are concerned with issues rarely covered by the mainstream media.

An average fanzine is likely to contain match reports plus opinion pieces discussing current controversies surrounding the club, from first-team playing matters to everyday issues affecting the experience of the paying fan, no matter how small. They're often stridently political in tone – usually from a left-of-centre, 'sticking up for the little man' perspective – and may be concerned with issues such as ticket prices, accessibility, the wishes of fans being met by the board, ownership issues and many other constructive criticisms or concerns.

Fanzines usually make an effort to avoid being too worthy, however, leavening the mix with irreverent humour, jokes and cartoons that poke fun at both their rivals and often their own club and players too.

Fanzines are published at various intervals during the season – some are monthlies, some only bi-annual, many are irregular – and fans usually sell them outside the ground before games, but it's usually possible to pay for a postal subscription. In recent years, with the advent of the Internet, many fanzines have been forced to fold, though many of the more popular titles have battled on.

The website of magazine *When Saturday Comes* – which started out as a fanzine in the mid 1980s – has a list of links to fanzines (www.wsc.co.uk).

Internet sites

Many club fanzines have now emigrated to the Web, where an online presence is cheaper and easier to maintain. The Internet also has the added advantage of being instantly reactive, unlike periodical fanzines.

On the whole these sites operate in much the same way as fanzines do: match reports, opinion pieces and jokes. But they also have forums and chatboards, allowing fans to discuss the latest action and news stories as and when they happen.

Forums and message boards

Most clubs, no matter how far down the league pyramid, have at least one online forum that fans can visit and have their say on.

Forums need not be linked to a fanzine with any other editorial content – many sites are standalone forums.

Each discussion topic is called a *thread* or *topic*. You can either start one yourself (by clicking a 'new thread' or 'new topic' button, giving it a title and posting a first entry) or reply to one that's already been started – you should be able to see a list of topics, click the one that interests you and post a response.

These forums can be quite addictive because fans usually have a lot to say about what's going on at their club at any one time. As you can imagine, passions can sometimes run high – so try to keep calm and address other posters as you would if you were talking face to face with a friend.

Some people post entries simply in order to wind other users up and start arguments – they might not even be fans of the club. (Such people are known as *trolls*.) This is sadly part and parcel of the medium, though some sites attempt to address this by fencing off part of the site for paid subscribers only. If you use chat sites a lot and want to discuss matters in a rational and intelligent manner, it may be worth subscribing to such a section. Prices are reasonable – the Manchester United site Red Issue's subscription section costs £10 per year – and worth paying if you want to weed out the trolls.

Branching Out into Books

Football hasn't always been brilliantly served by the world of publishing. For years all that was on offer were staid footballer autobiographies, the players mouthing platitudes, and a few reference tomes. Much has changed in the last 20 years or so, however, with publishers releasing some more thoughtful, honest and revealing player autobiographies as well as a huge range of well-written histories of clubs, countries and players.

The turning point – so the popular theory goes, anyway – was the publication in 1991 of a book called *Fever Pitch* by Nick Hornby. Treating the sport and its fans with intelligence, it sold by the bucketload, proving that books about football needn't be lowest common denominator.

The following list is by no means definitive – you can choose between hundreds of fantastic football books on the shelves – but my selection forms the basis of a very decent football library.

Most of the following books are still in print; you can easily and cheaply source the few that aren't at Internet second-hand bookshops.

Autobiographies

Footballing autobiographies don't usually involve a lot of 'auto', with the bulk of the work being undertaken by ghostwriters – usually sports journalists. Buyer beware: the magnitude of the star is by no means always a guide to the quality of the autobiography. A lot of dross exists out there, but the ones in this section are all worth a read.

Keane: The Autobiography (Roy Keane with Eamon Dunphy)

Roy Keane got in a lot of trouble when this book was released because he admitted to deliberately fouling Manchester City rival Alf-Inge Haaland during a tempestuous Mancunian derby. But Keane was nothing if not honest, and he also lifted the lid on the infamous row with Republic of Ireland manager Mick McCarthy that saw him sent home from the 2002 World Cup. A real page turner, and a must for Manchester United fans.

Full Time: The Secret Life of Tony Cascarino (Tony Cascarino with Paul Kimmage)

Player autobiographies are often blander than the paper they're written on, but like his former Republic of Ireland team-mate Roy Keane, Tony Cascarino pulls no punches here. Eschewing the opportunity to big himself up, Cascarino admits to his failings as a footballer and, occasionally, as a human being. Painfully honest.

With Clough by Taylor (Peter Taylor with Mike Langley)

Brian Clough and Peter Taylor were the most successful managerial partnership of the 1970s, winning the league at Derby County and the league and European Cup with Nottingham Forest. This book is a unique insight into how a top-level managerial duo operates, and a fascinating historical document because the two fell out soon after – *as a result of the publication of this book!*

Only a Game (Eamon Dunphy)

Like Cascarino, Eamon Dunphy was a Republic of Ireland international who knew his limitations. This is a diary of Dunphy's disillusionment as a Second Division player struggling for form at Millwall in the mid 1970s, the season going from bad to worse for the player. Anyone who likes this may also enjoy Garry Nelson's *Left Foot Forward*, a similar diary of a Charlton journeyman in the 1990s.

Captain of Hungary (Ferenc Puskás)

There have been few players in the history of the game as good as Ferenc Puskás. This book – published while Puskás was still playing – charts his rise as a player, describing Hungary's successes of the early 1950s in great detail. But it's the team's failure at the 1954 World Cup that makes for the most vivid read. A wonderful take on one of the most famous sides of all time, and a snapshot of how football used to be in the old days.

Biographies

As with autobiographies, the quality of biographies can be variable, particularly if they're written to cash in on temporary fame or notoriety. There are plenty of good ones, however.

Sir Alf (Leo McKinstry)

Despite winning the 1966 World Cup for England, Alf Ramsey is seen as a bit of a cold fish by football fans. (He didn't celebrate the victory, responding with a stereotypically British stiff upper lip.) This warm biography explains why he was the man he was and manages to make him more loveable while doing so. Even fans of Scotland are likely to warm to him!

Provided You Don't Kiss Me: 20 Years with Brian Clough (Duncan Hamilton)

Hamilton was a football journalist on a local Nottingham paper when Clough was winning leagues and European Cups at Forest. This is an affectionate memoir of his time reporting on the club – effectively a bird's eye view of how Clough kept going through the years despite knocking back prodigious amounts of whisky.

Bob Paisley: Manager of the Millennium (John Keith)

With three European Cup wins to his name, Bob Paisley is still the most successful manager at the very top level of the English game. But unlike the Matt Busbys, Brian Cloughs and Bill Shanklys, he has left a strangely low-profile legacy. This book tells the story of one of the lesser-known greats in English football history, a worthwhile read even for non-Liverpool fans.

Engineering Archie (Simon Inglis)

While the likes of Ramsey, Clough and Paisley built the teams, Archibald Leitch was busy building the stadiums. Leitch, a Scottish engineer operating between 1899 and 1929, designed eye-catching stands for Manchester United, Arsenal, Chelsea, Liverpool, Everton, Aston Villa – and Rangers, where his stand collapsed in 1902, killing 26 spectators, and where he earned his redemption with one of the grandest stands in the land 30 years later. A beautiful coffee table book.

Out of His Skin: The John Barnes Phenomenon (Dave Hill)

The story of how John Barnes signed for Liverpool in 1987 and quickly became the main man in the most attractive side the club had ever fielded. But the book is a social history as well because Barnes was the first-ever black player to become a first-team fixture at Anfield – causing racial tension to rise to the surface on Merseyside.

Club-specific books

Although the following books are all about a specific club, I chose them because they're just as interesting for non-fans – and are in no way blindly biased as some club specific books can be!

The Unforgiven: the Story of Don Revie's Leeds United (Rob Bagchi and Paul Rogerson)

Leeds were the most consistently successful team in England between 1965 and 1975, but never reached the levels of popularity enjoyed by the likes of Manchester United and Liverpool. This book tells their story from a Leeds perspective, turning several of English football's pariah figures into more sympathetic people.

The Glory Game (Hunter Davies)

During the 1971/2 season, the writer Hunter Davies was given unprecedented access to the inner workings of a top football club. Allowed behind the scenes at Tottenham Hotspur for an entire season, he showed how the managerial staff and players in a professional squad interact with each other. Highly revealing.

Barca: a People's Passion (Jimmy Burns)

The story of how Barcelona became one of the most important clubs in the world, and a byname for Catalan identity and nationalism. Some of the biggest names in football have played for the club, from Johan Cruyff to Diego Maradona – though not always successfully!

Bhoys, Bears and Bigotry (Bill Murray)

An even-handed history of the sectarian problems that have blighted the Old Firm duo of Rangers and Celtic. A lighter read than it sounds, it unearths some stories and straightens some misconceptions that are sure to delight and annoy fans of both clubs in equal turns.

Country specific books

Football is a world game, so broaden your horizons by reading up on the sport's development around the globe.

Tor! The Story of German Football (Uli Hesse Lichtenberger)

German football has a bad name in Great Britain – mainly because Germany always wins! Unfairly characterised as a nation of arrogant footballers, the country has in fact always been wracked by self-doubt, as this wonderfully written (and self-deprecating) history explains. It'll make you look at the German national team in a whole new light.

Calcio – a History of Italian Football (John Foot)

Few countries have as glamorous a footballing history as Italy. This comprehensive book tells the story of the style, the success, the teams, the players, the scandals and the tragedies that have shaped one of the most famous nations in the world. A very easy book to dip in and out of.

Futebol: a Brazilian Way of Life (Alex Bellos)

Football in Brazil is totally chaotic, yet despite it all the country is the most successful in the world. This book charts the history of the nation that gave us Pelé, Garrincha, Zico, Ronaldo and Kaká, explaining how failure at the 1950 World Cup made every Brazilian determined to reach the pinnacle of the sport.

Soccer in a Football World (David Wangerin)

Football has never quite taken off in the US, despite many attempts to establish the sport in the world's most prosperous nation. This book tells the fascinating story of aborted launches in the 1920s, the failure of world stars Pelé, Cruyff and Beckenbauer to publicise it in the 1970s and a renewed push in the 1990s.

All Played Out (Pete Davies)

The writer Pete Davies travelled to the 1990 World Cup, talking to both the England national team and its fans, at a tournament from which nothing was expected. But England reached the semi-finals, changing the mood of a nation.

General history

Football has a rich history, and you can use the books in this section to round out your knowledge of the game's past – and maybe get a glimpse of the future – as a cultural, social and economic phenomenon.

The Ball Is Round: a Global History of Football (David Goldblatt)

From the 'high industrial' football of Europe to the game under the auspices of Latin American generals, this is the definitive history of how football spread across the globe. This is a huge tome – over 900 pages, with no illustrations. But don't be intimidated by its size and scope: it's a breezy read, its 20 chapters easy to dip in and out of.

Inverting the Pyramid: a History of Football Tactics (Jonathan Wilson)

The story of how football progressed from a kickabout in the park, with seven players up front, to the highly strategic games of today. This wonderful book is effectively a potted history of football, as well as being an insight into the minds of some of the greatest managers and tactical thinkers the sport has known.

Kicking and Screaming (Rogan Taylor and Andrew Ward)

A series of very engaging transcripts of interviews from a BBC television series on the history of football in England. Many of the biggest names in the sport share their memories, from immediate post-war legends like Tom Finney and Len Shackleton to more modern heroes such as Gary Lineker and Ian Wright.

Football against the Enemy (Simon Kuper)

Simon Kuper travels to 22 countries to see how football is played and viewed across the world. An enlightening and witty book: among many observations, he notes that Britain is the only country that produces footballers willing to continue playing even if they've broken their heads.

100 Years of Football: the FIFA Centennial Book (various)

Produced to celebrate the centenary of the world governing body, this is a comprehensive, if fairly straightforward and uncontroversial, history of the game. It is, however, a gorgeous coffee table tome, with hundreds of glossy colour photographs of famous players, events, places and artefacts. A superb snapshot of a footballing century.

Reference

Facts and figures are part of football's life blood. You need to be able to reach for a range authoritative tomes if you're going to get to know the game in detail.

The Complete Book of the World Cup (Cris Freddi)

If you only read one book about the greatest tournament in the world, make sure it's this one. Every single match since 1930 is given its own separate report, with full team line-ups, scores, scorers and statistics. Totally comprehensive.

Sky Sports Football Yearbook (ed Jack and Glenda Rollin)

Formerly known as the _Rothmans Football Yearbook_, until legislation outlawed tobacco sponsorship in sport – and still referred to as 'Rothmans' by some – this annual contains nearly 1,000 pages of match and tournament information, with tournament winners stretching back to the game's inception.

50 Years of the European Cup and Champions League (Kier Radnedge)

A coffee-table sized book charting the history of the European Cup since its launch in 1955. The story of every season is given its own separate spread, and the final has another. The book has over 300 photographs, plus in-depth stats for each final, as well as the cover of every final programme.

Football Grounds of Great Britain (Simon Inglis)

Every single stadium in the country is lovingly described and captured in photograph in this book. The book charts the history of each ground, with stories not only of the bricks and mortar but also the development of each club and its social history. A treasure trove of fascinating stories from British football's archive.

When Saturday Comes: the Half Decent Football Book (various)

An A–Z (well, okay, an A–Y) from abandoned matches to youth football, this is an encyclopaedia of British football, written by fans, for fans. Opinionated and witty, it includes potted histories of every single club in the English and Scottish leagues.

Literature

For a subject which means so much to so many, football isn't that well served either by fiction or more literary memoirs. Some gems exist, however, and this section leads you through them.

Fever Pitch (Nick Hornby)

Arguably the most famous book ever written about football, _Fever Pitch_ is the autobiographical story of an Arsenal fan's devotion for football. The book is written as a diary, each entry referring to a specific game between the late 1960s and early 1990s and touching on a different aspect of being a supporter. A classic in the genre, it's sold over a million copies.

The Damned Utd (David Peace)

Peace – a novelist who'd previously written several bleak novels about life in 1970s Yorkshire – returned to the county to retell the story of Brian Clough's ill-fated 44 days in charge of Leeds United in 1974. A work of fiction based on fact, it caused some controversy – Clough's family denied he used to drink as heavily at the time as he did in the book – but remains a gripping story.

The Far Corner (Harry Pearson)

A regular columnist for *When Saturday Comes* and the *Guardian*, Pearson spends a season going to matches at various different levels in the north-east 'far corner' of England. A hilarious take on the joy and pain of being a supporter – he concentrates more on the banter in the stands than the action on the pitch – and probably the funniest book about football ever written.

My Favourite Year (various)

A selection of essays from fans about their club's greatest-ever season. Writers include Roddy Doyle, who tells the emotional story of the Republic of Ireland's 1990 World Cup campaign, and Nick Hornby, who remembers Cambridge United's shambolic efforts in 1983/4 when the team broke the league record for consecutive games without a win.

A Season with Verona (Tim Parks)

Novelist Parks goes around Italy, travelling with fans in support of Hellas Verona. Like *Fever Pitch*, the book shines a light on how football fans think and act, though this time as part of a totally different culture. A superb take on what it's like to be a supporter in one of the most passionate footballing countries in the world.

Chapter 18

Other Football-based Pastimes

So you've been to the match, bought a programme, eaten a pie, started a chant, switched on the TV, bought a bunch of DVDs, played a quick game of Cuju, committed the offside rule to memory, raised a glass to Pelé, Diego Maradona and Lily Parr, got fit, joined a team – and practised the Cruyff Turn, no doubt stepping on the ball accidentally and falling flat on your face.

And yet you've only just scratched the surface. You can get involved with football in hundreds, maybe thousands, of other ways. This chapter looks at just a few more of them, beginning with one of the sport's most traditional all-consuming passions.

Betting

Football and gambling have always gone hand in hand, ever since the launch of the Littlewoods football pools in 1923. The sport lends itself well to taking a punt – the absolutes of winning, drawing, losing and scoring goals are easy to understand and gamble on.

Having a bet on football can be great fun, and is one of the joys of following the sport. But be careful – you don't want gambling to become a problem. The main rule is: don't chase your losses. If you've decided to spend £10 on bets, assume before you begin that you'll lose that £10, and that you can afford that £10 loss. If you can't afford it, don't bet. If you can afford it and you lose the money, don't try to win it back: you've had your betting fun for the day. If you win something, it's a bonus. Keep everything in perspective, don't be greedy and you'll be okay.

Match fixing

Unlike other sports such as horse racing, cricket and formula one, football has remained relatively free of result fixing at the very top level of the game.

That's not to say problems haven't existed over the years. Recently, UEFA, the European governing body, was forced to investigate claims of match fixing in some Champions League and UEFA Cup fixtures. And in the 1990s betting syndicates from the Far East blew the floodlights at some FA Premier League matches in order to rig results; if their bet was winning, forcing a game to be abandoned after half time meant the result stood.

But the two big match-fixing scandals in English football history were both back in the midst of time. In 1965 three players were sent to prison for agreeing to fix results, even though it never actually happened. One of them, the Sheffield Wednesday defender Peter Swan, was almost certain to play for England in the 1966 World Cup – but he'd thrown his chance away.

That paled into insignificance compared to the seven players banned for life in 1915, after Manchester United's win over Liverpool was found to be rigged. Liverpool were safe in mid-table, United battling against relegation. A deal was struck between players, with many taking odds of 7/1 on a 2-0 win. That's how the game ended – after Liverpool's Jackie Sheldon, a former United star, shanked a penalty miles wide of goal. The two points won meant United stayed up at the expense of Chelsea.

The pools

Littlewoods first launched the football pools in 1923. The principle was simple: all the entry fees were put into a pool, between a quarter and half of the pool was given back as prizes and the rest went either into the Littlewoods coffers or those of the taxman. In those days, decades before the National Lottery, it was the only form of gambling that offered a very high jackpot: many thousands of pounds.

There have been some notable pools winners over the years. In 1961 a Yorkshire housewife called Viv Nicholson won just over £150,000 – the rough equivalent of £2 million in today's money – and promised to 'spend, spend, spend'. She did – and eventually lost it all. Elaine McDonagh was the first £1 million winner in 1987. A syndicate from Manchester won nearly £3 million in 1994 – coincidentally, on the same day as the very first National Lottery draw.

Millions of people played the pools – either with Littlewoods or the other two big companies, Zetters and Vernons – but the advent of the National Lottery in the 1990s, and the chance of vastly bigger prizes, saw entries dwindle. Where once nearly 10 million played, now less than a million take part.

Littlewoods Gaming now owns Zetters and Vernons, and a New Football Pools has been launched. You can find it at www.footballpools.com.

You can play many different games, with various combinations of predictions winning prizes, but the scoring principle remains the same:

- ✔ A score draw (1-1, 2-2, 3-3 and so one): 3 points

- ✔ A no-score draw (0-0): 2 points

- ✔ A home or away win: 1 point

So if you're playing the classic 'treble chance' game, you have eight selections from the Saturday fixture list. The person in the pool closest to the maximum of 24 points – eight fixtures multiplied by three points – wins the top-prize 'dividend'.

Players with fewer points can also win prizes. Depending on how many points people score, and how much of the 'pool' is left to share out, it's possible to win a very small dividend, sometimes less than £1! It is also possible to make complicated multiple stakes, covering very many permutations of results: these are known as *perms*.

Even though the pools is much less popular than it once was, it holds a special place in the hearts of football fans. Even now the results services on BBC and Sky on a Saturday afternoon are known as 'classified checks' – a hangover from the days the final scores doubled as a 'classified pools check'.

Fixed-odds betting

A much simpler proposition than the pools, you can place fixed-odds bets at any high street bookmaker, online betting site or telephone betting service. Coupons and websites list all the fixtures, with odds for a plethora of possible results, outcomes and occurrences. You can bet on a single outcomes or build the bet up into a multiple accumulator.

'Fixed odds' guarantees that the odds agreed don't change.

Tying your selections together into a multiple bet means you only have to place one stake, and may win a large amount of money. However, it drastically lessens your chances of winning: each selection in the accumulator has to win otherwise the whole thing loses.

Correct score

Predict the final score of the match. The most common results – 1-0, 1-1 and 2-0 – usually give out the most stingy odds.

If you think the score is going to be 0-0, bet instead on 'no goal-scorer' in the first goal-scorer market. Own goals do not count in the first goal-scorer market, so if the game ends 1-0 after a team scores an own goal, you get what's effectively a payout on a 0-0 prediction for free!

Odds made simple

In the UK you usually write betting odds out in fractional form: 2/1, 10/1, 11/2, 1/2.

The odds 2/1 – 'two to one' – means that if you place £1 and the bet wins you win £2. Betting convention means you also get your stake back, so the bookmaker gives you £3. Similarly, 10/1 gives you a £10 win for a £1 stake, with your £1 stake returned: £11 would be winging back into your pocket.

A price of 11/2 means you win £11 for every £2 staked – or £5.50 for every £1.

The price 1/2 – 'two to one on' – is a very *short price*: for every £1 staked you only get half of that back: 50 pence. (Plus, of course, your £1!) The more likely a result is, the *shorter* the price is. Conversely, an unlikely result gets *long odds*, such as 100/1.

First goal-scorer

Who'll score first? Bookies offer odds on each member of the team's likelihood of scoring the opening goal of the game. Strikers usually have the shortest odds, followed by goal-scoring midfielders.

Sometimes you can get good value on defenders who come up for corners and free kicks, with a hope of getting a header on target. Also keep in mind a team's regular penalty taker: sometimes this player isn't noted for scoring from free play and so their odds will be higher.

Half-time/full-time

Predict the state of play at the halfway stage and at full time. You have three options at both stage: either team will be winning, or the scores will be level.

You can often find value in a match the home side is expected to win easily. Occasionally, hot favourites struggle to score the first goal; it's quite often because away sides, setting their stall out to defend, hold out until half-time. A clever bet on the half-time/full-time market is therefore a draw/home win.

Specials

Betting firms often open 'special' markets on any football-related subject, however trivial they may seem. A market usually exists for offering odds on the next high-profile manager to be sacked, or how far certain teams may get in the World Cup. It's always worth a look to see what firms are advertising; some of their stranger bets can often be a lot of fun.

In-game betting

After kick off the markets move around as games take their shape. If a team suddenly takes a 3-0 lead within the first five minutes, the chances of them winning the game – and of them drawing and losing it – drastically alter. In-game betting reflects this. You can make new bets during the game, usually on websites or over phone accounts, unless you're in the bookies at the time!

Spread betting

A betting firm offers a *spread* of an eventuality. For example, the firm may think a player will score the first goal in a game between the 25th and 30th minute. It's the punter's task to decide whether to go higher than the prediction (buy) or lower (sell).

So if you decide that the spread is too low, and the first goal won't come until the second half, you should buy at the higher figure: in this example, you may 'buy at 30 minutes', placing a £1 unit stake.

If the first goal comes after 40 minutes, you win £1 for every minute higher than 30 minutes: £10. If the first goal comes on 90 minutes, you win £60 (£1 unit stake for every one of the 60 minutes higher than 30). However, if the first goal comes after 10 minutes – 20 minutes below the point at which you've 'bought' – you owe £20.

If you think the spread is too high, and the first goal will come before 25 minutes, you should 'sell' at 25 minutes. Exactly the same profit and loss risks apply, except in reverse.

Spread betting can win you large sums of money with one correct decision, but you can easily lose a fortune and quickly run up some very serious debts. Be careful – and don't risk what you can't afford.

The bookies or punter exchanges?

For all types of betting it's worth looking on betting exchange sites such as Betfair (www.betfair.com), where you're taking odds offered by other gamblers, not a bookmaking firm. Sometimes you find more favourable odds.

If you decide to give Betfair a spin, you can only help your chances by checking out *Winning on Betfair For Dummies*, by Alex Gowar and Jack Houghton (Wiley).

Taking Control with Fantasy Football

It's hard to believe for those old enough to remember the advent of fantasy football games but the original game was released nearly 20 years ago. Fantasy League was launched in 1991 in the United Kingdom, and by the middle of the decade had become a worldwide craze.

Initially the preserve of magazines and newspapers, fantasy football is now at home on the Internet, with hundreds of different games on offer.

The rules

The idea behind fantasy football games is a simple one. A fantasy manager – that's you – gets a fantasy budget to spend on 11 players. From a list of current stars – usually a complete list covering all teams from a specific league – the fantasy manager has to compile his team within his set budget.

Points are then accrued after each match, based on what happens to each player in the actual matches. Totals are added up and the fantasy manager's team is given a place in an overall league of all entrants.

Some games cost a small subscription to join and others are offered free of charge.

As well as entering the main competition players can enter into 'mini leagues' consisting solely of their friends and work colleagues.

With so many different types of game now available, many add additional rules to the basic set-up in order to differentiate them from competitors. For example, the *Sun* newspaper factors in the performance ratings that journalists give players in match reports. The following advice covers the basic principles that apply to most games.

How to choose your players

You must choose 11 players. You can't go over your budget, but you don't have to spend it all. You usually have to pick one goalkeeper, four defenders, four midfielders and two strikers. Sometimes you're allowed different tactical combinations, the most common being an option to select three midfielders and three strikers.

Some games now are squad based, which means you also have to pick a substitutes' bench.

You can make changes – transfers – to your team or squad as the season progresses. Most games limit you to one or two swaps per week, and you must stay within your budget.

You won't be able to pack your team with 11 star players – the budget and player list has been worked out so it's impossible.

Most players decide to choose one or maybe two 'big name' players. These eat up a vast proportion of your budget, so it's best to decide on them first and then fill in the other positions. The more big-name players you buy, the more cheaper players you need to select to balance your budget. It's a tricky balancing act: your team selection will take many drafts before you decide who to select!

Scoring points

Details vary considerably between formats – you have to read the scoring rules of any game you play carefully – but on the whole points are scored when players:

- ✔ **Play in a match.** Sometimes points are docked if players are substituted or go off injured.
- ✔ **Score a goal.** Bonus points are usually awarded for a hat-trick.
- ✔ **Making an assist.** If a player sets up a goal – the pass leading to the goal – they're rewarded.
- ✔ **Keeping a clean sheet.** This usually applies to both goalkeepers and defenders. Sometimes goalkeepers win extra points.

Depending on the game, players also pick up points if they save penalties, are made man of the match or cross a high-rating threshold in a match report.

Points are docked from player totals if they:

- ✔ **Concede a goal.** This usually only covers goalkeepers and defenders.
- ✔ **Get booked or sent off.** The penalties for a straight red, as opposed to two yellows, may be harsher.

Players also lose points if they miss penalties or score own goals.

Collecting memorabilia

Football has been going for over 150 years and has generated an awful lot of memorabilia and ephemera along the way. The bits and bobs you, your parents and their parents before them have picked up could be worth a lot of money – or even more importantly, could rekindle a lot of happy memories.

Cigarette cards

Cigarette cards were a practical invention: they stiffened soft packets of cigarettes, making it less likely the contents would get crushed in transit. Soon enough companies realised they could print pictures on these cards and by making the pictures part of a collectible set smokers would become loyal to the brand. The practice was introduced in the US in 1871, but didn't catch on in the UK until 16 years later.

Various companies printed many series – usually featuring staid objects such as ships, castles and steam trains – until in 1896 Marcus & Company, a small Mancunian tobacconists, released the first ever football range.

Ten years on Ogden's cigarettes printed the first colour football cards. They were a roaring success and many other companies copied the practice over the next 40 years, with lifelike paintings and drawings making way for cartoons and caricatures, which in turn were replaced by photographs. Sadly, the Second World War caused a paper shortage and the cigarette card eventually died out.

Cards can be very collectable these days, even if many of the players pictured would otherwise be forgotten. A single early Marcus & Company card fetches between £150 and £200. Even less rare cards from as late as the 1940s are worth between £3 and £5 each.

Stickers

Collecting football stickers in an album has been a rite of passage for many a young British football fan since in the 1970s. Since the Italian company Panini launched the first successful sticker book in the UK in 1978 – the logically titled *Football 78* – there has been an annual every year covering England's top division, plus issues for each major international tournament.

You can usually purchase retro stickers for between £1 and £5, and can often make savings for bulk buys. The cost of annuals varies wildly: a complete *Panini Football 84* annual fetches £50, yet a totally empty Italian version of the 1974 World Cup album costs £160.

Programmes

It's always worth holding onto your match day programme because you never know if it'll be worth something in the future. Most programmes from before the Second World War, for example, fetch at least £30, no matter what team is involved. Many pre-war programmes are priced upwards of £100. Extremely rare editions, before or after the war, can be worth thousands.

Check through your old pile at home because even relatively common recent match programmes fetch between £3 and £5.

One of the most expensive programmes is for the match between Manchester United and Wolverhampton Wanderers on Saturday 8 February 1958. The match was never played because the Munich air disaster occurred two days previously – but although most of the programmes, already printed, were pulped, some remain. The programme is now worth over £5,000.

Newspapers

It's always worth keeping a scrapbook, or a folder, containing newspaper clippings – even in today's digital age. Although nowadays you can source an old football report on the Internet, there's still something special seeing it printed next to the rest of the day's news.

So if your team registers a memorable result – a European Cup win, a promotion or maybe even an everyday league match you'll always want to remember – it's worth making a wise investment the day after by purchasing a newspaper or two (or three). It might not seem like it now, but in a few years you'll love flicking back through those papers.

Old shirts

If you have any old replica shirts lying around and you don't wear them any more, don't throw them out. Wash them, fold them up and store them somewhere the moths won't get to them – because in 10 or 20 years they could be worth a small fortune.

England and Scotland replica shirts from the 1980s can cost between £80 and £200 – even more if they're limited-edition World Cup shirts with extra embroidery. Manchester United's home shirt from 1988 will set you back £150 and Liverpool's grey away shirt from the same year costs another £50 on top.

More recent shirts are much cheaper – partly because less time has passed, but mainly because fewer replica strips were produced in the old days. But it's still worth holding on to these shirts if you have the room to store them.

It's common practice to frame shirts and hang them on walls. If you do this – especially if the shirt has been signed by a famous player – get sun-resistant glass in the frame so the colours of the shirt don't fade over time.

Autographs

How much an autograph is worth depends not only whose it is – you obviously get more money for 1966 World Cup winning captain Bobby Moore than 1996 Millwall midfield stalwart Bobby Bowry – but also what it's on – a classic shirt is more collectable than a scrap of paper.

However, even combinations of famous players, dead or alive, and classic memorabilia may not fetch as much as you think: a lot of famous players have signed an awful lot of autographs over the years.

The best autographs, anyway, are personal, and have a dedicated message to you. Some things are worth more than money, especially if it's the player you idolised as a child.

Visiting Grounds

If you can visit a church or a cathedral to admire the architecture, why can't you do the same with a football ground? They either have around a century's worth of history behind them or are shining new monuments to the beautiful game.

Even if a game isn't on it's worth having a nose around a ground. You usually find something football-related in the immediate environs – a statue, a plaque, a memorial or even a famous pub or meeting room – and there's a good chance a bigger ground has a stadium tour or museum.

The 92 club

Some fans based in the United Kingdom try to visit as many of the league grounds in England, or in both England and Scotland, as they possibly can. This is known as 'doing the 92', or 'doing the 132' if they roam north of the border.

Some self-imposed guidelines exist for reaching the full total of 92 or 132:

- ✔ **You have to see a league match played**. Friendlies don't count. And you have to watch the entire game.

- ✔ **A league club must currently use the ground.** If you've visited a ground but the club has since been relegated from the league, it doesn't count.

- ✔ **Old grounds don't count**. If a club has moved to a new stadium and you've been to the old ground but not the new one, that's tough luck.

Of course, all of this is strictly unofficial, and just a bit of fun. And very expensive. And possibly insane.

Playing Computer Games

Football was badly served on home computers during the 1970s and 1980s because the game was too complex to render on machines with small chips and slow processors. Even so, games like Match Day on the ZX Spectrum, and International Soccer on the Commodore 64 are nevertheless remembered by older gamers with great affection.

In the early 1990s the advent of comparatively powerful gaming machines like the Sega Megadrive and the Super Nintendo allowed computer whizzes to develop more advanced football games. Soon enough there was an intense video-game rivalry to match anything Real Madrid and Barcelona could manage . . .

PES and FIFA

The two biggest selling football action games are Konami's Pro Evolution Soccer (PES) series and Electronic Arts' (or EA Sports') FIFA series. Both series have been going in some form or other since the early 1990s, on various platforms. Pro Evolution Soccer originated from a Konami series called International Superstar Soccer, and the EA Sports FIFA franchise has been updated annually since 1993.

Both PES and FIFA have huge fanbases. Perhaps typically for games about football, supporters of one game are fiercely loyal and can often dislike the other title. More rational gamers are able to enjoy both!

As a generalisation, gamers consider FIFA to be more of an arcade-style game and PES a more realistic 'simulation'. Over the years PES has enjoyed a better reputation within the gaming community, although recently FIFA has made up some critical ground. Both series are, however, considered classics of the genre in their own way.

Championship Manager and Football Manager

For years the most popular strategic football game was Championship Manager. Essentially a more in-depth version of fantasy football games, Championship Manager – first launched in 1993 – allowed you to take over any of the country's sides and try to lead them to glory over a series of seasons.

The game developed first into a huge cult hit, then a mainstream smash. A notoriously addictive game, managerial 'careers' on Championship Manager could cost players hours, days and sometimes many weeks of their lives. The chance to take a small club up from the lower leagues, wheel and deal, set tactics, keep the chairman and press happy and win first the league championship, then the European Cup, was too good for many to miss.

However, in 2006 the game's creators split from the production company. Since then the company has retained the name Championship Manager while writing a completely new game. Meanwhile the old game is now marketed under the name Football Manager.

On the whole, fans of the original Championship Manager express a preference for the new Football Manager. However, the new Championship Manager has built a new fanbase and is now popular in its own right.

Joining Supporters' Clubs

You may want to meet up with other fans, either supporters of the same club, or those with similar interests. Plenty of organisations exist that you can join.

Regional clubs

Most clubs around the country have at least one out-of-town supporters association in another town or city, even if it's just London (which has a supporters' branch for nearly every club in the land).

If you've moved away from the club, or simply support it from afar, it's worth joining up. Not only does the supporters' club hold social events, allowing you to meet other local like-minded folk, it arranges travel to and from games, and might even be guaranteed an allocation of tickets from the club.

A quick search on the Internet should throw something up. Failing that, make a phone call to the football club; someone there will be able to furnish you with the relevant information and contact details.

Supporters' federations

Just because you support the team it doesn't necessarily mean the people who own or run the club are worthy of your loyalty. If they're doing something that's annoying you – perhaps they have suddenly raised ticket prices dramatically, are running up large debts or are planning to sell a beloved player, sack a popular manager or move the club out of town – You can join a groups to get politically active.

Nearly every club in the country has a supporters' federation of some sort. At times of crisis members are often highly visible at home matches – perhaps they're handing out leaflets or stickers of support – and they'll be happy to answer any questions you have.

Failing that, the Football Supporters Federation (www.fsf.org.uk) may be your first port of call. They may be able to point you in the direction of your club's supporters' group, or at least advise you on what to do next in the event of a problem.

Owning Your Own Club

Of course, you could go the whole hog and run a football club yourself. Naturally, the only way this is usually possible is if you have a spare few zeroes on your bank balance. However, in 2007 the folk behind website MyFootballClub came up with a plan.

If enough enthusiasts committed to paying a £35 annual membership for a share in the site, the money would be pooled to buy a non-league club – with every shareholder having a vote to decide on all club matters, right down to transfers and team selection!

Over 50,000 people signed up, and in early 2008 the proceeds were used to buy Kent side Ebbsfleet United. The club went on to win that season's FA Trophy for the first time. However, it wasn't a non-stop fairytale: many shareholders, the initial buzz of involvement having worn off, failed to renew their annual membership, placing Ebbsfleet in severe financial trouble.

Similar projects are, however, underway all across the world, in Brazil, Spain, Japan and the US. Only time will tell whether the business model is viable – but whatever happens in the long run, the move represents another landmark in the long and varied history of football.

Something else will be along to surprise us in a minute . . .

Part V
The Part of Tens

'He's not been able to sneak out for
a drink since his wife took up football.'

In this part . . .

Every *For Dummies* book includes a Part of Tens, chapters that each contain ten or so interesting pieces of information. So who were the greatest players of all time? The best teams? The most absorbing matches? Not everyone is going to agree with my choices – that's half the fun of choosing – but one thing I think we can agree on is that the ones I've picked are straight from football's top drawer.

Chapter 19

Ten Great Players

Ask a hundred football fans to draw up a list of the ten greatest players of all time, and the chances are no two lists will be the same. So I don't expect you to agree with the following list . . . but you'll give me Pelé and Maradona, right?

Pelé

Edson Arantes do Nascimento can't remember how he got his nickname. He certainly didn't like it as a child, getting into fights at school with friends who used it. But Pelé would become the most famous nickname in the history of sport. He was barely out of school before, in 1956 and at 15 years of age, he had joined Santos, one of the biggest clubs in Brazil. A year later he was playing for the national side. And another year had passed when he became the most famous player on the planet at the 1958 World Cup in Sweden.

Brazil had failed to impress in their first two games of the tournament, so in the third match against the USSR gave first-ever caps to the 24-year-old winger Garrincha and the 17-year-old Pelé. In the first minute, Garrincha hit the post. In the second, Pelé did the same. And in the third, the trouble the pair were causing gave Vava room to score. Brazil won, allowing Pelé to take centre stage for the rest of the competition. He scored the winner against Wales in the quarter-final, a hat-trick against France in the semi and two goals in a 5-2 win over hosts Sweden in the final. Brazil had won their first World Cup. The youthful Pelé, crying with joy at the final whistle, was the nation's hero.

An instant world star, Pelé and Santos toured the world, becoming World Club champions in 1962 and 1963. The next two World Cups weren't so successful for Pelé: Brazil won in 1962, but Pelé was injured in the first round, while in 1966 the Portuguese kicked him out of the tournament with some vicious tackling. Pelé announced his retirement from international football, saying he 'didn't want to end his years as a cripple'. But he was persuaded to return in 1970, for his – and football's – greatest moment: Pelé scoring in the final as the attacking verve of Brazil put defensive football, in the shape of Italy, to the sword.

This time Pelé really did retire from the international game. By now commonly regarded as the greatest player who ever lived, Pelé's achievements were outstanding: he'd scored 1,281 goals in 1,363 matches, coined the phrase 'the beautiful game' and even caused warring Nigerian factions to call a two-day ceasefire so everyone in Lagos could watch him play in an exhibition match in 1969. But he wasn't finished yet. In 1975 he joined the New York Cosmos in the North American Soccer League, leading his team to the 1977 Soccer Bowl while almost single-handedly establishing football as a serious sport in the United States. He retired in 1977, since when he has become a roving ambassador for Brazil, the United Nations and UNICEF.

Diego Maradona

So is Pelé the greatest player to have ever kicked a ball? Or is that man El Diego? The debate is likely to rage on for all time, though one thing is certain: Diego Armando Maradona may or may not be a better player than his Brazilian rival, but he's certainly more of a flawed genius.

Like Pelé, Maradona broke onto the international scene early, winning his first cap for Argentina as a 16-year-old. He was expected to make the Argentinian squad for the 1978 World Cup, but was left out by César Luis Menotti. The decision angered Maradona at the time – he refused to speak to his national manager for nearly a year – but he calmed down enough by 1979 to win the World Youth Cup with his country.

The 1982 World Cup was a personal disaster for Maradona: the midfielder lost his rag in a second-round match against Brazil and received a red card for crunching his studs into the groin of Brazil's Batista. He was transferred from Boca Juniors to Barcelona that summer for a world-record £3 million, though the stay in Spain wasn't a success either and ended with a spectacular brawl in the 1984 cup final against Atlético Bilbao, Maradona swinging haymakers and executing karate kicks in revenge for having his ankle broken earlier that season by Andoni Goikoetxea: the Butcher of Bilbao.

Maradona's excesses put him in danger of becoming a wasted talent, but now his fortunes changed dramatically. He transferred to Napoli for another world-record fee – this time $5 million – in the summer of 1984, and led the southern Italian club to two Serie A titles plus a UEFA Cup. It was an amazing achievement: Napoli had never won a major title before Maradona's arrival, nor have they won one since his departure.

If that wasn't achievement enough, Maradona single-handedly led Argentina to the 1986 World Cup, inspiring an otherwise average team with some of the greatest personal displays in the World Cup's history. He scored an amazing mazy goal in the semi-final against Belgium, and set up the winner in the final against West Germany. But it's his performance in the quarter-final with England that defines him: a blatant handball goal punched past goalkeeper Peter Shilton to open the scoring, followed two minutes later by his second of the match, a hypnotic dribble from inside his own half, considered by many to be the best goal of all time.

Maradona led Argentina to a runners-up spot in the 1990 World Cup, but then his career went into sharp, self-inflicted decline. He was sent home from the 1994 World Cup for failing a drug test. His top-flight career effectively over, his personal life descended into a blizzard of cocaine, though he eventually kicked the habit. If Maradona wasn't the greatest of all time – a title he has a claim to – he was certainly the most controversial.

Franz Beckenbauer

'Der Kaiser', as the swaggering sweeper Franz Beckenbauer was known, was captain of the great Bayern Munich team of the late 1960s and 1970s, but it could all have been so very different. Young Franz was a fan of another Munich team, Munich 1860, and planned to join his favourite club in the early 1960s. However, at a youth tournament he was slapped in the face by an 1860 player, and decided to join rivals Bayern instead. It was a brave decision because Bayern were in the second-tier Regionalliga Süd at the time, but within a year of Beckenbauer's 1964 debut Bayern were promoted to the Bundesliga, and a glorious career began.

Beckenbauer was soon picked for West Germany and in 1966, as a 20-year-old, he helped his team reach the final of the World Cup, scoring four goals from midfield along the way. England beat the Germans in the final, but four years later Beckenbauer – by now bossing the game from central defence with a peerless arrogance born of his comfort on the ball – had his revenge, his long-range effort inspiring West Germany to come from two goals down in the quarter-final against the English to win 3-2. His luck ran out in the semi-final, though, as he was forced to play on with a dislocated shoulder as Italy won a classic, 4-3 in extra time.

The 1974 World Cup was his crowning achievement. Now captain of West Germany, the team struggled initially, losing a politically embarrassing match against the communists of East Germany in the group stage. Manager Helmut Schön suffered what amounted to a minor nervous breakdown, forcing Beckenbauer to assume full control of the team. Under Beckenbauer's auspices, West Germany were reborn, eventually beating the much-fancied Dutch team of Johan Cruyff in the final.

Meanwhile with Bayern Beckenbauer led his team to three consecutive European Cup wins between 1974 and 1976, four Bundesliga titles and four German Cups. In the late 1970s and early 1980s he spent four years in the United States with the New York Cosmos, winning a championship alongside Pelé, before coming back to Germany for a last hurrah – and a final Bundesliga title – with Hamburg.

As if that wasn't enough, Beckenbauer became only the second man after Brazil's Mário Zagallo to win the World Cup as player and manager, leading his country to victory in 1990. And never once, in all those years, did he appear to break sweat.

Johan Cruyff

Although Beckenbauer was the most decorated of the great 1970s' players, the Dutch legend Johan Cruyff – in his native language, Johannes Cruijff – remains the most celebrated. Dutch football in the 1960s and 1970s was famous for *Total Football* – the idea being that every player on the pitch could do each other's job, switching around as the game went on – and Cruyff was the concept's icon.

Cruyff was a centre-forward by trade, but as a Total Footballer he spent many a game on the left wing, or the right or deep in midfield, if he so chose. He broke into the Ajax team as a 17-year-old in 1964; within seven years the team had become the greatest in Europe, winning three consecutive European Cups between 1971 and 1973. After Ajax's third European Cup, Cruyff moved to Barcelona for a world-record $922,000, instantly inspiring a struggling mid-table side to a 5-0 win over their arch rivals Real Madrid, leading the Catalan side straight up the table to their first championship since 1960.

Meanwhile with Holland Cruyff was setting the 1974 World Cup alight, with some majestic displays. The tournament showcased his brazen individuality. A piece of skill down the wing against Sweden – sending the ball back between his legs with his instep and then changing direction in an instant to scamper off – became known as the *Cruyff Turn*. And while his team-mates all wore kit manufacturer Adidas's trademark three stripes on their shirts, Cruyff had a bespoke shirt with only two stripes – because he had a personal deal with Puma!

Holland failed at the final hurdle in the final that year, surprisingly losing to hosts West Germany, but in many eyes the Dutch were the moral victors of the championship. Cruyff refused to play in the 1978 finals, concentrating instead on his new career in the United States with the LA Aztecs and the New York Cosmos, before heading back to Holland where he won another couple of titles with Ajax. In a final flourish, after arguing with Ajax over the terms of an improved contract, he joined the Amsterdam club's arch rivals Feyenoord in a fit of pique and won one last title at the age of 37. Few players have been so individually determined as this Dutch master.

Garrincha

Garrincha – real name Manuel Francisco dos Santos – was born into extreme poverty in 1933. Childhood illness left his spine deformed and both of his legs badly bent; surgeons thought it would be a miracle if he was able to walk unaided, never mind play football. But despite his left leg curving outwards and his right leg inwards, he became Brazil's greatest-ever winger.

Known as Little Bird, he broke into the Botafogo team as an 18-year-old in 1953, scoring a hat-trick from the right wing on his debut. He helped his team win the Rio state championship in 1957, and won a place in the Brazil squad for the 1958 World Cup finals. After Brazil had played two poor games without Garrincha, manager Vicente Feola asked the team psychiatrist if the winger was ready to play for his country in their next game against the USSR. 'It would be a disaster,' came the reply, because the psychiatrist considered Garrincha to be a simple man with no interest whatsoever in tactics. Feola decided to play him anyway and Garrincha caused havoc, hitting the post within 60 seconds as Brazil beat the Russians easily.

Garrincha, along with Pelé, helped his team win the 1958 World Cup – and when Pelé was injured during the 1962 tournament it was down to Little Bird to inspire Brazil to victory alone. And he did, the explosive winger scoring two goals apiece in both quarter- and semi-finals.

The 1966 tournament was the beginning of the end for Garrincha. He scored a thumping free kick against Bulgaria, but Brazil's second match was his last in the famous yellow shirt. With a 3-1 defeat by Hungary, it was the only time he'd lost while playing for his country. Pelé was missing that day, maintaining the record that Brazil had never lost while the two players were in the team together. Naive and innocent away from the football field, Garrincha became a lost soul. He died in 1983, his final years lost to alcoholism and penury.

Zinedine Zidane

For a while it looked like Zinedine Zidane, despite his rich talent, wasn't going to make it to the very top. The midfield play-maker had already been anointed as the greatest French player of his generation by the time of Euro 96, that summer securing a move from Bordeaux to Italian giants Juventus, but the great tournament people expected him to have never materialised. Two Italian titles in the following two years with Juve gave him his first medals of note, but even those achievements were tempered by high-profile failures in the 1997 and 1998 Champions League finals.

But then it all suddenly took off. In the 1998 World Cup finals Zidane went from zero to hero – and how. Against Saudi Arabia he was sent off for stamping on an opponent. Suspended for two matches, France struggled and nearly went out. They hung on in there, though, and Zidane's return was the catalyst for an upturn in form that culminated in a 3-0 win in the final over Brazil, Zidane heading home the first two goals. As well as being the star player, Zidane – born to Algerian parents – became the symbol of France's multi-ethnic team. (The French projected 'Merci, Zizou!' onto the Champs Elysées the night of the 1998 win.)

Zidane's career then went stratospheric. He was the star of the tournament at Euro 2000, as France added that trophy to their roll of honour. He then moved to Real Madrid, becoming the world's most expensive footballer at £47 million – and he repaid the club by scoring the greatest-ever goal in a Champions League final: an unstoppable volley against Bayer Leverkusen in 2002.

Zidane had one last hurrah in 2006. Almost single-handedly, the 34-year-old dragged France to their second World Cup final with some performances that rolled back the years. After scoring the opener against Italy with the cheekiest of chipped penalties, he was sent off in extra time for headbutting Marco Materazzi in the chest. It was his last act on a football field, a bittersweet one that symbolised the yin and yang of his temperament: the most aesthetically beautiful player of the 1990s and 2000s, he was sent off 11 times for violent conduct.

Alfredo di Stéfano

No transfer has been as controversial, or changed the course of football history as much, as the one that brought the Argentinian midfielder Alfredo di Stéfano to Real Madrid in 1954. It was complicated, too, and steeped in political intrigue.

In 1949 di Stéfano was playing for River Plate of Buenos Aires when all professional players in Argentina went on strike. The clubs decided to use amateur players to complete the season, so the talented di Stéfano joined Bogota side Millonarios in a fit of pique. The problem was, the Colombian league was at the time outlawed by FIFA. So when Real Madrid bought di Stéfano from Millonarios in 1954, the world governing body pointed out that the player was still – in their eyes – owned by Boca Juniors. Who had just sold him to . . . you guessed it, Real's arch rivals, Barcelona.

The matter was eventually settled in the Spanish courts. In a decision heavily weighted in Real's favour – the Madrid club's biggest supporter being General Franco – the court ruled that Barcelona and Real should take turns with di Stéfano each season. Barca flounced off, leaving di Stéfano to move to Madrid, and the player went on to star in all five of Real's winning European Cup finals between 1956 and 1960.

A box-to-box midfielder who could defend as well as he could attack, many old-timers (including Bobby Charlton) would tell you he was better than both Pelé and Maradona. But despite playing for both Argentina and Spain, he never featured in the World Cup finals, a fact that counts against him in some eyes to this day.

Ferenc Puskás

When Hungary visited Wembley in 1953 to play England, one of the home side pointed to a small, slightly podgy inside-left in a red Hungarian shirt during the warm up. 'Look at that little fat chap!' laughed the unidentified English international. 'We'll murder this lot!' Ninety minutes later, England had been thrashed 6-3, their first defeat at Wembley by a side from outside Britain. And, of course, the little fat chap – Ferenc Puskás – was the architect of Hungary's triumph, one that would go down in history as one of the most famous matches of all time.

Puskás gave the game its defining moment, too, pulling a ball back with the sole of his boot, sending England captain Billy Wright sliding hysterically off the pitch while his tormentor simply changed feet and hammered the ball into the roof of the net from a tight angle. In one of the most famous lines in the history of football journalism, the *Times* newspaper described Wright as 'like a fire engine speeding off to the wrong fire'.

Hungary had already won the 1952 Olympics, Puskás the star of a team that would become known as the Magical Magyars. They followed up their 6-3 win in England with a 7-1 victory over the same opposition in Budapest, and were huge favourites to win the 1954 World Cup. But Puskás was injured as Hungary beat West Germany 8-3 in a group game, and his tournament went from bad to worse. First, after Hungary beat Brazil in the quarter-final, an opponent accused the non-playing Puskás of smashing a bottle over his head during a dressing-room brawl between the two teams. Then, returning from injury in the final against the rejuvenated West Germans, he scored the opening goal only to see his team lose 3-2. Even then, the hobbling Puskás had 'scored' an equaliser in the dying seconds only to see the ref rule it out for a very dubious offside.

The Hungarians had been denied the prize the world had thought was theirs for the taking, but Puskás still had personal glory, and his greatest triumphs, to come. He defected from the east after the 1956 Hungarian revolution (at one point he was reported to have been killed in fighting on the streets of Budapest) and after serving a suspension ordered by FIFA for absconding from his former club side Honvéd, eventually signed with Real Madrid. He formed an instant understanding with Alfredo di Stefano, one which peaked in the famous 7-3 win over Eintracht Frankfurt in the 1960 European Cup final, Puskás scoring four times (a feat unequalled to this day). Puskás went on to play for Spain – in those days you could switch countries after a certain period of residency – but he never reached the heights of his Hungarian pomp when he scored an amazing 83 goals in 84 matches.

George Best

The greatest British player of all time, George Best was the first player in Europe – and arguably the world – to become a celebrity as well as a football star. This would be both the making of him, and his ruination.

Best broke into the Manchester United team at the age of 17 in 1963, and by the time he'd completed his first full season he'd won the league title. In 1966 he scored two goals in a European Cup quarter-final tie with Benfica, the press in Lisbon giving him the nickname El Beatle thanks to his pretty-boy looks and moptop hair.

Manchester United couldn't get past the semi-finals of the European Cup that season, but won the league again in 1966/67 and reached the final of the 1968 European Cup. Best proved to be the star of the show, walking in what was effectively the decisive goal in a 4-1 win over Benfica.

Having won the European Cup, many older players at Manchester United felt their job was done. Best, however, was only 22, and he became frustrated and disillusioned as the club drifted. His glitzy personal life didn't help: he began drinking heavily and spending more time in nightclubs with various models and Miss Worlds than on the training pitch. On New Year's Day 1974 an overweight Best played his last game for the club at Queens Park Rangers. Papers reported that he was 'a sad parody' of the player he'd once been. Come the end of the season, Best was turning out for non-league Dunstable Town while United were amazingly relegated. He was still only 27.

Best's later career was a slow decline: an entertaining if directionless stint at Second Division Fulham, followed by spells in the United States with the Tampa Bay Rowdies, Scotland with Hibernian and back in England with Bournemouth. Best's high living eventually caught up with him, first as he went to jail in 1986 for drink driving and then tragically in 2005 when, despite a liver transplant, the booze killed him. Few players wasted their talent like Bestie – but then precious few players have had talent like his to throw away.

Gerd Müller

Without question, the Bayern Munich and West Germany striker Gerd Müller is the least spectacular player on this list of ten, and probably the least technically talented. That, however, matters little – because Müller was almost certainly the most lethal goal-scorer in the history of the sport.

To quote the German football writer Uli Hesse-Lichtenberger, 'Müller scored with his shin, his knee and his backside, and sometimes even with his feet . . . he scored in cup games against lowly opposition and on the world stage marked by the best defenders there were.' And sure enough, his record stands up to scrutiny: in 427 league games he scored 365 goals. He scored 62 goals in 68 German Cup games, netted 66 times in 72 club appearances in Europe and in 62 appearances for the West German national team he scored an unbelievable 68 times.

'I am not putting that little elephant in among my string of thoroughbreds,' the Bayern Munich coach Zlatko ⬚ajkovski said upon first clapping eyes on Müller in 1964, when the club was still in the regional leagues. But he eventually relented and Müller's goals took Bayern first to promotion, then the German Cup and then the European Cup Winners' Cup within three seasons. Two more seasons passed and Bayern won their first-ever Bundesliga title. Then in 1974 came the club's first European Cup.

In 1974 Müller retired from international football – at the very top. His final meaningful act in a German shirt was to twist on the spot and hook home the winning goal in the World Cup final. Müller went on to win two more European Cups with Bayern before enjoying a stint in the United States with the Fort Lauderdale Strikers. Since his retirement in 1982, nobody's scored goals with such intense regularity. But then again, nobody did before Müller started out either.

Chapter 20

The Ten Greatest Teams of All Time

*T*hroughout history hundreds and hundreds of teams have made their mark on the game. Here are some of the greatest, but when you can only pick ten, some famous teams miss out. So, with a heavy heart, I've no room some truly great sides. Still, these guys aren't half bad . . .

Preston North End (1881–1890)

In 1881 a Preston cotton mill administrator called William Sudell joined the board of a newly founded local football team, Preston North End, and soon became the team manager. Between them, club and manager spent the rest of the decade making headlines and shaping the future of a sport still in its infancy.

His first job was to assemble a team. Most clubs at the time picked their side from local lads, but Sudell decided that wasn't the best way to go. Noting that the Scottish national team were giving their English counterparts a regular going-over – between 1878 and 1882, Scotland recorded 5-1, 6-1 and 7-2 victories against the Auld Enemy – he decided to fill his team with Scots. Problem was, how to entice them down to Preston? Football was still an amateur sport at the time – professionalism was outlawed – so paying them was out of the question. Sudell simply circumvented this problem by giving them spurious 'jobs' at his mill.

This decision inadvertently revolutionised the game. In 1884 the Football Association disqualified the side from the FA Cup, accusing Preston of professionalism. Sudell simply shrugged his shoulders and organised a boycott, telling the FA that if professionalism wasn't legalised, Preston and a coalition of powerful Lancashire clubs would form their own football association. The FA crumbled, and amateurism was gone for ever.

Preston became the most powerful side in the country. In 1887/88, they won 42 out of 43 games they played, winning one FA Cup tie 26-0 (against Hyde, still an English record). However, they failed in the one match that really mattered. At the FA Cup final, Preston requested their team be photographed with the trophy – before the match had started! 'Hadn't you better win it first?' the referee (perhaps apocryphally) replied. West Bromwich Albion won 2-1.

But the season after saw Preston remembered as one of the most famous sides of all time. Thanks to the goalscoring exploits of Fred Dewhurst, Jimmy Ross and John Goodall – 54 goals between them in 27 matches – they won the first-ever Football League championship, going the entire season unbeaten. They also won the FA Cup, a perfect season that earned them the sobriquet The Invincibles.

The glory days didn't last much longer. Preston won the league again the following year, but have yet to win it since. Meanwhile, four years later Sudell was jailed for embezzling £5,000 from his mill owners to fund Preston's team-building.

Austria (1931–1934)

Austria weren't much of a side at the start of the century – their record defeat was an 11-1 thumping at home by England in 1908 – but all that changed in the 1920s when the team was managed by Hugo Meisl, an administrator at the Austrian FA. Meisl was a student of the international game, and particularly liked the Scottish passing style (many teams of the era were either dribbling the ball or hoofing it long).

Scotland had famously trounced England 5-1 in 1928 (they went down in history as The Wembley Wizards) but they in turn were thrashed by Austria, who announced themselves on the world stage with a 5-0 win in 1931. The team were built around the striking skills of Matthias Sindelar – known as Der Papierene (The Paper Man) – and quickly became the number one side in the world. Their quicksilver all-out attack proved too much for Germany (5-0 and 6-0), Switzerland (2-0 and 8-1), Italy (2-1 and 4-2) and Hungary (8-2 and 5-2).

Austria were hot favourites to win the 1934 World Cup, especially as they could now also boast the goals of Josef Bican (who in his career scored at least 805 times in official matches, more than any other player in the history of the sport). But in the semi-final a thuggish Italian side viciously set upon them and they lost 1-0 when the referee, said to have been threatened by the dictator Benito Mussolini, turned a blind eye when keeper Peter Platzer was bundled illegally into the goal while holding the ball.

Nevertheless, it was Austria, not eventual world champions Italy, who were remembered fondly: known forevermore as Wunderteam, a title that needs no translation.

Torino (1943–1949)

Few teams, if any, have dominated their domestic scene like the Torino side of the mid-to-late 1940s did in Italy. Known as Il Grande Torino, they won five Serie A championships in a row between 1943 and 1949 – a record the club still holds jointly to this day with their Turin city rivals Juventus – and would surely have won more had the league not been suspended for two years towards the end of the Second World War. During those seasons they scored 483 goals, while letting in only 165.

The team's star player was their captain Valentino Mazzola, a powerful attacking midfielder who once scored 29 goals from midfield in a single season – but they were far from a one-man team. In May 1947, 10 out of the 11 players who made up the Italian national side against Hungary were from Il Grande Torino – and coach Vittorio Pozzo only left out goalkeeper Eusebio Castigliano because he thought it would demotivate players all around the country if Italy was 100 per cent Torino!

Il Grande Torino's attacking style meant Italy – at the time the reigning world champions – were favourites to win the 1950 World Cup, retaining the trophy they'd won before the war in 1934 and 1938. But tragedy struck. Flying back from a friendly in Portugal on 4 May 1949, the team's plane hit a basilica standing on a hill in Superga, near Turin, as it came in to land under heavy fog. The entire team was killed instantly.

Torino were awarded that year's championship – which they were on the verge of winning anyway – but the club didn't win another until 1976. Italy, meanwhile, somewhat understandably decided to travel to the 1950 World Cup in Brazil by boat, instead of plane. The trip took two weeks and, unable to train, an unfit team were knocked out after their very first match.

Hungary (1950–1954)

The countries from the Eastern Bloc had an added advantage in the Olympic Games during the Cold War: under communism, all the top players were technically amateur, and so unlike Western professionals were eligible to compete in the Games. That, however, doesn't wholly explain Hungary's gold medal win in 1952, because the team – with its crown jewel Ferenc Puskás up front alongside the equally prolific Sandor Kocsis – were exceptional, and had already gone two years unbeaten in friendlies.

Hungary's performance at the 1952 Olympics earned them an invitation to a prestigious friendly against England, seen as one of the top teams in the world. They played the match in November 1953 and the Hungarians – now three years into an unbeaten run and with deep-lying forward Nándor Hidegkuti now added to the mix – put England to the sword, thrashing them 6-3 at Wembley. At a return match in Budapest the following February they humiliated England even further, winning 7-1.

Hungary were short-priced favourites for the World Cup, and won their group matches against South Korea and West Germany 9-0 and 8-3. They then beat the 1950 runners up, Brazil, 4-2 in the quarter-finals, before repeating the same score in the semis to knock out reigning champions Uruguay. But Puskás had been injured, and though he played (and scored) in the final against a rejuvenated West Germany, Hungary's now four-year unbeaten run came to a juddering halt in the biggest game of all. The team threw away a 2-0 lead to lose 3-2, although the ref controversially ruled out a last-minute equaliser.

Hungary went on another long unbeaten run of 18 matches, until losing again to Turkey in 1956, but the team was beginning to show its age. Then in 1956 came the Hungarian revolution, and with fighting raging on the streets of Budapest many players defected to the west. The team had failed to win the World Cup expected of it, but would be forever known as *Aranycsapat* – Hungarian for The Golden Team.

Real Madrid (1955–1960)

Real Madrid had only won the Spanish league twice when goalscoring midfielder Alfredo di Stéfano and flying winger Francisco Gento signed for the club in 1953. And those two championships were back in the 1930s. But within a year, the pair had helped Madrid win their first title for 21 years, sparking an unprecedented run of success. By the end of the decade Real Madrid was, by a long chalk, the biggest club in the world.

The team retained their championship in 1955 and entered into the first-ever European Cup. They reached the final, where they faced Reims of France. Despite falling 2-0 down in ten minutes, Madrid landed the cup, winning 4-3 after a di Stéfano-inspired comeback. Adding Reims' star player Raymond Kopa to their team, Madrid went on to win the next four European Cups as well. They beat Fiorentina in 1957, Milan in 1958 and Reims again in 1959. At that point Kopa returned to France, but by now his creative genius had been eclipsed by an even greater talent.

Ferenc Puskás had defected from Hungary in 1956, receiving a ban from UEFA at the request of his former club, Honvéd of Budapest. Madrid showed an interest in signing him, and used their political influence – they were supported by Generalissimo Franco – to persuade UEFA to lift the ban. Puskás joined, and went on to score 240 times in 260 matches, a phenomenal record.

The team had one last European Cup left in them – which they won in the 1960 final, still considered by many to be the greatest of all time. Puskás scored four, di Stéfano three, as they murdered Eintracht Frankfurt 7-3. It was di Stéfano's crowning glory: all in all he won five European Cups, scoring 49 goals in the process. Puskás scored another hat-trick in the 1962 final, though Real Madrid lost 5-3 to Benfica. Madrid didn't win another European Cup until 1966 – when Gento, the only survivor of the great side of the 1950s, picked up his sixth title.

Celtic (1967)

When Jock Stein took over as Celtic manager in 1965, the famous Glasgow club were suffering a terrible slump. They hadn't won a league title for 11 years, and nothing whatsoever since 1957. The transformation Stein effected on Celtic was both immediate and outstanding. Within weeks of his arrival, Stein led Celtic to the 1965 Scottish Cup, their first trophy for eight seasons. The following year saw Celtic win their first championship since 1954. And then, in 1966/67, came the greatest season in the club's history.

The team – which included captain and central defender Billy McNeill, talented yet hard-working midfield duo Bertie Auld and Bobby Murdoch, and tricky winger Jimmy 'Jinky' Johnstone – won every single competition they entered that year. They won the Scottish League, the Scottish Cup, the Scottish League Cup and even the Glasgow Cup – but it was in Europe where they tasted their greatest success.

Celtic reached the European Cup final in Lisbon, but weren't expected to beat Internazionale of Milan, who had won the trophy in 1964 and 1965 with a defensive brand of football called *catenaccio* (literally 'door bolt'). Stein's side, on the other hand, were swashbuckling and adventurous. Which was just as well, because they went 1-0 down early in the game. But Inter shut up shop, allowing Celtic to launch wave after wave of attack, turning the game around in the second half to win 2-1. Attack had beaten defence, and Celtic became the first-ever British team to win the biggest club prize of all, the team earning the epithet *The Lisbon Lions*. Amazingly, every single player of the side was born within a 48-km (30-mile) radius of Glasgow.

Brazil (1970)

The Brazilian side that won the 1970 World Cup is probably the most famous, and certainly the most revered, international team of all time. Brazil had won the 1958 and 1962 World Cups playing some exciting attacking football, but had literally been kicked out of the 1966 finals in England, crashing out in the first round after some rough treatment by their opponents. Pelé was carried off the pitch against Portugal that year, vowing to retire from international football. 'I do not want to end my life as a cripple,' he announced afterwards. It appeared the new cynical and defensive style of football had triumphed over Brazil's carefree approach.

Brazil's cause – a commitment to attack and free-flowing football – looked even more lost in 1968, when West Germany, Czechoslovakia, Mexico (twice) and Paraguay all beat them. For a country on top of the world a mere six years earlier, five defeats in a calendar year was a catastrophe. But then, under new manager João Saldanha, and then his replacement Mário Zagallo, Brazil threw caution to the wind with the most attack-minded front line of all time – Pelé, Jairzinho, Tostao, Rivelino and Gerson – and the decision paid rich dividends.

Brazil won all of their qualifiers for the 1970 World Cup and then matched the feat in the finals themselves, winning all six matches. They scored 19 goals while doing so, beating reigning world champions England, the dangerous Uruguayans and the super-defensive Italians in the final.

But despite those 19 goals, it is perhaps two missed chances that the side is best remembered for. Against Czechoslovakia, Pelé was inches away from scoring from inside his own half, while against Uruguay he famously let the ball drift past one side of an advancing keeper while running round his other side then nearly whipping the ball into the empty net from an acute angle. Brazilians have since longed for a side to play a similar brand of carefree football, but apart from their 1982 vintage of Zico, Falcão and Socrates, none have come close.

Netherlands (1974–1978)

Holland so very nearly failed to reach the 1974 World Cup finals. Had the ref not erroneously ruled out a perfectly good goal by Belgium for a non-existent offside, the Dutch side that invented Total Football would never have made it to the greatest stage of all. But the gods smiled on them, and the team amazed the world with a totally new way of playing.

The principle behind Total Football was simple enough: any of the players on the pitch, excluding the goalkeeper, could play in any position during the match, moving around as they saw fit. So, for example, if the left back decided to scamper up the wing, the central defender may drop into the vacant position. In turn, the striker might temporarily play in central defence!

But you needed great players to be able to do this – and Holland had them in abundance. Star man was winger-come-striker Johan Cruyff, who had helped Ajax of Amsterdam win three European Cups in a row between 1971 and 1973. He was ably assisted by goalscoring midfielders Johan Neeskens and Johnny Rep, defensive lynchpin Arie Haan, striker Rob Rensenbrink and ball-playing defender Ruud Krol.

The side ripped through the world's best in the 1974 finals, humiliating Argentina 4-0 and beating reigning world champions Brazil. But they froze in the final against West Germany, despite taking a 1-0 lead right at the start without their opponents even touching the ball. Nevertheless, they are remembered as one of the all-time classic sides.

Holland reached the final again in 1978, despite Cruyff having retired from international football. They were the width of a post away from beating hosts Argentina and winning the trophy, Rensenbrink rolling the ball onto the woodwork in the dying seconds of normal time with the scores 1-1. The ball bounced clear and Argentina won in extra time.

Milan (1987–1994)

One of Italy's biggest clubs, Milan were at the lowest point in their history during the early 1980s. Implicated in a match-fixing scandal, the club were demoted to Serie B – the Italian second division – for the very first time in their history. If that wasn't shameful enough for the proud giants, after winning immediate promotion, they were relegated again – though this time it was simply because the team wasn't good enough. Milan bounced straight back to the top flight again but were drifting aimlessly – and then in 1986 local businessman Silvio Berlusconi bought the club.

Berlusconi's first act was to employ little-known Parma coach Arrigo Sacchi, whose Serie B side had knocked Milan out of the 1986 Coppa Italia. Sacchi bought some rising Italian stars – midfielders Roberto Donadoni and Carlo Ancelotti – and more importantly three Dutch players in Ruud Gullit, Marco van Basten and Frank Rijkaard. The team won the Italian championship in 1988 and then the European Cup in 1989, beating Real Madrid 5-0 in the second leg of the semi-final, then Steaua Bucharest 4-0 in the final. They retained the trophy a year later with a 1-0 win over Sven-Göran Eriksson's Benfica.

But they were about to hit even greater heights. Sacchi took over the Italian national team, making way for Fabio Capello. Under Capello, Milan won three titles in succession in the early 1990s, winning the 1991/92 title without losing a single game. By now attack was less important than defence. Where once the Dutch players had been the stars, now it was defenders Franco Baresi, Paolo Maldini and Alessandro Costacurta who took centre stage: in the 1993/94 title-winning season they only scored 36 goals in 34 games!

Barcelona (2009)

While Real Madrid won the first five European Cups, between 1956 and 1960, and added another in 1966, their arch rivals Barcelona sat jealously on the sidelines. It wasn't until 1992 that the Catalan giants finally landed the biggest club trophy of all. The side that broke Barca's duck went down in history as The Dream Team. It featured world-famous names such as striker Hristo Stoichkov, winger Michael Laudrup and the man who scored the winning goal against Sampdoria in the final, defender Ronald Koeman – but the fans' favourite was defensive midfielder Pep Guardiola, a local boy made good.

Guardiola returned as manager in the summer of 2008, and had an immediate impact on the club. He got rid of big-name attacking players who'd helped Barcelona win a second European Cup in 2006 – and placed his faith in the attacking triumvirate of Samuel Eto'o, Thierry Henry and Lionel Messi. With Andrés Iniesta pulling the strings in midfield, and new signings Gerard Pique and Daniel Alves shoring up the defence, Barcelona embarked on the greatest season in their history.

They won the Spanish championship with ease, and added the Spanish Cup, securing a domestic double. And after reaching the Champions League final with a spectacular and dramatic injury-time winner by Iniesta against Chelsea, they added the greatest prize in Europe to their season tally, rolling Manchester United over in the final.

They had become the first-ever Spanish side to win a Treble – joining an elite band of clubs who've won a domestic league-and-cup double as well as the European Cup in the same season.

Chapter 21

Ten Great Matches

*J*ust about anything can make a match live long in the memory: a last-minute goal, a dramatic turnaround, a point-blank save, even the odd controversial refereeing decision. These time-honoured classics tick all the boxes . . .

Arbroath 36, Bon Accord 0 (Scottish Cup, 1885)

Even now, over a century later, Saturday, 12 September 1885 stands as without question the most amazing – and as you'll see, plain odd – day in the history of Association Football. It was the first round of the Scottish Cup, and Dundee Harp recorded a quite outstanding result in their tie against Aberdeen Rovers: they won 35-0! The referee was sure the actual score was 37-0, but admitted he might have lost count somewhere along the line. Anyway, the Dundee Harp club secretary sportingly assured him his side had 'only' scored 35 goals – and anyway, it was clearly a world-record score, so what difference did an extra couple make? The Scottish FA recorded Dundee Harp's win.

It was an especially good result for Harp defender Tom O'Kane, who'd been playing his first game for the club since moving from Arbroath. After the match he sent a telegram to his old team-mates, informing them of Harp's world-record feat. O'Kane received an immediate reply, which said Arbroath had gone one better: a 36-0 win in the Cup against another gaggle of Aberdonian halfwits, Bon Accord. O'Kane considered the reply to be a hilarious joke.

He wasn't laughing later, though. Still a resident of Arbroath, he returned home to find that his old side had indeed won 36-0, their 18-year-old striker having scored 13 goals (a record that has since been equalled, but never beaten). The morning after, O'Kane ran the 18 miles to Dundee to break the bad news to his new club: it was Arbroath who held the world-record score, not Dundee Harp. The club secretary immediately regretted sportingly chalking off those two goals – although it later transpired Arbroath had seen another *seven* goals disallowed for dubious offside decisions, so justice was probably done.

Brazil 1, Uruguay 2 (World Cup, 1950)

The 1950 World Cup was the only staging of the tournament not to have a final. Instead, there was a final pool, a mini-league containing four teams – Spain, Sweden, Uruguay and hosts Brazil – who all played each other, the table-toppers taking the pot. But as it turned out, the final match in the pool was effectively the 'final' to all intents and purposes. To secure the title Brazil, who'd won their first two matches (scoring 13 goals in doing so!), only had to draw with Uruguay, who'd struggled to win one and draw the other. The Uruguayans could themselves still take the trophy home if they won, but few gave them a chance of beating the pre-tournament favourites on their own patch.

Nobody in Brazil did, anyway. On the morning of the match, one Brazilian newspaper printed a photograph of their national team on the front page, with the headline 'CHAMPIONS!'. The mayor of Rio, not to be outdone, took to the pitch before kick-off and gave a congratulatory address: 'You who in less than a few hours will be hailed as champions by millions of compatriots! You who will overcome any other competitor! You who I already salute as victors!' Meanwhile the Brazilian FA minted personally engraved gold medals for each squad member and commissioned a celebratory samba to be performed at the final whistle.

All seemed to be going to plan. Brazil dominated the first half, though they failed to score. Just after the restart Friaca put the hosts one up. With Uruguay having been non-existent as an attacking force up until then and now needing two goals to win, the game looked up. But with a world-record crowd of over 200,000 in the Maracanã, Brazil became jittery. And when Juan Schiaffino equalised midway through the second half, the home fans became nervous. It was too much for their team, who crumbled with 11 minutes to go, the full-back Bigode allowing Alcide Ghiggia to skate past him and beat the despairing keeper Moacyr Barbosa at his near post. At the final whistle the crowd fell into almost total silence. FIFA bigwig Jules Rimet handed over the trophy that bore his name and then observed that the atmosphere was 'morbid' and 'too difficult to bear'.

Brazil played that day in their first-choice white shirts for the very final time; now considered unlucky, they never played in white again and within three years had adopted their trademark yellow, green and blue kit.

England 3, Hungary 6 (Friendly, 1953)

People often cite this game as the first time a non-British team beat the English national side on home soil. But that's not actually true: four years earlier the Republic of Ireland beat England 2-0 in a friendly at Everton's Goodison Park ground. Even so, you can't underestimate the cataclysmic effect of Hungary's famous thrashing of England in 1953.

Hungary had won the 1952 Olympic title, bursting onto the international scene with a whole new way of playing. At the time teams played with five men up front, with the central striker furthest upfield, leading the line. Hungary dispensed with that idea, allowing their nominal centre-forward, Nándor Hidegkuti, to drop deep into space. England, stuck in a tactical rut, found Hidegkuti's movement impossible to counter.

Before the start of the game English players took one look at their opponents – the Hungarians were going through a complex warming-up routine, they wore lightweight boots and one of their forwards, Ferenc Puskás, was slightly over-weight – and blithely told each other they'd steamroller a team who 'didn't even have proper kit' and fielded 'a little fat chap'. They were soon disabused of this notion.

Within a minute Hidegkuti – whom nobody had bothered to follow into the space behind the front men – went on a run and walloped in Hungary's first. England equalised but Hidegkuti soon added a second, before Puskás scored a third, sending the England captain sliding off the field with an embarrassed look on his face as he did so. After 63 minutes Hungary had scored six times to England's two, and they eased off the gas. Alf Ramsey scored a consolation penalty right at the death, but England's humiliation had long been complete.

Charlton Athletic 7, Huddersfield Town 6 (English Second Division, 1957)

On the opening day of the 1957/58 English Second Division season, Huddersfield found themselves 3-0 down at half-time at home to Charlton Athletic. In an inspired second half they replied with three goals of their own to force a draw. Normally, that performance would have been enough to earn the title Comeback of the Season. But in the return match Charlton turned the tables on Huddersfield in the most amazing manner imaginable.

It was a freezing day at Charlton's Valley ground, four days before Christmas, and there wasn't much cheer for the home side's captain Derek Ufton, who dislocated his shoulder after 17 minutes and had to leave the field of play.

In those days substitutes didn't exist, so Charlton had to play the majority of the game with ten men. Defeat looked inevitable – especially when Huddersfield made it two before half-time.

During the interval Charlton winger Johnny Summers' favourite boots, which he'd been wearing for years, finally fell to pieces. Reluctantly, he pulled on a brand-new pair, trotted back out and pulled a goal back just after the start of the second half, but the effort looked futile because Huddersfield ran in three more to go 5-1 up with just under 30 minutes to play.

It was then that Summers' new boots began to work their comic-strip magic. Summers whipped in a cross for Johnny Ryan to score, then scored Charlton's third himself a minute later. On 73 minutes he completed his hat-trick, before levelling the scores at 5-5 with his fourth of the match on 78 minutes – then putting his team ahead on 81 minutes with his *fifth* of the game: 6-5! Huddersfield threatened to ruin the story with an equaliser on 86 minutes, but Summers wouldn't be denied, sending over another peach of a cross for Ryan to score the winner in injury time.

Magic boots? Well, probably not. Though consider this: Summers was infamous for only being able to play with his left foot, and he scored all five of his goals here with his right!

Real Madrid 7, Eintracht Frankfurt 3 (European Cup, 1960)

For a while it looked like Glasgow belonged to Eintracht Frankfurt in the spring of 1960. First they beat Rangers 6-3 at Ibrox in the second leg of their European Cup semi-final, completing a 12-4 aggregate win over the Glaswegian giants. The victory saw them return to Glasgow for the final, held at Hampden Park, where they played reigning European champions Real Madrid. After 18 minutes of the match, having looked thoroughly composed, Frankfurt went a goal ahead through Richard Kress. And then the Clydeside sky fell in on them.

Madrid had won all four European Cups held to date, and were about to make it five in a row with a display that would go down in history as the team's signature performance – and perhaps the best of all time. A huge Hampden crowd of 135,000 – containing a young Alex Ferguson – oohed and aahed as Francisco Gento tore down the left wing time and again at breathtaking speed, while Alfredo di Stefano began to dictate play from the centre of the park. Di Stefano scored twice in three minutes to put Real ahead before they reached the half-hour mark, and then Ferenc Puskás took over. He added Real's third just before half-time, walloping an unstoppable shot into the roof of the net from an impossible angle, and scored two more to complete his hat-trick before the hour.

Puskás added Real's sixth and his personal fourth before a stunning team effort from Real sandwiched two late Erwin Stein consolation goals, di Stefano finishing a flowing five-pass move straight from the restart. On the final whistle Puskás picked the ball up. His four goals meant it was his, though he didn't keep it, shoving it into Stein's chest after the German striker had the audacity to pester him for the souvenir. Stein may have made off with the ball but Puskás took the plaudits – he's still the only player to score four in a European Cup final.

England 4, West Germany 2 (World Cup, 1966)

Alf Ramsey had promised from the outset that England would 'most certainly' win the World Cup. 'I'm certain of success,' he said on the eve of the tournament, though he did add one caveat: 'We have deficiencies, and one is finishing.' Just a minor problem, then – but one that the team would solve in spectacular fashion by the end of the tournament.

Star striker Jimmy Greaves hadn't found the net in the group games, and what was worse, his leg had been badly cut open against the French. He was to be out for the quarter-final.

Geoff Hurst took Greaves's place and seized his opportunity, scoring the winner against Argentina then setting up the winner in the semi-final against Portugal. Greaves had recovered by the morning of the final, but in the days before substitutes the manager didn't name him for the team. Hurst, controversially, kept his place.

Ramsey's choice of Hurst over Greaves wasn't the final controversial decision of the day, either. The 1966 World Cup final between England and West Germany was the most contentious of all time. The Germans went ahead early on through Helmut Haller, only for Hurst to justify his selection with an equaliser. With 12 minutes to go Martin Peters poked home what looked like the winner – until Wolfgang Weber scrambled a last-gasp equaliser for West Germany.

'You've won it once, now go and win it again,' Ramsey told his men before extra time. And win it they did, though they needed a large slice of luck when Hurst's shot came down off the crossbar and landed on the line. It wasn't a goal, but the Azerbaijani linesman gave it anyway. Hurst became the only man to complete a hat-trick in a World Cup final in the dying seconds. BBC commentator Kenneth Wolstenholme soundtracked the goal with the immortal words: 'They think it's all over – it is now!'

Manchester United 4, Benfica 1 (European Cup, 1968)

This was the happy ending to the most bittersweet of footballing odysseys. Manchester United had been the first English team to compete in Europe, manager Matt Busby ignoring a Football League diktat ordering United not to play in the new European Cup, a trophy the small-minded bureaucrats considered beneath English clubs. His young side reached the semi-finals that year, 1956/57, and were expected to go all the way the following season. Fate intervened, though, and tragically so: on February 6 1958 a plane transporting the 'Busby Babes', as they were known, back home after their quarter-final win against Red Star Belgrade crashed on a snowy Munich runway. Seven of the team were immediately killed and their star man Duncan Edwards died in hospital 15 days later. Red Star asked UEFA to name United as 'Honorary Champions' that year, but they denied the request.

Busby himself was at death's door for a while but pulled through and within seven years had built his second great side. That team, built around George Best, Scottish striker Denis Law and Munich survivor Bobby Charlton, reached the 1968 European Cup final where they faced Euesbio's Benfica. Law missed the final with a knee injury, but Best and Charlton provided the decisive blows.

After a goal-less first half, Charlton opened the scoring with a very rare header. Benfica equalised with 12 minutes to go through Jaime Graça. Eusebio was clean through right at the death and arrowed a shot goalwards, but United keeper Alex Stepney somehow smothered it. Eusebio could do nothing but stand and applaud Stepney for his amazing save.

The match went into extra time, and within eight minutes United had sewn it up. First Best scored what was effectively the winner by rounding the Benfica keeper and walking the ball into the net. The 19-year-old Brian Kidd – on his birthday – added another, before Charlton scored his second and United's fourth. Busby and Charlton had reached their holy grail ten seasons after the Busby Babes had perished.

Brazil 4, Italy 1 (World Cup, 1970)

Many consider the Brazilian side that won the 1970 World Cup to be the greatest ever in the history of the game, boasting the attacking quintet of Pelé, Gerson, Tostão, Rivelino and Jairzinho. So amazing is this side's story that even their qualifying campaign was the stuff of legend.

Brazil had been struggling in 1968 and were under intense pressure from the media. So to shut the newspapers up the Brazilian FA appointed a journalist as manager! João Saldanha was an instant success, gathering what would become the 1970 side together and winning all six of their qualifiers, scoring 23 goals along the way.

Saldanha didn't take the team to the finals in Mexico, though – having threatened a newspaper critic with a loaded gun! He was replaced by Mario Zagallo, who led the team to the ultimate glory. In Mexico, Brazil won every game; the only team who didn't let in at least three goals were reigning champions England, who conceded a solitary effort in a 1-0 defeat.

Brazil faced Italy in the final, their attacking verve up against the meanest defence in world football. Under a scorching sun, the Brazilians danced through the Italian defence time and again; their *pièce de résistance* was captain Carlos Alberto's thrashing strike to seal a 4-1 win. Pelé had opened the scoring, marking his last international with a goal, while Jairzinho became the only man to score in every game of the finals.

Nigeria 3, Argentina 2 (Olympics, 1996)

Nigeria claimed Africa's first prize, at the 1996 Atlanta Olympics' football tournament. Their star man was Kanu, who'd won the 1995 Champions League with Ajax and was now playing at Italian giants Internazionale, but their squad also boasted the likes of Jay Jay Okocha, Daniel Amokachi and Celestine Babayaro.

Even so, people expected the team to lose their semi-final against reigning world champions Brazil, whose side contained World Cup winner Bebeto, Ronaldo, Rivaldo and Roberto Carlos. But in an amazing match, which saw Brazil 3-1 up with 12 minutes to go, Nigeria turned it round in the most dramatic manner. Victor Ikpeba pulled one back before Kanu scored twice in the final minute to pull off an amazing 4-3 win.

Could lightning strike twice in the final against an Argentina side featuring Hernán Crespo, Ariel Ortega, Claudio López and Diego Simeone? It certainly could: once again Nigeria trailed with the clock against them. But from 2-1 down with 16 minutes left, Amokachi equalised before Emmanuel Amunike scored another last-minute winner. Nigeria won the gold medal, Africa their first major title. Can the continent add a second at the 2010 World Cup?

Liverpool 3, Milan 3 (Champions League, 2005)

Before the final of the 2005 Champions League, Liverpool could already claim to have been involved in the greatest European final of all time, a wild rollercoaster win – 5-4! – over Spanish minnows Alaves to claim the 2001 UEFA Cup. Few thought they could ever surpass this victory in terms of sugar-rush drama – but that's exactly what was about to happen. And how.

At the outset of the 2004/5 Champions League, people considered Liverpool to be one of the outsiders for the tournament. Their odds of 33/1 to win looked about right when, against Olympiakos in their final first-stage group match, they needed three goals in the second half to progress to the knockout stages. They got them, though, with captain Steven Gerrard scoring the crucial third with four minutes to go, a famous piledriver from outside the box. Continuing to battle against the odds, Liverpool then beat Bayer Leverkusen, Italian champions Juventus and English champions Chelsea to reach the Istanbul final.

Milan lay in wait, and were everyone's favourite to win the trophy. Liverpool's squad couldn't compare with the Milanese man for man: the Rossoneri could boast Brazil's top midfielder Kaka, Argentinian striker Hernán Crespo, Ukrainian goal machine Andriy Shevchenko and Italian playmaker Andrea Pirlo. Those pre-match predictions looked sage when, within 50 seconds of kick-off, veteran Milan defender Paolo Maldini hooked the ball home for his side's opening goal. By half-time a totally dominant Milan had added two more through Crespo, with Kaka running the show from the middle of the park.

But new Liverpool manager Rafael Benitez didn't panic. He brought on Dietmar Hamann to smother Kaka, allowing Gerrard to roam free upfield. And in six crazy second-half minutes, first Gerrard, then Vladimir Smicer and then Xabi Alonso amazingly levelled the scores. Milan were shellshocked, though they managed to slowly claw their way back into the game. The match went to extra time and with less than two minutes remaining crack hitman Shevchenko found himself alone with the ball two yards out, but somehow Liverpool keeper Jerzy Dudek made a point-blank double save and the destiny of the trophy seemed written. Sure enough, after a penalty shootout that Liverpool always led, the Reds had won their fifth European Cup.

Part VI
Appendixes

'They keep getting relegated.'

In this part . . .

This Part contains the Appendixes. In many books, Appendixes consist of reams of dusty footnotes and worthy, shelf-bending bibliographies. Not here. In this book, the two appendixes are collections of vital information.

The first appendix is a roll of honour. It tells you the winners of the major football tournaments – and who they beat, where they beat them, and when. The second appendix, the glossary, is one you'll find yourself turning to time and again when you want to refresh your memory about the meaning of football's lingo.

Appendix A

Roll of Honour

· ·

*T*he first football match between two clubs was played in 1860, while the first game contested by two countries was in 1872. Were I to list every single major trophy win, at both club and international level, I'd need to publish at least another 173 volumes of this book. Try carrying *those* home from the shops!

Instead, here are a select few of the most significant results in football history.

For those of you interested in delving deep into the record books, may I recommend the peerless website of the Rec Sport Soccer Statistics Foundation: www.rsssf.com. It has absolutely *everything*, even the winner of the 1956 Guatemalan league (that was Comunicaciones, since you ask).

World Cup

The World Cup is the biggest football tournament in the world. All of FIFA's 208 member states are eligible to enter. It's held every four years, with the winners earning the right to call themselves champions of the world.

World Cup finals (1930 – 2006)

Year	Hosts	Winner	Runner-up	Score
1930	Uruguay	Uruguay	Argentina	4-2
1934	Italy	Italy	Czechoslovakia	2-1 aet
1938	France	Italy	Hungary	4-2
1950	Brazil	Uruguay	Brazil	2-1*
1954	Switzerland	West Germany	Hungary	3-2
1958	Sweden	Brazil	Sweden	5-2
1962	Chile	Brazil	Czechoslovakia	3-1
1966	England	England	West Germany	4-2 aet

(continued)

World Cup finals (1930 – 2006) *(continued)*

Year	Hosts	Winner	Runner-up	Score
1970	Mexico	Brazil	Italy	4-1
1974	West Germany	West Germany	Netherlands	2-1
1978	Argentina	Argentina	Netherlands	3-1 aet
1982	Spain	Italy	West Germany	3-1
1986	Mexico	Argentina	West Germany	3-2
1990	Italy	West Germany	Argentina	1-0
1994	USA	Brazil	Italy	0-0 aet (Brazil win 3-2 on penalties)
1998	France	France	Brazil	3-0
2002	South Korea and Japan	Brazil	Germany	2-0
2006	Germany	Italy	France	1-1 aet (Italy win 5-3 on pen-alties)
2010	South Africa			
2014	Brazil			

* The 1950 tournament had no official final, but a final pool involving four teams: Uruguay, Brazil, Spain and Sweden. However the final match between Uruguay and Brazil was effectively a 'final', as it was the decisive game.

Total World Cup wins (1930 – 2006)

Wins	Team	Years
5	Brazil	1958, 1962, 1970, 1994, 2002
4	Italy	1934, 1938, 1982, 2006
3	(West) Germany	1954, 1974, 1990
2	Uruguay	1930, 1950
2	Argentina	1978, 1986
1	England	1966
1	France	1998

European Championship

The European Championship – or Euros, as they're colloquially known – is held every four years, midway between World Cups. It was known as the European Nations Cup until 1968. The winners have the right to call themselves European champions.

European Championship finals (1960 – 2008)

Year	Hosts	Winner	Runner-up	Score
1960	France	Soviet Union	Yugoslavia	2-1 aet
1964	Spain	Spain	Soviet Union	2-1
1968	Italy	Italy	Yugoslavia	2-0 (replay after 1-1 draw)
1972	Belgium	West Germany	Soviet Union	3-0
1976	Yugoslavia	Czechoslovakia	West Germany	2-2 (Czechoslovakia win 5-3 on penalties)
1980	Italy	West Germany	Belgium	2-1
1984	France	France	Spain	2-0
1988	West Germany	Netherlands	Soviet Union	2-0
1992	Sweden	Denmark	Germany	2-0
1996	England	Germany	Czech Republic	2-1 aet *
2000	Belgium and Netherlands	France	Italy	2-1 aet *
2004	Portugal	Greece	Portugal	1-0
2008	Austria and Switzerland	Spain	Germany	1-0
2012	Ukraine and Poland			

* Both the 1996 and 2000 finals were settled by a Golden Goal in sudden-death extra time.

Total European Championship wins (1960 – 2008)

Wins	Team	Years
3	(West) Germany	1972, 1980, 1996
2	France	1984, 2000
2	Spain	1964, 2008
1	Soviet Union	1960
1	Italy	1968
1	Czechoslovakia	1976
1	Netherlands	1988
1	Denmark	1992
1	Greece	2004

Copa America

The Copa America is the oldest international tournament in the world. It decides the champions of South America. It has had a chequered history, being played irregularly and structured erratically since the first official staging in 1916 – but since 1987 it has taken the same format, an entire tournament staged in one country. It is now staged every four years.

Recent Copa America finals (1987 – 2007)

Year	Hosts	Winner	Runner-up	Score
1987	Argentina	Uruguay	Chile	1-0
1989	Brazil	Brazil	Uruguay	1-0
1991	Chile	Argentina	Brazil	3-2
1993	Ecuador	Argentina	Mexico	2-1
1995	Uruguay	Uruguay	Brazil	1-1 (Uruguay win 5-3 on penalties)
1997	Bolivia	Brazil	Bolivia	3-1
1999	Paraguay	Brazil	Uruguay	3-0
2001	Colombia	Colombia	Mexico	1-0
2004	Peru	Brazil	Argentina	2-2 (Brazil win 4-2 on penalties)
2007	Venezuela	Brazil	Argentina	3-0
2011	Argentina			

Total Copa America wins (1916 – 2007)

Wins	Team	Years
14	Argentina	1921, 1925, 1927, 1929, 1937, 1941, 1945, 1946, 1947, 1955, 1957, 1959, 1991, 1993
14	Uruguay	1916, 1917, 1920, 1923, 1924, 1926, 1935, 1942, 1956, 1959, 1967, 1983, 1987, 1995
8	Brazil	1919, 1922, 1949, 1989, 1997, 1999, 2004, 2007
2	Paraguay	1953, 1979
2	Peru	1939, 1975
1	Colombia	2001
1	Bolivia	1963

Africa Cup of Nations

This is the pinnacle of African football, with the winners earning the right to name themselves African champions. The tournament has been held on a regular basis since 1957, and is now held every two years.

Africa Cup of Nations finals (1957 – 2008)

Year	Hosts	Winner	Runner-up	Score
1957	Sudan	Egypt	Ethiopia	4-0
1959	Egypt	Egypt	Sudan	after final group
1962	Ethiopia	Ethiopia	Egypt	4-2
1963	Ghana	Ghana	Sudan	3-0
1965	Tunisia	Ghana	Tunisia	3-2
1968	Ethiopia	Congo Kinshasa	Ghana	1-0
1970	Sudan	Sudan	Ghana	1-0
1972	Cameroon	Congo	Mali	3-2
1974	Egypt	Zaire	Zambia	2-0 (replay after 2-2 draw)

(continued)

Africa Cup of Nations finals (1957 – 2008) *(continued)*

Year	Hosts	Winner	Runner-up	Score
1976	Ethiopia	Morocco	Guinea	after final group
1978	Ghana	Ghana	Uganda	2-0
1980	Nigeria	Nigeria	Algeria	3-0
1982	Libya	Ghana	Libya	1-1 (Ghana win 7-6 on penalties)
1984	Ivory Coast	Cameroon	Nigeria	3-0
1986	Egypt	Egypt	Cameroon	0-0 (Egypt win 5-4 on penalties)
1988	Morocco	Cameroon	Nigeria	1-0
1990	Algeria	Algeria	Nigeria	1-0
1992	Senegal	Ghana	Ivory Coast	0-0 (Ghana win 11-10 on penalties)
1994	Tunisia	Nigeria	Zambia	2-1
1996	South Africa	South Africa	Tunisia	2-0
1998	Burkina Faso	Egypt	South Africa	2-0
2000	Ghana and Nigeria	Cameroon	Nigeria	2-2 (Cameroon win 4-3 on penalties)
2002	Mali	Cameroon	Senegal	0-0 (Cameroon win 3-2 on penalties)
2004	Tunisia	Tunisia	Morocco	2-1
2006	Egypt	Egypt	Ivory Coast	0-0 (Egypt win 4-2 on penalties)
2008	Ghana	Egypt	Cameroon	1-0
2010	Angola			
2012	Gabon and Equatorial Guinea			
2014	Libya			

Confederations Cup

This is contested by the champions of all six FIFA confederations – Europe, South America, North and Central America, Africa, Asia, and Oceania – plus the World Cup winners and the host nation. It is yet to be considered a truly prestigious tournament, though its profile is rising sharply.

Confederations Cup finals (1993 – 2009)

Year	Hosts	Winner	Runner-up	Score
1993	Saudi Arabia	Argentina	Saudi Arabia	3-1
1995	Saudi Arabia	Denmark	Argentina	2-0
1997	Saudi Arabia	Brazil	Australia	6-0
1999	Mexico	Mexico	Brazil	4-3
2001	South Korea and Japan	France	Japan	1-0
2003	France	France	Cameroon	1-0 aet
2005	Germany	Brazil	Argentina	4-1
2009	South Africa	Brazil	USA	3-2
2013	Brazil			

Note: the 1993 and 1995 tournaments were called the King Fahd Cup and staged by Saudi Arabia. FIFA took over the tournament in 1997 and renamed it.

Olympic Games

The Olympic football tournament was, up until 1980, an amateur tournament, fitting in with the Olympic ideal. After several tweaks, professionals have since been admitted, though only players under 23 years old can play. It is now a de facto Under-23 World Cup.

Olympic Games football finals (1908 – 2008)

Year	Hosts	Winner	Runner-up	Score
1908	London	England	Denmark	2-0
1912	Stockholm	England	Denmark	4-2
1920	Antwerp	Belgium	Czechoslovakia	2-0
1924	Paris	Uruguay	Switzerland	3-0
1928	Amsterdam	Uruguay	Argentina	2-1 (after 1-1 draw)
1936	Berlin	Italy	Austria	2-1
1948	London	Sweden	Yugoslavia	3-1
1952	Helsinki	Hungary	Yugoslavia	2-0
1956	Melbourne	Soviet Union	Yugoslavia	1-0

(continued)

Olympic Games football finals (1908 – 2008) *(continued)*

Year	Hosts	Winner	Runner-up	Score
1960	Rome	Yugoslavia	Denmark	3-1
1964	Tokyo	Hungary	Czechoslovakia	2-1
1968	Mexico City	Hungary	Bulgaria	4-1
1972	Munich	Poland	Hungary	2-1
1976	Montreal	East Germany	Poland	3-1
1980	Moscow	Czechoslovakia	East Germany	1-0
1984	Los Angeles	France	Brazil	2-0
1988	Seoul	Soviet Union	Brazil	2-1
1992	Barcelona	Spain	Poland	3-2
1996	Atlanta	Nigeria	Argentina	2-0
2000	Sydney	Cameroon	Spain	2-2 (Cameroon win 5-3 on penalties)
2004	Athens	Argentina	Paraguay	1-0
2008	Beijing	Argentina	Nigeria	1-0
2012	London			

Women's World Cup

The Women's World Cup was founded in 1991, and has exploded in popularity over its brief life. The tournament is held every four years. The winners earn the right to call themselves champions of the world.

Women's World Cup finals (1991 – 2007)

Year	Hosts	Winner	Runner-up	Score
1991	China	USA	Norway	2-1
1995	Sweden	Norway	Germany	2-0
1999	USA	USA	China	0-0 (USA win 5-4 on penalties)
2003	USA	Germany	Sweden	2-1 aet*
2007	China	Germany	Brazil	2-0
2011	Germany			

* Final decided by sudden-death golden goal

European Cup / Champions League

The Champions League – formerly the European Cup – is the biggest and most prestigious club championship in the world. The winners are crowned champions of Europe.

European Cup and Champions League finals (1956 – 2009)

Year	Winner	Runner-up	Score	Stadium
1956	Real Madrid	Reims	4-3	Parc des Princes, Paris
1957	Real Madrid	Fiorentina	2-0	Santiago Bernabeu, Madrid
1958	Real Madrid	Milan	3-2	Heysel, Brussels
1959	Real Madrid	Reims	2-0	Neckar, Stuttgart
1960	Real Madrid	Eintracht Frankfurt	7-3	Hampden, Glasgow
1961	Benfica	Barcelona	3-2	Wankdorf, Berne
1962	Benfica	Real Madrid	5-3	Olympic, Amsterdam
1963	Milan	Benfica	2-1	Wembley, London
1964	Internazionale	Real Madrid	3-1	Prater, Vienna
1965	Internazionale	Benfica	1-0	San Siro, Milan
1966	Real Madrid	Partizan Belgrade	2-1	Heysel, Brussels
1967	Celtic	Internazionale	2-1	Nacional, Lisbon
1968	Manchester United	Benfica	4-1 aet	Wembley, London
1969	Milan	Ajax	4-1	Santiago Bernabeu, Madrid
1970	Feyenoord	Celtic	2-1 aet	San Siro, Milan
1971	Ajax	Panathinaikos	2-0	Wembley, London
1972	Ajax	Internazionale	2-0	De Kuijp, Rotterdam
1973	Ajax	Juventus	1-0	Red Star, Belgrade
1974	Bayern Munich	Atletico Madrid	4-0 (after 1-1 draw)	Heysel, Brussels
1975	Bayern Munich	Leeds United	2-0	Parc des Princes, Paris
1976	Bayern Munich	St Etienne	1-0	Hampden, Glasgow
1977	Liverpool	Borussia Monchengladbach	3-1	Olimpico, Rome

(continued)

European Cup and Champions League finals (1956 – 2009) *(continued)*

Year	Winner	Runner-up	Score	Stadium
1978	Liverpool	Bruges	1-0	Wembley, London
1979	Nottingham Forest	Malmo	1-0	Olympia, Munich
1980	Nottingham Forest	Hamburg	1-0	Santiago Bernabeu, Madrid
1981	Liverpool	Real Madrid	1-0	Parc des Princes, Paris
1982	Aston Villa	Bayern Munich	1-0	De Kuip, Rotterdam
1983	Hamburg	Juventus	1-0	Olympic, Athens
1984	Liverpool	Roma	1-1 (Liverpool win 4-2 on penalties)	Olimpico, Rome
1985	Juventus	Liverpool	1-0	Heysel, Brussels
1986	Steaua Bucharest	Barcelona	0-0 (Steaua Bucharest win 2-0 on penalties)	Sanchez Pizjuan, Seville
1987	Porto	Bayern Munich	2-1	Prater, Vienna
1988	PSV Eindhoven	Benfica	0-0 (PSV win 6-5 on penalties)	Neckar, Stuttgart
1989	Milan	Steaua Bucharest	4-0	Nou Camp, Barcelona
1990	Milan	Benfica	1-0	Prater, Vienna
1991	Red Star Belgrade	Marseille	0-0 (Red Star win 5-3 on penalties)	San Nicola, Bari
1992	Barcelona	Sampdoria	1-0 aet	Wembley, London
1993	Marseille	Milan	1-0	Olympiastadion, Munich
1994	Milan	Barcelona	4-0	Olympic, Athens
1995	Ajax	Milan	1-0	Ernst-Happel, Vienna

Year	Winner	Runner-up	Score	Stadium
1996	Juventus	Ajax	1-1 (Juventus win 4-2 on penalties)	Olimpico, Rome
1997	Borussia Dortmund	Juventus	3-1	Olympiastadion, Munich
1998	Real Madrid	Juventus	1-0	Amsterdam Arena, Amsterdam
1999	Manchester United	Bayern Munich	2-1	Nou Camp, Barcelona
2000	Real Madrid	Valencia	3-0	Stade de France, Paris
2001	Bayern Munich	Valencia	1-1 (Bayern won 5-4 on penalties)	San Siro, Milan
2002	Real Madrid	Bayer Leverkusen	2-1	Hampden, Glasgow
2003	Milan	Juventus	0-0 (Milan won 3-2 on penalties)	Old Trafford, Manchester
2004	Porto	Monaco	3-0	AufSchalke, Gelsenkirchen
2005	Liverpool	Milan	3-3 (Liverpool won 3-2 on penalties)	Ataturk, Istanbul
2006	Barcelona	Arsenal	2-1	Stade de France, Paris
2007	Milan	Liverpool	2-1	Olympic, Athens
2008	Manchester United	Chelsea	1-1 (United won 6-5 on penalties)	Luzhniki, Moscow
2009	Barcelona	Manchester United	2-0	Olimpico, Rome

Total European Cup / Champions League wins (1956 – 2009)

Wins	Team	Years
9	Real Madrid	1956, 1957, 1958, 1959, 1960, 1966, 1998, 2000, 2002
7	Milan	1963, 1969, 1989, 1990, 1994, 2003, 2007
5	Liverpool	1977, 1978, 1981, 1984, 2005
4	Ajax	1971, 1972, 1973, 1995
4	Bayern Munich	1974, 1975, 1976, 2001
3	Manchester United	1968, 1999, 2008
3	Barcelona	1992, 2006, 2009
2	Benfica	1961, 1962
2	Internazionale	1964, 1965
2	Nottingham Forest	1979, 1980
2	Juventus	1985, 1996
2	Porto	1987, 2004
1	Celtic	1967
1	Feyenoord	1970
1	Aston Villa	1982
1	Hamburg	1983
1	Steaua Bucharest	1986
1	PSV Eindhoven	1988
1	Red Star Belgrade	1991
1	Marseille	1993
1	Borussia Dortmund	1997

Appendix B

Glossary

Advantage: When the referee decides to let play continue after a foul has been committed, as stopping play would benefit the team who have committed the foul.

Amateur: A player who plays without being paid.

Assistant manager: The second-in-command of a football team, after the manager. Does not pick the team, but assists the manager in whatever way is seen fit. Often a friend to the players, bridging the gap between the big boss and the team.

Assistant referee: Formerly known as linesmen or lineswomen, the assistant referees run along the touchline, helping the referee officiate the game. Their main responsibilities are determining if a ball has gone out of play, who touched it last, and whether a player is offside, though they will also act as a second pair of eyes to any incident on the field, and advise the referee wherever necessary.

Back heel: Playing the ball with the heel, usually sending it in a backwards direction. The move can be utilised as either a pass or a shot.

Bench: Substitutes, manager, assistant manager, physio, and whoever else is associated with the team but not currently playing. So called because they are usually sitting on a bench!

Bicycle kick: A difficult manoeuvre where the player jumps, leans backwards, and moves their legs as though pedalling a bicycle to kick the ball. The ball is sent over the head of the kicker, in a backwards direction.

Booking: A caution for foul play. The player is shown a yellow card. Two yellow cards will result in a sending off.

Box: The penalty area, or penalty box.

Captain: The on-field leader of the team, as designated by the manager. They are responsible for keeping up morale, communicating with the referee, and making minor tactical changes as the game progresses. (Captains are only permitted to make on-the-spot tactical changes if the manager has given them the authority.)

Caution: Punishment for foul play. The player is shown a yellow card. Two yellow cards will result in a sending off.

Centre spot: The mark directly in the centre of the pitch, used to position the ball for kick-offs.

Chip: A delicate pass, clipped up into the air and dropped towards a precise spot.

Clean sheet: A final score of no goals conceded. If a team lets in no goals during a match, the goalkeeper is said to have *kept a clean sheet.*

Clearance: A ball being kicked or headed away from any particular danger zone. A clearance can be made to avert an immediate goal threat – a ball hoofed off the goal line by a defender is a *goal line clearance* – or more generally away from a team's defensive third.

Club: An organisation which exists to put out football teams for the purposes of competition. A club will have at least a basic set-up of a first team, a reserve team, and a youth team. The first team will fulfil the club's competitive fixtures.

Coach: 1. The team manager in the USA. 2. The trainer, a member of the managerial team who puts the players through their fitness drills and tactical practices.

Corner: A kick taken by the attacking side, after the ball has been put out behind the goal line by the defending side. It is taken from the left or right corner of the pitch, on the side of the field the ball went out of play. It is usually sent straight into the penalty area, in the hope that an attacking player can get a shot or header on target.

Cross: A ball sent into the penalty area by an attacking player, from either the left or right side of the field.

Dead ball: The ball is considered *dead* when it is not in play, but still on the field. This means it has been positioned for a free kick, a corner or a penalty.

Defender: One of the players whose first responsibility to his team is to ensure goals are not scored against them. They play in a formation at the back of the team, hoping to nullify the threat of the opposition attackers. They may be asked to follow a particular opponent around – man-to-man marking – or take care of a certain area of the pitch – zonal defending.

Direct free kick: A free kick from which a player can take a direct shot at goal.

Dissent: The act of arguing with the referee or the referee's assistants. Dissent is often punished with a yellow card. Extreme cases of dissent can see a player sent off, usually for swearing or aggressive behaviour.

Draw: 1. If two teams end the game with the same amount of goals, the result is a draw. 2. The method to group or pair teams in a competition; teams are *drawn* randomly to determine who will play each other in a specified round of a tournament.

Dribble: Keeping control of the ball with the feet, and retaining possession, while running.

Drop ball: A method of restarting a game if the referee has had to stop it without the ball having gone out of play. This is usually for an injury. The ball is dropped to the ground by the referee, at which point players on both sides can touch the ball and get on with the game.

Dummy: Making to kick the ball, or move in a particular direction, but not doing so, confusing the opposition in the process.

Equaliser: A goal which levels the score of a game. If a team was losing 1-0, and scores to make it 1-1, they have scored an equaliser.

Extra time: Two 15-minute periods of play contested when teams finish the 90 minutes drawn, but a winner on the day is required. (This usually occurs in cup competitions, where a replay would be impossible – or unfair – to stage.)

Fair play: Sportsmanship. Both teams and players can win Fair Play awards for good behaviour.

Far post: The goalpost further from the ball.

Final: The last tie in a knockout tournament between the two teams yet to be knocked out. The decisive game.

Final whistle: The referee's blast on the whistle that signals the end of the game.

Formation: The tactical arrangement a manager or coach sets his team in. A formation is a numbered combination of the ten outfield players, reading from the back to the front of the pitch. So the classic 4-4-2 formation has four players at the back, four in midfield, and two up front.

Forward: A primarily attacking player. A forward's job is to score goals, or create them by combining with another forward player. They are also known as goalscorers, or strikers. Forwards can also play on the wings, or as attacking midfielders, but this is a much looser definition of the term.

Foul: An infringement of the Laws of the Game.

Fourth official: An official whose task is to help the referee and his two assistants, usually from the stand or the technical area. They will oversee substitutions, keep the two benches in line, and announce the amount of stoppage time at the end of a match.

Free kick: A dead-ball kick taken by an attacking team, after a player has been fouled.

Friendly: A match which is not part of an official competition, counting for nothing in particular. Usually an exhibition game, either between clubs who rarely play each other, or two countries.

Full back: Either a left back or right back; that is, a defender who plays on either the left or right wing of the pitch.

General manager: A behind-the-scenes administrator who assists the manager in transfers and other club-related business. Often a former professional player or manager. Rarely considered at fault when the team is playing badly.

Goal: 1. The ultimate aim of football. A goal is scored when the entire ball crosses the goal line, under the crossbar and between the goal posts. 2. The area in which the goal is scored.

Goal kick: Method of restarting the game when the attacking team put the ball out of play over the goal line (but not in the goal). Usually taken by the goalkeeper, but occasionally by one of their team-mates.

Goal line: The lines that run between each touch line at either end of the pitch. The goal is situated in the middle of the goal-line.

Goal mouth: The area directly in front of the goal.

Goalkeeper: The only player on the pitch allowed to use their hands – but only in the penalty area – the goalkeeper's job is to ensure the opposing team does not score.

Golden goal: A sudden-death goal, scored in extra time, which wins the match immediately.

Ground: 1. The surface of the pitch. 2. A stadium.

Half time: The period between the first and second halves.

Half volley: A kick or shot made immediately after a dropping ball hits the ground.

Hand ball: A foul by a player who handles the ball with their arm or hand on purpose. Goalkeepers can only be called for this foul outside the penalty box.

Hat-trick: Three goals in a game by the same player. A perfect hat-trick is a trio of goals, one scored by a left-footed shot, another by a right-footed shot, and a third with a header.

Header: Propelling the ball using one's head.

Indirect free-kick: A free kick from which a player can not take a direct shot at goal.

Injury time: Time added on by the referee at the end of each half, to account for any stoppages in play. Also known as stoppage time.

Inswinger: A shot, pass or usually a cross which curves in towards the goal from wherever it has been hit.

Interval: Another word for half-time.

Keeper: A colloquialism for goalkeeper.

Kick-off: A kick from the centre spot which starts the game or the half, or restarts the match after a goal.

Linesman: The old-school term for Assistant referee. It was changed to become gender neutral in the early 2000s.

Manager: The person who runs the team, picks the players, chooses the tactical approach, and makes in-game decisions such as tactical rethinks and substitutions. They also determine which players to buy and sell.

Man-to-man marking: A system where each defender tracks a specific opponent, and stays with them all game, usually following their every move around the pitch.

Match: A game.

Midfielder: A player who spends most of their time in the centre of the pitch. They are usually the most influential players in the side, contributing to both attack and defence, and dictating the speed and direction of play.

Near post: The goalpost nearest to the ball.

Nutmeg: A move in which a player kicks the ball between the legs of an opponent. The kick can be a pass to another team-mate, or a "pass" to themselves, the player running round their confused opponent and carrying on their way.

Obstruction: Deliberately getting in the way of another player with no intention of playing the ball.

Officials: 1. The referee, the referee's assistant, and the fourth official. 2. Representatives of a club. For example, newspaper reports may say "officials of Manchester United were talking to Player X about a transfer".

Offside: A player is offside when they are nearer to their opponents' goal than the second-to-last opponent – *at the time the ball is played forward by a team-mate*.

Offside trap: A defensive tactic used to lure opponents into being caught offside. All defenders move up the field at the same time, leaving opponents stranded.

One touch: A kick or pass made using the player's first touch upon receiving the ball.

Outswinger: A shot, pass or usually a cross which curves away from the goal from wherever it has been hit.

Overlap: When a defender runs down either wing, past their midfield or attacking players, to become part of the attack.

Own goal: A goal accidentally scored by a player into their own net. The own goal counts as a goal for the opposition.

Pass: How a player moves the ball to another, using either their feet or head.

Penalty: A free shot from 12 yards in the penalty area, upon the award of a direct free kick in the box. Also known as a penalty kick.

Penalty area: The 18x44 yard area around each goal, in which the goalkeeper is allowed to handle the ball, and fouls by the defending team are punished with a penalty kick.

Physio: The physiotherapist, team doctor, or man carrying a bucket of water and sponge.

Pitch: The playing area.

Playmaker: A player – usually a midfielder – whose job it is to dictate the way the entire team plays, and at what tempo. This is usually meant in a creative sense, with the player influencing the game through clever passing.

Professional: A player who is paid, and earns their living, from playing football.

Red card: A card shown by a referee to a player who has committed a serious offence, usually violent or cynical. The player is sent off, and no longer able to take part in the game. The player cannot be replaced.

Referee: The official who is in charge of the game, and makes decisions according to the Laws of the Game.

Restart: Another word for kick-off.

Save: A shot or header blocked, caught or parried by the goalkeeper, which otherwise would have been a goal.

Semi-professional: A player who is employed by a club on a part-time basis, but must also hold down a day job to make ends meet. Semi-pros are usually found in the lower leagues, at small clubs who cannot afford full-time salaries.

Set piece: A free kick, corner, throw-in or goal kick.

Shot: A kick towards the goal. A shot at goal is off target, a shot on goal is on target.

Side: A team.

Soccer: Shorthand for Association Football. Often erroneously claimed to be an Americanism, when in fact the word was coined by British university students in the late 1800s.

Square pass: A pass played to a team-mate standing alongside – rather than ahead, or behind – that player. Often used pejoratively, to suggest a lack of creativity or attacking gung-ho on the part of the passer.

Stoppage time: Time added on at the end of the game for injuries, arguments, substitutions, and so on.

Striker: Another word for forward. Often used for a player whose sole purpose is to score goals.

Substitute: A replacement player who can be swapped for a player on the pitch.

Tackle: A defensive motion in which a player uses their foot to take the ball off an opposing player, or block their progress.

Target player: A forward, usually a tall or bulky one, who is the target of passes and crosses – usually of the long variety. The target player is usually an adept header of the ball, and very strong.

Through pass: A pass that goes between and past the last line of defence, allowing an attacker to run into space and receive the ball.

Throw-in: The method by which a ball that has gone out of play over the touch line is deposited back into play, a player throwing it in over their head using both hands.

Time wasting: Deliberately taking unnecessary amounts of time to restart the game from dead-ball situations in order to run down the clock. This is only ever done by teams who are winning the game, and are looking to close out the match. This is technically an offence, but is not always punished by the referee as it can be very subjective.

Touch line: The lines running down both sides of the pitch, from each goal line.

Trainer: 1. A team's medical expert. 2. A manager or coach, usually specialising in tactics or fitness.

Transfer: The method by which players change the teams and clubs they play for.

Unsportsmanlike behaviour: Conduct that brings disgrace to the game.

Volley: Kicking the ball when it has been sent flying through the air, before it has hit the ground again.

Wing: Either side, or flank, of the field. Wingers are the attacking players who are positioned on either side of the field.

Yellow card: A card shown by a referee to a player who has committed an offence that requires them to be put on a warning. A second yellow card results in the player being sent off.

Zonal defence: A tactic where defenders look after a designated section of the field, or penalty area, rather than concentrating on a particular opponent.

Index

• C •

• G •

• *N* •

• Q •

• R •

• S •

• Y •

• Z •

FOR DUMMIES®

Making Everything Easier!™

UK editions

BUSINESS

978-0-470-51806-9

978-0-470-74381-2

978-0-470-71382-2

FINANCE

978-0-470-99280-7

978-0-470-71432-4

978-0-470-69515-9

HOBBIES

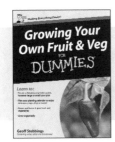

978-0-470-69960-7

978-0-470-74535-9

978-0-470-75857-1

British Sign Language
For Dummies
978-0-470-69477-0

Business NLP For Dummies
978-0-470-69757-3

Competitive Strategy For Dummies
978-0-470-77930-9

Cricket For Dummies
978-0-470-03454-5

CVs For Dummies, 2nd Edition
978-0-470-74491-8

Digital Marketing For Dummies
978-0-470-05793-3

Divorce For Dummies, 2nd Edition
978-0-470-74128-3

eBay.co.uk Business All-in-One
For Dummies
978-0-470-72125-4

Emotional Freedom Technique For
Dummies
978-0-470-75876-2

English Grammar For Dummies
978-0-470-05752-0

Flirting For Dummies
978-0-470-74259-4

Golf For Dummies
978-0-470-01811-8

Green Living For Dummies
978-0-470-06038-4

Hypnotherapy For Dummies
978-0-470-01930-6

IBS For Dummies
978-0-470-51737-6

Lean Six Sigma For Dummies
978-0-470-75626-3

FOR DUMMIES®

A world of resources to help you grow

UK editions

SELF-HELP

978-0-470-01838-5

978-0-7645-7028-5

978-0-470-74193-1

Motivation For Dummies
978-0-470-76035-2

Overcoming Depression For Dummies
978-0-470-69430-5

Personal Development All-In-One For Dummies
978-0-470-51501-3

Positive Psychology For Dummies
978-0-470-72136-0

PRINCE2 For Dummies
978-0-470-51919-6

Psychometric Tests For Dummies
978-0-470-75366-8

Raising Happy Children For Dummies
978-0-470-05978-4

Sage 50 Accounts For Dummies
978-0-470-71558-1

Succeeding at Assessment Centres For Dummies
978-0-470-72101-8

Sudoku For Dummies
978-0-470-01892-7

Teaching English as a Foreign Language For Dummies
978-0-470-74576-2

Teaching Skills For Dummies
978-0-470-74084-2

Time Management For Dummies
978-0-470-77765-7

Understanding and Paying Less Property Tax For Dummies
978-0-470-75872-4

Work-Life Balance For Dummies
978-0-470-71380-8

STUDENTS

978-0-470-74047-7

978-0-470-74711-7

978-0-470-74290-7

HISTORY

978-0-470-99468-9

978-0-470-51015-5

978-0-470-98787-2

08049_p2

FOR DUMMIES®

The easy way to get more done and have more fun

LANGUAGES

978-0-7645-5194-9

978-0-7645-5193-2

978-0-471-77270-5

MUSIC

978-0-470-48133-2

978-0-470-03275-6
UK Edition

978-0-470-49644-2

SCIENCE & MATHS

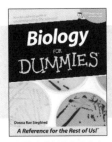

978-0-7645-5326-4

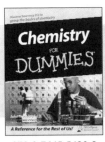

978-0-7645-5430-8

978-0-7645-5325-7

Art For Dummies
978-0-7645-5104-8

Bass Guitar For Dummies
978-0-7645-2487-5

Brain Games For Dummies
978-0-470-37378-1

Christianity For Dummies
978-0-7645-4482-8

Criminology For Dummies
978-0-470-39696-4

Forensics For Dummies
978-0-7645-5580-0

German For Dummies
978-0-7645-5195-6

Hobby Farming For Dummies
978-0-470-28172-7

Index Investing For Dummies
978-0-470-29406-2

Jewelry Making & Beading
For Dummies
978-0-7645-2571-1

Knitting For Dummies, 2nd Edition
978-0-470-28747-7

Music Composition For Dummies
978-0-470-22421-2

Physics For Dummies
978-0-7645-5433-9

Schizophrenia For Dummies
978-0-470-25927-6

Sex For Dummies, 3rd Edition
978-0-470-04523-7

Solar Power Your Home For Dummies
978-0-470-17569-9

Tennis For Dummies
978-0-7645-5087-4

The Koran For Dummies
978-0-7645-5581-7

Wine All-in-One For Dummies
978-0-470-47626-0

FOR DUMMIES®

Helping you expand your horizons and achieve your potential

COMPUTER BASICS

978-0-470-27759-1

978-0-470-13728-4

978-0-470-49743-2

DIGITAL PHOTOGRAPHY

978-0-470-25074-7

978-0-470-46606-3

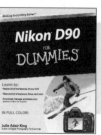

978-0-470-45772-6

MAC BASICS

978-0-470-27817-8

978-0-470-46661-2

978-0-470-43543-4

Access 2007 For Dummies
978-0-470-04612-8

Adobe Creative Suite 4 Design
Premium All-in-One Desk Reference
For Dummies
978-0-470-33186-6

AutoCAD 2010 For Dummies
978-0-470-43345-4

C++ For Dummies, 6th Edition
978-0-470-31726-6

Computers For Seniors For Dummies ,
2nd Edition
978-0-470-53483-0

Dreamweaver CS4 For Dummies
978-0-470-34502-3

Excel 2007 All-In-One Desk Reference
For Dummies
978-0-470-03738-6

Green IT For Dummies
978-0-470-38688-0

Networking All-in-One Desk Reference
For Dummies, 3rd Edition
978-0-470-17915-4

Office 2007 All-in-One Desk Reference
For Dummies
978-0-471-78279-7

Photoshop CS4 For Dummies
978-0-470-32725-8

Photoshop Elements 7 For Dummies
978-0-470-39700-8

Search Engine Optimization
For Dummies, 3rd Edition
978-0-470-26270-2

The Internet For Dummies,
11th Edition
978-0-470-12174-0

Visual Studio 2008 All-In-One Desk
Reference For Dummies
978-0-470-19108-8

Web Analytics For Dummies
978-0-470-09824-0

Windows Vista For Dummies
978-0-471-75421-3

**Available wherever books are sold. For more information or to order direct go to www.wiley.com
or call +44 (0) 1243 843291**

08049_p4